Nichiren

南無妙法蓮華經　日蓮

南無上行菩薩
南無無辺行菩薩
南無浄行菩薩
南無安立行菩薩
南無釈迦牟尼仏
南無多宝如来
南無文殊師利菩薩
南無普賢菩薩
南無舍利弗尊者
南無迦葉尊者

大日天王
大梵天王
第六天魔王
大月天王
大明星天王
帝釈天王
大龍王
阿闍世王
十羅刹女
伝教大師
鬼子母神
天照太神
八幡大菩薩
転輪聖王
阿修羅王
大広目天王
大毘沙門天王
大持国天王
大増長天王

若悩乱者頭破七分
有供養者福過十号

昭和四十一年十一月一日

佛滅後二千二百三十余年之内未曾有之大曼荼羅也

日達在判

Asian Studies at Hawaii, No. 26

Nichiren:
Selected Writings

By Laurel Rasplica Rodd

ASIAN STUDIES PROGRAM
UNIVERSITY OF HAWAII
THE UNIVERSITY PRESS OF HAWAII

Library of Congress Cataloging in Publication Data

Nichiren, 1222-1282.
  Nichiren, selected writings.

  (Asian studies at Hawaii; no. 26)
  Bibliography: p.
  Includes index.
  1.   Nichiren (Sect)–Collected works.   I.   Series.
DS3.A2A82   no. 26   [BQ8349.N57]   950'.08s   [294.3'92]
ISBN 0-8248-0682-4   79-17054

Opposite the title page is one of the *honzon,* or symbolic representations of the Teaching, written by Nichiren for his followers. The bold characters in the center read "Namu Myōhōrengekyō," (Homage to the Sutra of the Lotus of the Wonderful Law), Nichiren.

The names of various buddhas, bodhisattvas, and gods which flank this *honzon* illustrate that all beings share in the Buddha-nature as promised in the Lotus Sutra. This *honzon* is distributed to believers by the Nichiren Shōshū.

for Greg

Contents

Preface

Nichiren does not appear in historical documents of his time, and there is no biography by any of the disciples who knew him. *Goden dodai*ᵃ, the earliest biography, is by Nichidōᵇ (1282–1342), who was born the year Nichiren died. His work contains no information not found in Nichiren's own writings. Two hundred years later Nitchōᶜ (1422–1500) wrote a more extensive biography, *Gensō kedōki*ᵈ, which was first printed in 1666. This includes most of the legendary material that has become part of Nichiren's story.

Several modern biographers have tried to exclude facts which cannot be verified by reference to Nichiren's writings. Among the best of these biographies are *Nichiren: sono kōdō to shisō* (Tōkyō: Hyōronsha, 1973) and *Nichiren to sono montei* (Tōkyō: Kobundō, 1965), both by Takagi Yutaka; *Nichiren no shōgai to shisō* (Tōkyō: Shunshūsha, 1972), volume two of the series Kōza Nichiren edited by Tamura Yoshirō and Miyazaki Eishū; and *Yogenja no bukkyō* (Tōkyō: Chikuma shobō, 1967), by Tamura Yoshirō, volume thirteen of the Nihon no Bukkyō series.

The most recent critical edition of Nichiren's writings, the *Shōwa teihon Nichiren shōnin ibun,* published from 1959–1963, contains collated texts of 523 complete writings and 248 fragments of letters attributed to Nichiren. Debate over the authenticity of some works attributed to Nichiren began fifty years after his death. *Nikkō yuikai okibumi*ᵉ, written in 1333, warns, using one of Nichiren's favorite metaphors, that those who make forgeries and include them among the authentic writings are "parasites in the body of the lion."[1] The splintering of Nichiren's following into opposing factions within a few years of his death encouraged the composition of forged documents, over many of which scholars and devotees are still arguing.

Fortunately, many works in Nichiren's autograph survive: there are today ninety complete works and one hundred thirty fragments. Besides these, there were twenty-eight complete works and six fragments which had been collected at Kuonji, the main temple of the branch of the Nichiren sect located on Mount Minobu, where Nichiren lived the last decade of his life. These letters were lost in a fire in the late nineteenth century. For this study I have relied on the writings generally considered authentic which are included in volumes I and II of *Shōwa teihon Nichiren shōnin ibun*.

Annotation in the following volumes was most helpful in making the translations and preparing the accompanying notes: *Nichiren* (Tōkyō: Chūōkōronsha, 1970) by Kino Kazuyoshi; *Nichirenshū* (Tōkyō: Chikuma shobō, 1969) edited by Tamura Yoshirō; *Nichiren shōnin zenshū* (Tōkyō: Nichiren shōnin zenshū kankōkai, 1925), seven volumes, edited by the Nichiren shōnin zenshū kankōkai; *Nichiren* (Tōkyō: Iwanami shoten, 1970) by Tokoro Shigemoto and Takagi Yutaka; and *Shinranshū Nichirenshū* (Tōkyō: Iwanami shoten, 1964) edited by Nabata Ōjun and others.

Among the useful discussions of Nichiren's doctrine are *Nichiren no shisō to Kamakura bukkyō* (Tōkyō: Fūzanbō, 1965) by Tokoro Shigemoto; and *Nichiren goroku* (Tōkyō: Shunshūsha, 1973), volume five of *Kōza Nichiren*, edited by Tamura Yoshirō and Miyazaki Eishū.

I have used the following rules in transliterating names, book titles, and technical terms: Chinese names are given in Chinese romanization; names of buddhas and bodhisattvas are given in romanized Japanese; names of other Indian figures are in romanized Sanskrit, or, in the case of some fictional characters, in Japanese transliteration; Buddhist terms are given in romanized Japanese, except for Sanskrit terms that have been adopted into English; book titles are romanized, with the exceptions of those commonly known by their English titles; and sutras are given their Japanese titles. Words found in *Webster's Third New International Dictionary* are not in italics, and diacritical marks have been removed. The appendixes include Chinese characters for Buddhist terms, characters and dates of historical figures, and characters and Taishō numbers of sutras and religious writings.

Dates are cited by year of the Western calendar, followed by month and date according to the lunar calendar; for example, 1276/9/13 is the thirteenth day of the ninth moon of the year 1276.

The following abbreviations appear in notes. Complete documentation appears in the bibliography.

Ch'en   *Buddhism in China*
Chih-i   Hurvitz, Leon, *Chih-i*
Hurvitz   Hurvitz, Leon, *Scripture of the Lotus Blossom of the Fine
              Dharma*
Kern   Kern, H., *Saddharma-puṇḍarīka*
NKBT   Nabata Ōjun et al., *Shinranshū Nichirenshū*
STH   Risshō daigaku Nichiren kyōgaku kenkyūjo, *Shōwa teihon
              Nichiren shōnin ibun*
T   Takakusu Junjirō et al., *Taishō shinshū daizōkyō*

NOTE

1.   Tamura Yoshirō, "Kamakura shinbukkyō to Nichiren shisō," in Miyazaki
      Eishū and Motai Kyōkō, eds., *Nichiren shōnin kenkyū* (Kyoto: Heirakuji
      shoten, 1972), p. 280.

      [a] 御伝土代
      [b] 日道
      [c] 日朝
      [d] 元祖化導記
      [e] 日興遺誡置文

Acknowledgments

Special thanks are due Professor William Sibley for his suggestions and patience and to Miss Naomi Fukuda of the Asia Library at The University of Michigan for helping me to obtain and use materials on which this study is based.

Part I
NICHIREN

CHAPTER 1
The Man

In Kominato, a remote fishing hamlet on the Pacific coast of the Chiba peninsula across from Tōkyō, Tanjōji temple commemorates the birth of the founder of the Lotus sect of Japanese Buddhism. Nichiren was born in Kominato in 1222.[1]

All that is known of Nichiren's family and childhood is preserved in a few scattered sentences of his letters. "I am the son of an outcast, a man who lived by the sea in the Tōjō district of Awa, in Japan's barbaric east."[2] "In this life I was born a humble and poor man."[3] "I am the son of a fisherman."[4] "I am not a man from the central provinces of Japan, nor am I the son of a provincial warrior, but rather a child of the people from a remote province."[5]

Modern scholars point out that the term "fisherman" referred to a broad class of society. Kino Kazuyoshi has suggested that Nichiren's father could have been head of a small group of fishermen and responsible for the group to local authorities.[6] Takagi Yutaka, who has written some of the best studies of Nichiren's life and followers, believes the father must have been a manorial functionary *(shōkan),* for Nichiren sided with the manor lords in their feuds with *bakufu* officials and he was sent to the temple for an education, a privilege usually reserved for the sons of higher classes.[7] During the Kamakura period, manor lords struggled to protect their holdings against steady encroachment by the appointed stewards *(jitō)* of the *bakufu.*[8] In the clashes between the manorial family, to whom Nichiren's family was indebted,[9] and the *jitō* Tō-jō Kagenobu, it was natural that the family should have sided with the manor on which Kominato was located.

Nichiren's lowly origins were unique among the religious leaders of the Middle Ages in Japan; Hōnen, Shinran, Dōgen, and Eisai all came from noble or samurai families. Moreover, Nichiren was born far from the centers of political or religious influence while the others were all from Kyoto or the surrounding provinces. Such a birth was a handicap in a society in which the religious hierarchy was based upon social status, and the great centers of Buddhism lay in the western provinces of Japan.[10] On the other hand, this background attracted many of Nichiren's followers down to the present day.[11]

STUDY AT KIYOZUMIDERA

In the gentle, wooded mountains less than ten miles to the north of Kominato the temple Kiyozumi nestles almost at the summit of the peninsula's highest peak, overlooking the ocean. Here the eleven-year-old Nichiren came to study.[12]

He grew to love his teacher, the priest Dōzen.[13] From him he learned to read and write, to pray to the Buddha Amida and esoteric deities, and to understand the basic Tendai doctrines.[14] He studied Chinese language as well as the Buddhist scriptures Dōzen revered—the Amida sutras[15] and the Lotus Sutra.

In the thirteenth century, Kiyozumidera belonged to the esoteric Sanmon branch of Tendai,[16] and the chief object of worship was the bodhisattva Kokūzō (Ākāśagarbha), the central figure in the Taizōkai (matrix) mandala. This bodhisattva of wisdom vast as space, who sits upright upon a lotus, holding the sword of wisdom and the jewel of the cessation of desires, played the central role in the visions and dreams of Nichiren, who later wrote: "From the time I was very young I prayed to the bodhisattva Kokūzō to make me the wisest man in Japan.[17]

Nichiren also absorbed from Dōzen and the other monks the dissatisfaction with life and consciousness of its uncertainty which were widespread in his time.[18]

I knew man's life was uncertain and I wanted to study the Buddha's teachings. When you breathe out, you do not know whether you will breathe in again. Not even dew in the breeze disappears as quickly as man. Whether wise or foolish, old or young, it is man's lot to be ever changing. Therefore, one must prepare first for the hour of death and leave other matters till later.[19]

In 1237 Dōzen ordained his young pupil and gave him the name Zeshō-bō Renchō[m]. The youth had learned all he could from the country monks and limited library of his provincial temple. He had absorbed "the doctrines of all the writings of Shan-tao and Hōnen"[20] and had come to realize the limitations of his master, whose main Buddhist practice was to "recite 'Homage to the Buddha Amida' because that practice was widespread in Japan."[21]

Kiyozumidera was "a remote place. Moreover, although it was called a temple, there was no one well versed in Buddhist practices."[22] At sixteen Nichiren set off on a study tour.

> I traveled to study at the temples of different provinces, in Kamakura, Kyoto, at Mount Hiei, Mount Kōya, Onjōji, Tennōji, and others . . . . I had one wish: that I might learn all the teachings of the Buddha which had been brought to Japan, all the discussions by bodhisattvas and commentaries by teachers. Not only were there the Kusha, Jōjitsu, Ritsu, Hossō, Sanron, Kegon, Shingon, and Tendai schools, but also the ones called Zen and Jōdo. Since I wanted to learn at least the central teachings, even if I did not understand the complexities of doctrine of each school, I traveled extensively . . . .[23]

The first stage of the quest took Nichiren to Kamakura, the new political center of Japan, where he "heard the teachings of Jōdo and Zen,"[24] the two new schools of Buddhism with which he would later contend. Jōdo was just spreading to Kamakura: Kōmyōji was founded the year Nichiren arrived, and the construction of the giant statue of Amida called the Daibutsu had begun the year before, in 1238. Zen had been introduced in 1202 when the Jūfukuji was constructed for Eisai, and Eisai's disciples were preaching a combination of Zen meditation and esoteric Buddhist practice.

Worship of Amida was the first Buddhist practice Nichiren discarded as he pursued his investigation of Buddhist philosophy.[25]

A journey to Mount Hiei near Kyōto, site of the Enryakuji, the center of Tendai and the largest Buddhist monastery of the day, was the next step for the young priest who was attracted to the Tendai teachings.[26] He found that the established sects were chiefly controlled by the aristocracy. From the Heian period younger sons of noble families had made vocations of the priesthood so that the upper levels of the Buddhist hierarchy were closed to those without secular status. Probably Nichiren was not admitted to the circles of disciples gathered around famous teachers.[27] Thus while Nichiren could attend the public lectures he was forced to draw his own conclusions from scriptures and commentaries as he might not have done had he been directed by one of the masters. Perusal and comparison of texts filled his days as he formed scholarly habits that remained with him all his life.[28]

As he read, Nichiren became uncomfortably aware of the contradictions among the sutras and the claims of each to superiority.

> There are ten clear mirrors which should reflect the sacred teaching for this world. These are the sects called Kusha, Jōjitsu, Ritsu, Hossō, Sanron,

> Shingon, Kegon, Jōdo, Zen, and Tendai . . . . Scholars of this world think
> each of these ten mirrors reveals the Buddhist Path . . . . But, as one gains
> knowledge of them, believing they will bring one's own salvation and guide
> others as well, one finds all seven of the Mahāyāna sects praising them-
> selves. "Only my sect has the teaching. Believe in it," they say . . . . Each
> of these sects teaches that certain sutras and certain commentaries will pro-
> vide understanding of the whole Buddhist scripture and complete compre-
> hension of the Buddha's meaning . . . . But my doubts are difficult to
> dispel. When I look at this world, I see each sect praising itself, but a coun-
> try has only one king . . . . Is not the Buddhist scripture the same? Which
> sutra should one believe? Which is the king of all sutras?[29]

At last he fastened upon two scriptural passages that allayed all his
doubts. In the *Nehangyō* he read: "Follow the teaching, not men; the
meaning, not the word; true wisdom, not shallow understanding."[30] Nichiren realized he could rely on the doctrine he learned in the sutras and
that he did not need a teacher to interpret them. The *Nehangyō* convinced him of the truth of the words of the Buddha Śākyamuni in the
Muryōgikyo,[31] the introduction to the Lotus Sutra:

> I knew that the natures and desires of all living beings were not equal. As
> their natures and desires were not equal, I preached the Law variously. It
> was with tactful power that I preached the Law variously. In forty years
> and more, the truth has not been revealed yet.

Truth was to be found solely in the Lotus Sutra.
Studies completed, faith decided, Nichiren returned to Kiyozumidera
with his message.

> In order to repay my debt to the bodhisattva Kokūzō, on 1253/4/28, on the
> south side of Dōzen's worship hall at Kiyozumidera in the Tōjō district of
> the province of Awa, I first spoke to Jōken and a few others.[32]

The events of that spring morning have been dramatized over the centuries, and Nichiren Buddhists today regard this sermon as seminal in the
history of their sect. Nichiren himself did not believe his ideas were new.
He wrote:

> I am not the founder of a sect. Nor am I one of the tip leaves of the tree. I
> am not one who keeps the precepts nor yet one who breaks them but only a
> simple priest without precepts. I do not have wisdom nor yet do I lack wis-
> dom. I am an oxlike, a sheeplike man. Why have I begun to preach? I am
> merely a forerunner who began to chant "Homage to the Lotus Sutra" as
> though sleep-talking.[33]

Not new doctrine but reform of Tendai Buddhism was Nichiren's message: other scriptures should be abandoned in favor of the Lotus Sutra,
the embodiment of the absolute truth according to Tendai philosophy.

He soon made enemies of those who worshipped Amida as he taught that the teachings of the Lotus Sutra superseded those of the Amida sutras. Kagenobu, the *jitō,* was a devotee of Amida and nursed ill feeling for Nichiren's family who had been allies of the manorial lord. He was also trying to extend his prerogatives to the control of Kiyozumidera: "Tōjō Saemon Kagenobu, an evil man, hunted the tame deer kept at Kiyozumi and tried to make all the priests of the Dharma become followers of those who chant the *nenbutsu.*"[34] When this powerful local official exerted pressure on the priests to evict Nichiren, Dōzen and some of the others were sympathetic but fearful. Nichiren refused to modify his reformist stance, though urged to do so by his family and teachers.[35] "Fearing the *jitō,* they pretended to be my enemies and hate me, even though they felt sympathetic in their hearts,"[36] Nichiren wrote. In time, they slipped Nichiren out of the province to prevent Kagenobu from murdering him.

THE KAMAKURA YEARS

In 1254 Nichiren returned to Kamakura, where he lived quietly for five years, collecting a library of Buddhist scriptures and Chinese and Japanese classics, studying, preaching, and performing Tendai services with other priests in his home and in temples and homes to which he was invited.[37] He settled in Nagoe in the southeast section of the city, at the foot of the hills overlooking the Pacific Ocean.[38]

By winter of 1254 Nichiren had his first disciple, a Tendai priest named Jōben whom he had known at Mount Hiei. A year older than Nichiren and known as an outstanding student at Enryakuji, Jōben was an encouraging convert. He took the name Nisshō, borrowing one syllable of Nichiren's name, and soon sent for his twelve-year-old nephew to become Nichiren's second disciple. The boy, given the name Nichirō, became the dearest of all Nichiren's disciples, he was the son Nichiren never had.

Nichirō was the first disciple personally ordained by Nichiren. The established Buddhist sects maintained official ordination halls, such as the Tendai *kaidan* on Mount Hiei, where Nichiren probably was accepted officially into the community of monks.[39] Nichiren made no distinction between disciples who were ordained at Mount Hiei and those whom he himself ordained. It was strength of faith in the Lotus Sutra and success in converting others that mattered, not vows which might or might not be kept. Often Nichiren wrote that he and his disciples were priests "without vows *(mukai).*[40]

Nevertheless, Nichiren believed the doctrine he was preaching was a return to the original Tendai teachings, and much of his effort was directed toward Tendai priests. Those who had studied at Enryakuji and Onjōji and had read the same texts as Nichiren were most sympathetic to his ideas and were the easiest to persuade. Most of the lay converts in Kamakura were *myōshū,* lower- or middle-rank vassals of the *bakufu,* who had small landholdings and lived on their land when not on duty in Kamakura. Such lay devotees provided alms and economic support in return for spiritual guidance, and many gave shelter to Nichiren's disciples, or established chapels in their homes, thus becoming the nuclei of congregations in the eastern provinces of Suruga, Sagami, Kai, Shimōsa, Musashi, Awa, Izu, and Kōzuke.[41]

To his followers Nichiren explained that all the sutras were accommodations and preliminary teachings which prepared the way for the Lotus Sutra. He reminded them that in the Lotus Sutra the Buddha Śākyamuni promised that the Lotus would be taught to all during the last centuries of the Dharma *(mappō),*[42] and claimed that Chih-i, Miao-lo, and Saichō, the great Tendai leaders of the past, had also predicted that the Lotus Sutra would be widely taught during the *mappō.*[43]

As he read the Lotus Sutra, Nichiren chose the name by which we now know him. He kept the character *ren*[x], meaning "lotus," from his earlier religious name Renchō, and wrote before it the character *nichi*[y], "sun." The new name was a symbol of his dedication to the bodhisattva ideal, using images from similes found in the Lotus Sutra. "As the bright light of the sun and the moon can clear away all darkness and obscurity, so he who can keep to this sutra, going through the world, can lighten the darkness of all beings,"[44] Nichiren read and felt called by the Buddha to witness. He hoped to become a bodhisattva who "has well learned the bodhisattva-path and is untainted by worldly dharmas, like the lotus blossom in the water"[45] unsullied by the mud from which it grows.

Nichiren's compassion and concern were aroused by an onslaught of calamities that began in Kamakura the very year he arrived: there were plagues, droughts, famines, typhoons, fires, earthquakes, political plots, uprisings, and such terrifying astronomical events as an eclipse and a comet. Between 1254 and 1260 the era name was changed four times following the traditional belief that such name changes could influence the course of events. Nevertheless, 1258 and 1260 were the worst years of a bad decade. Famine and plague took their toll throughout Japan.[46] Nichiren, who had a literal belief in the Tendai teaching that all beings could attain Buddhahood and paradise in this very life,[47] looked on in horror as the suffering increased from year to year.

He wrote that on 1257/8/23, in the

late evening, there was an earthquake worse than any ever before experienced. On 1258/8/1, there was a typhoon; in 1259, a terrible famine; in

1260, a plague; and in 1261, an epidemic which lasted through all four seasons of the year without relief. More than half the populace died. Meanwhile, the rulers, aghast at the suffering, had various rites and services performed, following both Buddhist and non-Buddhist practices. Nevertheless, there was not the slightest sign of a result and the famine and plague worsened.[48]

The destruction brought by the earthquake, followed by years of famine and disease, left eastern Japan near ruin. "Oxen and horses lay fallen at the crossroads; skeletons were heaped in the streets. More than half the people died."[49] Buddhism seemed to be flourishing. Public ceremonies and services were common; philanthropy was increasing under the leadership of the Ritsu reform movement.[50] The common people were more involved in Buddhist practice and faith than ever before. Yet still there was suffering.

From Buddhism's introduction to Japan in the sixth century, it had been accepted as a political tool as well as a means to individual salvation. Several of the sutras, including the Lotus Sutra, were known as "nation-protecting sutras" *(chingo kokka kyō)*.[51] These sutras promise the protection of various gods to the country that reveres the sutra. Saichō, like other early Japanese Buddhist leaders, had emphasized the *chingo kokka* role of the Lotus Sutra, since it drew state support to his sect.

Nichiren, rather than reject the present world as hopelessly filled with suffering, dreamed of the accession of an ideal ruler, a wise Confucian-Buddhist king, who believed in the Dharma and would lead the country to faith.[52] Behind this concept lay the Confucian notion of rule by sages, which held that the national morality was dependent on the ruler's morality. If the ruler would convert, Nichiren felt, the country would become a true Buddhist nation. "In the world governed by the sage king, morality will prevail. In the world governed by the foolish king, immorality will triumph."[53] For Nichiren, two obligations coalesced: the Confucian duty of putting his wisdom to the use of the ruler, and the bodhisattva course of working for the salvation of all living beings. He set about composing a memorial to the *bakufu* in which he would recommend the *chingo kokka kyō* which promised to be most effective for the times: the Lotus Sutra.

The first essays Nichiren wrote were doctrinal expositions intended to explain the Dharma to a trained audience of priests. But the *Risshō ankokuron*[54] represents the type of writing in which Nichiren excelled and for which he is famous: the explication of doctrine for an individual, with anecdote, analogy, and detail chosen to appeal to that one person. The essay consists of a series of questions and answers comprising a dialogue between a Buddhist scholar and his visitor. During the conversation the scholar leads his guest to a correct understanding of the relationship between the establishment of the true Buddha Dharma *(risshō)* and the peace of the country *(ankoku)*. The dialectic form had often been used for essays in China and in earlier Japanese Buddhist doctrinal expositions.[55] Nichiren himself had used the style in some earlier compositions, but never with such skill and effect. The dramatic presentation suits Nichiren's spirit, and the lively, conversational form allows for presentation of other doctrines which may be effectively refuted.[56]

The essay was intended for Hōjō Tokiyori, who had resigned the office of regent to the shogun *(shikken)* in 1255 but continued to control the *bakufu* as head of the Hōjō clan.[57] Nichiren was shrewd about the locus of authority but perhaps less realistic about his chance of winning the *bakufu* to his position. Tokiyori was renowned for his intelligence and concern with good government and had sponsored many Zen priests and scholars, but it was unlikely that he would extend his patronage to an unknown priest who was not a member of the Buddhist hierarchy and not even a resident of any of the great temples. Nichiren had only a small congregation and few converts with secular influence.

Moreover, the position he was urging was one of repression: "If we hurry to stop alms to heretics and give alms instead to monks and nuns of the true faith, if we cleanse the kingdom of the teaching of these bandits,"[58] Japan will be transformed into a Buddhist utopia, he promised. The priests and devotees of other sects could hardly have been expected to take being branded as heretics quietly. Whatever his expectations, Nichiren was ignored. "There was no audience, I was not questioned, and my proposals were not adopted,"[59] he lamented.

The Amidists, whose faith was singled out by Nichiren for criticism as "heretical, evil teaching" and "slander of true Buddhism," soon learned of this memorial suggesting their faith be outlawed. The most prominent Jōdo priests in the anti-Nichiren movement in Kamakura, Dōkyō and Nōan,[60] challenged Nichiren to a debate, only, according to Nichiren, to be summarily defeated. Jōdo devotees fought back with slander, rumors, and ambush in the streets.[61] Six weeks after Nichiren submitted his memorial, his house on the outskirts of Kamakura was burned to the ground.

> The *nenbutsu* priests and their followers and the rulers were all in agreement, so in the middle of the night several thousand of them attacked my hut intending to murder me; but somehow I escaped harm. Since everyone was in sympathy with them, those who attacked me were not punished.[62]

For a few months Nichiren took refuge in Shimōsa province, where his convert Toki Tsunenobu lived. In the spring of 1261 he returned to Kamakura. Almost immediately he was arrested and put aboard a boat for the Izu Peninsula, across the bay to the south of Kamakura.[63] Apparently there was no trial. Nichiren believed Hōjō Shigetoki,[64] an Amidist, had instigated his exile.

Exile in Izu

For a month after being thrown upon the Izu shore, Nichiren found shelter in Kawana, a small fishing town, where the villagers were sympathetic. Funamori no Misaburō and his wife, who sheltered the exile, were "like my father and mother reborn in Izu."[65] When the *jitō* fell ill and Nichiren's prayers for him were followed by recovery, he converted, and the remainder of the two years of exile passed in relative comfort in the town of Itō.

During his exile Nichiren found in the scripture the strength he would need to face persecution for his teaching. He was impressed by two passages from the Lotus Sutra which seemed to apply to his life. In one the Buddha warns, "This scripture has many enemies even now when the Tathāgata is present. How much worse it will be after his nirvana."[66] The other foretells three types of enemies to appear "after the Buddha's passage into extinction, in a frightful and evil age": "ignorant men," "monks of twisted wisdom, their hearts sycophantic and crooked," and "prideful hermits, who say of themselves that they are treading the True Path, holding mankind cheaply because they covet profit and nourishment."[67] Nichiren recognized these three among his enemies and felt the prophecy of the sutra was being realized in his life, that he was "reading" the sutra with his every action. He exulted in his role:

> For more than 240 days, I have lived the Lotus Sutra each day and night. It is for the sake of this scripture that I was born into the world and suffer exile. It is precisely being born and suffering for the sutra which is called reading and practicing the sutra while walking, sitting, standing, and lying down . . . . Though others who were born as men exert themselves to waken the *bodhi* mind and hope for salvation in the next life, common men are diligent in their practice only two to four hours of every twenty-four. However, even when I am not conscious of thinking of the sutra, I am reading the sutra. Even when I am not looking at the sutra, I am living its words. During the *mappō* there has rarely been a person who practiced the teachings of the sutra twenty-four hours of the day, even if that practice was without conscious effort, as mine is.[68]

In Japanese Buddhist practice, a person who keeps a sutra, particularly the Lotus Sutra, always by him to read is called a *jikyōsha*, "one who keeps the sutra." Nichiren felt his ties to the Lotus Sutra were more intimate, that he was a *gyōja,* "one who lives the sutra," fulfilling its predictions in his life.

Hōjō Shigetoki, father of the regent, fell ill soon after Nichiren's banishment. Rituals and prayers brought a brief recovery, but in 1261/11, only six months after Nichiren had been sent to Izu, he died. Nichiren was sure this influenced the decision to release him on 1263/3/22: "Only Tokiyori realized the meaning of this event and he quickly arranged my freedom."[69] Whether Tokiyori might have implemented Nichiren's program will never be known, for in the eleventh month of the same year he died at the age of thirty-six. Nichiren was discouraged: "After Tokiyori passed away, I saw no hope for a good end to the situation. I felt I must flee this world as quickly as possible."[70]

He had not been home for ten years, not since he was driven away by the *jitō* Kagenobu.

> While living in Kamakura, I longed for Awa, the place where I was born. But though I was born there, the hearts of the people seemed set against me, and time passed without my traveling home.[71]

Possibly hoping he would now find sanctuary and some peace there, Nichiren returned to Kominato.

His father was dead and his mother ill. Nichiren prayed for her recovery, with a literal belief in the word of the Buddha that "this sutra is the medicine needed to cure the ills of the people of the world,"[72] and she and other villagers converted. Hoping to lead his first teacher Dōzen from his trust in Amida to faith in the Lotus Sutra, Nichiren visited Kiyozumidera, where Dōzen wept to see his pupil again but remained unconvinced. However, new converts were added to the number who had heard Nichiren's first sermon of 1253.

The number of Nichiren's enemies grew, too. On 1264/11/11, as Nichiren walked with ten of his followers along the road through Matsugahara, a part of the estates administered by Kagenobu, they were ambushed. It was just dusk.

> Arrows fell like rain and swords flashed like lightning. One of my disciples was killed and two were badly wounded. I received a blow on the forehead. There seemed to be no chance, but somehow I escaped death. My faith in the Lotus Sutra grows deeper.[73]

Again Nichiren had to flee. Probably he spent a few years preaching in Awa, Kazusa, and Shimōsa provinces.[74] The ambush had only strengthened his belief in his mission, and he announced to his disciples:

> There are many in Japan who read and study the Lotus Sutra and there are many who are beaten for coveting other men's wives or for stealing, but

there is no one else who is punished because he reveres the Lotus Sutra. None of those who claim to keep the precepts of the sutra have lived the predictions it contains. Only I read the sutra with my life.[75]

As the number of lay converts grew Nichiren began to encourage them to recite the *daimoku* (title), *Namu Myōhōrengekyō* or "Homage to the Sutra of the Lotus of the Marvelous Law," as a substitute for recitation of the *nenbutsu*.[76] The simple expression of faith was believed to suit the lesser beings of the *mappō* far better than studying difficult philosophy and keeping the rules of discipline. Reading a chapter or verse of the Lotus Sutra as a substitute for the whole had long been a part of the worship of the Lotus Sutra, based on such passages in the sutra as this:

> If again there is a man who offers a thousand millionfold world full of the seven jewels to Buddhas, great bodhisattvas, pratyekabuddhas, and arhants, the merit gained by him shall not match that of one who holds of this Scripture of the Dharma Blossom so much as a single four-foot *gāthā* [verse], for the latter's merit shall be the greatest.[77]

Nichiren's contribution was to urge the recitation as the sole practice necessary to salvation in the same way the Amidists had recommended the *nenbutsu* to their less educated followers.

The Mongol Threat

Nichiren had begun preaching again in Kamakura by early 1268 when Kublai Khan sent the first of his letters to the Japanese "king." The message, offering a delicately stated alternative between paying tribute to the Khan or suffering invasion by the Mongol forces, which had already pushed the Chinese court into exile and taken control of Korea, was taken first to the *bakufu* at Kamakura and then to the imperial court at Kyōto.

Unable to reach a consensus despite a series of frenzied conferences, the Japanese made no reply at all. Both the *bakufu* and imperial court ordered prayers to be offered at temples and shrines throughout the country. In addition, Hōjō Tokimune, the brash seventeen-year-old *shikken*, hastened plans for the defense of southwestern Japan where the brunt of an attack would fall. Expecting the invasion within months, the government mobilized the samurai and roused the people. A court noble, Konoe Motohira, wrote in his diary, "This is a unique event in Japanese history and a desperately serious one. All Japanese are appalled and despairing."[78]

Nichiren realized he had predicted just such an invasion in his memorial, *Risshō ankokuron*. Nor was his foresight ignored by his converts. As rumors excited the city, word of Nichiren's prediction reached new ears, and his reputation as a prophet swelled. The number of his followers increased in proportion.

Perhaps the person most astonished by the apparent accuracy of his prophecy was Nichiren himself. In the light of this singular threat of foreign invasion, Nichiren reviewed the *Risshō ankokuron* and extended his interpretations of the scriptures. With varying measures of humility and vaunt he sought to bring his predictions to the attention of prominent political and religious leaders. Again no one acknowledged his efforts.

Months passed. Nearly two years after the initial letter another threatening message from the Mongols was delivered by Korean messengers, and a second panic ensued. Nichiren desperately recopied his *Risshō ankokuron* and dispatched it to Taira Yoritsuna,[79] asking him to bring it to Tokimune's attention. He added a preface: "I submit this again as I did six years ago. So far my predictions have proven themselves. Will the future not bear me out as well? This essay contains prophecy."[80]

As Nichiren's anxiety grew, he renewed the attack on Hōnen's Amidist teachings begun in the *Risshō ankokuron* and now added Zen and Ritsu practice to his list of heresies which were causes of the disasters crushing Japan.[81] In 1271 the Kantō plain, the eastern area of Honshū, was devastated by drought, and the *bakufu* ordered the Shingon-Ritsu priest Ninshō[82] to perform rites for rain. Soon Ninshō, Dōkyō, and other priests were complaining to the *bakufu:* Nichiren had challenged them to produce rain within the month.[83] If rain fell, he had vowed to become Ninshō's disciple. If not, they were to become devotees of the Lotus Sutra. Although Ninshō gathered hundreds of priests for services, there was no rain. Humiliated, Ninshō became one of Nichiren's most active enemies; Nichiren was to see his hand in nearly every repression of his teaching.

A letter from the priest Gyōbin,[84] in 1271, accused Nichiren and his followers of ten misdeeds, including teaching that all sutras except the Lotus Sutra were useless in finding salvation, teaching that the precepts were deceptive and led to rebirth in hell, teaching that Zen practice would only increase the burden of bad karma, teaching that the *nenbutsu* would lead to rebirth in hell, burning images of Amida and Kannon and tossing others into the river, harboring a band of rebels, and gathering weapons and going about armed.

Evidently Nichiren's disciples were translating his words into action. Nichiren responded to Gyōbin with a challenge to debate before *bakufu* arbitrators.[85] He did not deny any of the charges. Even bearing arms, he insisted, was necessary in order to defend the Lotus Sutra. However, in preparation for war the *bakufu* had ordered suppression of unruly elements in lands held by *bakufu* retainers.[86] They found Nichiren and his teachings clearly seditious.

Exile to Sado

Soldiers took Nichiren into custody in the late afternoon of 9/12:

> I was led through the alleys of Kamakura like a traitor. They destroyed the room in my hut in which I enshrined the teachings of the Buddha and where I worshipped Śākyamuni. Several of them trampled the statue of Buddha and the scrolls of the scriptures into the mud. They even took the scrolls of the Lotus Sutra which I held and beat me with them. There had been no provocation which should have led to this; I had committed no crime. I was guilty only of spreading the Lotus Sutra.[87]

Taken before Taira Yoritsuna, Nichiren announced:

> In casting me aside, Japan throws down its pillar of support. Any day there will be rebellion and fighting and warriors from other countries will come and kill and take prisoners. The Kenchōji, Jūfukuji, Gokurakuji, Daibutsu, Chōrakuji—all the *nenbutsu* and Zen temples—should be burned to the ground and their priests beheaded at Yuigahama, or Japan will be destroyed.[88]

Sentenced to exile on the island of Sado, Nichiren was led out of Kamakura at two in the morning.[89] The road to Echi, where they would break the journey, led by the execution grounds at Tatsunokuchi, and Nichiren was convinced his journey would end there.[90] When they passed by, he felt a miracle had stayed the hand of the executioner.[91]

While Nichiren was held at Echi, the *bakufu* sought out his followers and imprisoned or exiled them.[92] "The cowardly gave up their faith and apostatized."[93] Some took whole congregations with them: "The disciples called Shōbō, Notobō, and Nagoeama and others were cowards at heart and foolish, though they called themselves wise. When they learned of my arrest, they led many others to give up their faith."[94] Many who had been faithful for years now turned their backs.[95]

In Echi, Nichiren pondered the meaning of his persecution and exile. Three days after his arrest he wrote to encourage his disciples in Kamakura.

> It is natural for you to grieve, but you must not. This was certain to happen. I had expected it from the start and was disappointed that I was not beheaded long ago. If I had been martyred in a past life for the sake of the Lotus Sutra, I would not have been born as such a miserable being in this world. As the sutra explains, "Again and again he will be cast out and many times censured," and by that his grave sins will be erased and he will achieve Buddhahood. Therefore, I must suffer.
>
> It is through my punishment by the government that my faith in the Lotus Sutra is revealed. When the moon disappears, we know it will fill

again; when the tides wane there is no doubt they will wax. Just so do I know that if I am persecuted, I have virtue. Why should anyone grieve?[96]

It was a walk of twelve days for Nichiren and his guard from Echi to the harbor of Teradomari. The journey would end at the remote island of Sado, miles from the northern coast of Honshū and weeks of travel from Kamakura. Already winter storms had blown up, and it was more than a week before the sea was calm enough to sail.

When at last they were able to cross to Sado, Nichiren was left in an abandoned temple in a desolate graveyard called Tsukahara. He and his few companions were ill-equipped to survive the winter.[97]

> When I was living in Kamakura in Shimōsa, I imagined the change of seasons must be the same in all the provinces, but during the two months I have been in the northern province of Sado, the freezing winds have blown continually and, while there are still days when there is no frost or snow, we never see the sunshine. In this very life I am experiencing the suffering of the eight cold hells. Here the hearts of men are like those of animals. They know neither ruler, lord, nor parent. How could they tell the difference between heresy and truth, between good teachers and bad . . . . You can ask the man I am sending back about the countryside here and about the place where I am living. I cannot describe it.[98]

At first the aging Nichiren found no sympathy among the local farmers and fishermen.

> The distance between Kamakura in Sagami and this northern country of Sado is more than one thousand leagues. They are further separated by mountains and sea, the mountains craggy and the sea rough. Wind and rain never cease. The mountains are full of robbers; the seas abound in pirates. In each house and each inn, the hearts of the people are savage as tigers or wild dogs. I imagine I am suffering the pain of the three evil destinies in this very life.[99]

Even in such adverse circumstances, however, Nichiren managed to make new friends and win converts; gradually his confidence and spirits returned. Two months after he arrived on Sado, he was so well known Amidist priests challenged him to debate. In 1272, "on the sixteenth and seventeenth of the first month, several hundred Amidists came to my home, led by the priest Inshōbō, their pillar and support."[100] Nichiren must have turned the debate to his own advantage, for soon he had a number of followers on Sado.[101]

In the next month another prediction made in the *Risshō ankokuron* proved accurate, further restoring Nichiren's confidence in his teaching. On 2/11, Tokimune learned that his illegitimate elder brother, Hōjō

Tokisuke, was plotting against him. Tokimune quickly moved to quash the rebellion and execute the leaders, but Hōjō had fought Hōjō, fulfilling the prophecy of internal rebellion and internecine fighting Nichiren had found in the sutras.

Not long after, Nichiren's imprisoned followers were released. Nichiren believed the abortive uprising to be the cause of their pardon.

> On the twelfth of the ninth month I was sentenced; on the eleventh of the second month of the next year there was a rebellion and military men whose duty it was to keep peace in Japan were put to death. This was punishment from heaven. Amazed by this the military government pardoned my disciples.[102]

In Kamakura the disciples renewed their preaching and, against Nichiren's wishes, their efforts to obtain his release.[103] Several disciples and lay supporters from the Kantō area felt it safe to travel to Sado and others sent servants.[104] In return, Nichiren dispatched a steady stream of letters and essays filled with sermons and encouragement.

After six months on Sado, Nichiren was moved to the town Ichinosawa and the home of Ichinosawa *nyūdō* (lay priest), a well-to-do farmer and Amidist. The move, which occurred after the rebellion of Tokisuke, may have reflected the easing of official attitudes against Nichiren. Soon he had worried them again, however. Although he never managed to convert Ichinosawa, Nichiren won many others and began to seem to be a threat again. Nichiren believed his old nemesis Ninshō instigated the warning of 1272 sent to those in charge at Sado to keep closer watch on Nichiren and his adherents and their plots.[105]

Although Nichiren still had many enemies, sentiment in Kamakura mellowed somewhat after the thwarted Tokisuke rebellion. The disciples made influential converts. One of these may have been Hōjō Tokimori, a minor member of the ruling clan. Early in 1274 this man, known as Lord Migenta, sent Nichiren a pair of swords as testament to his faith. Nichiren responded promptly as usual.

> Well now, I am the most unshakable man in Japan. I have never stopped warning that faith in Yakushi, Dainichi, and Amida, whom you have held dearer than lord or parent, would lead to the disasters foretold by the sutras, to the ruin of the people and the country, and to descent into hell in the next life. For this I have suffered much. I was a moth flying into the fire; a mouse running in front of the cat . . . . Stones are pulverized because they contain jewels; deer are killed for their hide and meat; fish are caught for their flavors . . . . Because I am the one who lives the Lotus Sutra, I have three kinds of enemies and I suffer at their hands. For you to become my disciple is an unexpected boon; there must have been karmic

> causes. If you believe well and truly, you will surely be born in the Vulture
> Peak paradise.
>
> You have sent me an offering of long and short swords . . . . When my
> lord wore them, they were instruments of destruction, but now they serve
> the Buddha for good.[106]

Word of pardon was already on its way as the swords arrived. Issued on
2/14, the pardon reached Sado on 3/8.[107] Nichiren was on his way back
to Kamakura on the thirteenth, once more hoping that he would be heed-
ed and Japan saved.[108]

RETREAT TO MINOBU

On 1274/3/16, Nichiren and the disciples pardoned with him were
greeted in Kamakura by those who had worked for their release. Three
years had passed since most had seen Nichiren. Followers flocked to him.

Within three weeks Nichiren was summoned by the *bakufu*. Taira Yoritsuna, head of the retainers' bureau and chief administrator of the Hōjō household, seemed ready to listen at last.

> On the eighth of the fourth month I was summoned by Taira no Yoritsuna.
> I told him that, since I had been born in the land of the emperor, I must act
> according to his law, but I could not accept it in my heart or mind. There is
> no doubt that the *nenbutsu* leads to hell or that Zen is the work of devils.
> And the Shingon rituals cannot be expected to ensure the defeat of the pow-
> erful Mongol nation.[109]

Yoritsuna would seem to have agreed with Nichiren's prediction that
the Mongol invasion, which had been expected momentarily since 1268,
would come within the year, but he and Nichiren could not agree on the
defensive action most necessary. For Yoritsuna the problem was political, diplomatic, and military. For Nichiren it was religious only: the invasion was to be punishment for heresy; only a return to the true religion
could avert it. Nichiren cited the defeat of the former Emperor Gotoba,
backed by Shingon rites and prayers but defeated nonetheless, in the
Jōkyū rebellion of 1221. "Heaven forbid that the Shingon teachers be
trusted to defeat the Mongols. If their rites are performed worse troubles
will befall us."[110]

To have supported the war effort with prayers and ritual, as did the
other sects, would have meant peace in his old age, influence, and official recognition of his teachings, but Nichiren could not compromise,
and Yoritsuna, with invasion threatening, could hardly have considered
outlawing those sects which were cooperating.

"Since they would not heed my words, I was powerless,"[111] Nichiren
wrote. He was discouraged and he was also afraid. All his predictions

based on the sutras had been borne out. He had no doubt that Japan would be crushed by the Mongols.

Counting this his third warning as a loyal Confucian to his ruler, Nichiren prepared to follow the precedent such Confucian ministers had set and retire to the mountains.[112] On 5/12, two months after his triumphant return, he left Kamakura alone with no destination in mind. For five days he traveled west along the Tōkaidō, spending the night of the seventeenth with Nanbu Sanenaga, Lord of Hakii in the Minobu district. To Toki he wrote: I have become a lone wanderer. If ever I do settle somewhere, we shall see each other again."[113] Nanbu persuaded him to stay and built a hermitage on Mount Minobu which became Nichiren's home for the last nine years of his life.

At first Nichiren was alone. He sent away the followers who wanted him to return to Kamakura.[114] Soon, however, converts from the nearby provinces began sending alms, visiting, and staying for instruction; within a few months there were forty to sixty disciples at Minobu.[115] Weakened by years of exile and sobered by the latest frustration of his hopes, Nichiren realized he had at most a few years left to preach the Lotus Sutra.

In 1274/10, five months after Nichiren retired to Mount Minobu, the Mongols invaded Japan. Their forces easily captured the small islands of Tsushima and Iki, slaughtering peasants and samurai defenders. When invasion of the main islands began at Hakata in Kyūshū, the Japanese were no match for the battle-seasoned Mongols, but a typhoon, seemingly the answer to months of prayer, sank a large part of the invaders' fleet and sent the rest back to Korea to recoup the losses and plan a second attack.[116]

The invasion fulfilled Nichiren's prophecy and promised punishment for the heretics against whom he had long inveighed. He even called the invaders saints, instruments of heaven.[117] The Mongols were merely the agents of destruction; the cause of it was the Japanese heretics. Still Nichiren feared for the safety of his believers: "Next time they attack, destruction will not be limited. Kamakura and Kyoto will fall like Iki and Tsushima. Before that happens, prepare yourselves and flee somewhere,"[118] he warned. Nichiren's time during his last years was devoted to helping various lay devotees cope with persecution by family, feudal lords, or governmental officials. The conflicts of secular and religious loyalties and the bloody competition between competing Buddhist factions in the Kamakura period come to life in the Minobu period letters.

The problems of Ikegami Munenaka, a samurai who lived in Musashi province, illustrate the pressures on Nichiren's converts in an era of strongly autocratic family organization. The father was an adherent of

Ninshō and insisted his sons accept his faith. Munenaka was equally anxious that his father convert to Nichiren's teachings. Twice the father disinherited Munenaka in favor of a younger son. Nichiren asserted that religious principles outweigh secular ones: true filial behavior consists of disobedience in cases of conflict between parental orders and religious precepts.[119]

Shijō Yorimoto was similarly endangered with becoming an outcast in feudal society. He was a hereditary retainer of Ema Mitsutoki of Nagoe and was converted by Nichiren during the latter's banishment to the Izu Peninsula.[120] In 1271, when Nichiren was sent to Sado and many of his followers were disinherited or lost their feudal ranks, Yorimoto's lord protected him and kept him in his service. Despite this protection, or because of the jealousy it aroused, quarrels between Yorimoto and other Ema retainers recurred during the 1270s. Yorimoto was ready to leave Ema's service,[121] but Nichiren persuaded him to repay his debt by converting his lord. True loyalty, Nichiren wrote, is not limited to this life but extends into the next: Yorimoto must help save Mitsutoki from rebirth in hell.[122]

A third instance of persecution illustrates the conflict between religious factions in Kamakura-era Japan. During the late 1270s Nichiren's lay converts increased rapidly, forming congregations and becoming more visible; pressure on the followers increased accordingly. The worst incident was the Atsuhara *hōnan* ("religious persecution") of 1279. For several years the Tendai Amidists at Ryūsenji, Jissōji, and Shijūkuin[123] and resident priests who were disciples of Nichiren had been fighting for control of the temples and their congregations.[124] After several years of intrigue within the temples and violence which involved both priests and lay believers, a series of petitions and counterpetitions were presented to the *jitō*.[125] Finally, twenty of Nichiren's followers, all farmers, were arrested, probably for violence rather than for religious beliefs, and taken to Kamakura, where several of the peasants were executed. In his letters Nichiren was careful to treat the *hōnan* as an attack on all believers, for he understood how opposition can increase the tenacity of faith.

The second Mongol attack was delayed until 1281, by which time the Japanese had completed a defense wall, trained soldiers to man it, and constructed a fleet of small warships. The invasion came in late spring. For some weeks the Japanese held the invaders at bay, until a typhoon again swept them away.

There are few letters to show Nichiren's reactions to the *kamikaze*. In one he snappishly asks why Kublai Khan's head had not been taken if the Japanese had really won the battle and points out that the danger is not over. Another attack will come, and another, until Japan converts to the

True Teaching or is destroyed: "When they come from that country, Japan will be like a frog in a snake's mouth or a carp or tuna on a chopping block."[126]

Nichiren's health was failing. In 1277 he had been stricken by a debilitating diarrhea, which recurred intermittently. In 1281 he wrote:

> For eight years I have been wasting away. My body has grown weak and my mind senile. This year, especially, since spring I have had spells of illness. During the autumn and winter my health deteriorated steadily and every night I was worse. For ten days I have been almost unable to eat. Snow has piled up and the winter cold grips us here. My body is cold as a stone and my spirit like ice.[127]

In the ninth month of 1282 Nichiren was persuaded to leave Minobu. Probably the destination was a hot spring in Hitachi. Accompanied by Hakii's son and riding Hakii's horse, he made his way to Ikegami. From there Nichiren wrote Hakii: "I had intended to return to Minobu along this road, but my suffering makes that uncertain . . . . Wherever I die, see that I am buried at Minobu."[128]

On 10/8 Nichiren called together six disciples—Nisshō, Nichirō, Nikkō, Nikō, Nitchō, and Nichiji—to ask them to cooperate in leading his followers. Around eight in the morning on the thirteenth he died. He was cremated and his bones sent to Minobu. His disciples scattered to preach and teach.

NOTES

1. The traditionally accepted date first appeared in *Goden dodai,* the earliest biography of Nichiren, written by Nichidō (1283–1341), where it is given as "the sixteenth day of the second month of the first year of Jōō." However, the change of era name took place on 4/13 that year, so that 2/16 would have been in the fourth year of Jōkyū. It seems safe to assume this birthdate was assigned after Nichiren's death. Tamura Yoshirō and Miyazaki Eishū, eds., *Kōza Nichiren,* volume 2, *Nichiren no shōgai to shisō* (Tokyo: Shunshūsha, 1972), p. 18.
2. *Sado gokangi shō*[a], STH, p. 511. The term Nichiren uses to characterize his social class, *sendara,* corresponds to the Sanskrit *caṇḍāla,* the untouchable caste, which includes those who take life or deal with animal products. Hirata Atsutane, writing in the early nineteenth century (see note 11, this chapter), interpreted Nichiren's term *sendara* to mean *eta,* the Japanese outcaste class. Contemporary scholars are unanimous in their contention that Nichiren was exaggerating the lowliness of his origins to establish sympathy with his followers.
3. *Sado gosho*[b], STH, p. 614.
4. *Honzon mondō shō*[c], STH, p. 1580.
5. *Nakaoki nyūdō goshōsoku*[d], STH, p. 1714. Later embellishments added to Nichiren's family tree include that of the mid-Muromachi *Nichiren shōnin chūgasan*[e], which claims Nichiren's father was Nukina Shigetada, the grandson of a Heike samurai from Tōtōmi province, who was exiled to Awa. In mid-Edo the

Honge betsuzu bussō ryūki[f] traced Nichiren's ancestry still farther back to Fujiwara Fuyutsugu. Other biographies purport to trace the family to the imperial
family. Kino Kazuyoshi, *Hairyū no michi* (Kyoto: Tankōsha, 1973), pp. 60–61.

6.   Kino, *Hairyū,* p. 60.

7.   Takagi Yutaka, *Nichiren to sono montei* (Tokyo: Kōbundō, 1965), pp. 1–2.

8.   See Jeffrey P. Mass, *Warrior Government in Early Medieval Japan* (New
Haven, Connecticut: Yale University Press, 1974); *idem, "Jitō* Land Possession
in the Thirteenth Century: The Case of *Shitaji Chūbun,"* in John W. Hall and
Jeffrey P. Mass, eds., *Medieval Japan: Essays in Institutional History* (New
Haven, Connecticut: Yale University Press, 1974), pp. 157–183, for a description
of this conflict which compounded many of the quarrels attributed to religious
differences in the thirteenth century.

9.   Nichiren expressed only a "great debt," for "her kind favor" *(Niiama gozen
gohenji*[g], *STH,* p. 869), but commentators suggest that she sponsored Nichiren's
studies at Kiyozumidera.

10.   Takagi Yutaka, *Nichiren: Sono kōdō to shisō* (Tokyo: Hyōronsha, 1970), p. 15.

11.   For example, even the national studies scholar Hirata Atsutane: (1771–1843)
praised Nichiren: "Was he not an honest priest! It is striking that he described
his origins just as they were with no dissimulation . . . . Because the original in-
tent of Buddhism was to revere those who were strong in virtue whether they
were noble or humble men, Nichiren was not the least ashamed of being the child
of *eta* . . . . This is based on the original concept of Buddhism: in the Buddha
Dharma there is no aristocrat and no commoner. Not understanding this, men
have concocted various lineages for Nichiren. In the end, this elevation of his
status can be called subversion by his own supporters." Cited in Tamura Yoshirō, *Yogenja no bukkyō* (Tokyo: Chikuma shobō, 1967), p. 9. Adherents of Nichiren Shōshū and other Nichiren sects in the twentieth century also have been
attracted by the commoner who achieved so much.

12.   *Honzon mondō sho, STH,* p. 1580.

13.   Nichiren's effort to convert his teacher to his own understanding of Buddhism
continued unsuccessfully until Dōzen's death in 1276. In *Hōonshō*[h], *STH,* pp.
1192–1250, Nichiren explained that his unflagging desire to convert Dōzen arose
from his sense of debt to his master; he had tried to repay the debt not by bowing
to Dōzen's mistaken beliefs but by leading him toward salvation.

14.   Kanazawa Bunko holds a copy of *Juketsu endaragi shūtōketsu*[i], an early
Japanese Tendai essay on the innate Buddha nature written by Enchin, which
was copied by Nichiren in the cell of his master Dōzen in 1238.

15.   The three sutras which treat Amida and the Western Pure Land Paradise *(jōdo)*
are *Muryōjukyō, Amidakyō,* and *Kanmuryōjukyō.* In these sutras the Buddha
Śākyamuni reveals the vows of Amida to establish a land of bliss wherein all beings can be freed from their suffering and to refuse nirvana until he has led
everyone to salvation. Tendai doctrine is all-encompassing and many Tendai
priests worshipped Amida as well as performing other religious practices. However, the *nenbutsu,* or recitation of Amida's name in hope of rebirth in his western paradise, was banned at Enryakuji in 1240, and a division into two sects,
Tendai and Jōdo, was well under way in Nichiren's time.

16.   The third chief priest of the Tendai sect in Japan, Ennin (792–862), had
emphasized the esoteric teachings which he had studied in China. After his death
a split occurred between the two main Tendai temples, Enryakuji and Onjōji.
The Enryakuji branch became the Sanmon, or Mountain, Order, while the Onjōji branch was called the Jimon, or Church, Order. The split stemmed mainly

from a succession dispute, but the divisive doctrinal point was the amount of emphasis to be given the mystic, esoteric side of Buddhism, which Ennin had made predominant at Enryakuji. Kiyozumidera is now a Shingon temple.

17.   *Zenmui sanzō shō*[j], *STH,* p. 473.

18.   Nichiren may also have studied under the two monks, Gijō and Jōken. They were among his later converts at Kiyozumidera and were the recipients of several of Nichiren's letters (for example, *Kekajōju gosho*[k], *STH,* p. 1500, and *Honzon mondōshō, STH,* p. 1573).

19.   *Myōhō amagozen gohenji*[l], *STH,* 1535.

20.   *Zenmui sanzō shō, STH,* p. 475. Shan-tao (613–681), a Chinese patriarch of the Pure Land sect, is regarded by Amidists in Japan as an incarnation of Amida, and his works are accepted as having scriptural authority. Hōnen (1133–1212), founded the Japanese Jōdo, or Pure Land, sect of Amidism.

21.   *Nanjō Hyōeshichirō dono gohenji*[n], *STH,* p. 1883.

22.   *Honzon mondōshō, STH,* p. 1580.

23.   *Myōhō bikuni gohenji*[o], *STH,* p. 1553.

24.   *Rakan nado o yaburu gosho*[p], *STH,* p. 1283.

25.   His first doctrinal treatise, *Kaitai sokushin jōbutsugi*[q] (*STH,* p. 1), dismisses worship of Amida as a provisional Mahāyāna teaching intended solely to lead those of inferior understanding and ability to the true teaching found in the Lotus Sutra.

26.   Sources for Nichiren's years of study are scarce. He mentions visits to temples of various sects in Kyōto and Nara. In 1251, in Kyōto, he was permitted to copy an esoteric text, the *Gorin kuji mitsu shaku*[r] by Kakuban. The *Riseiin kechimyaku*[s] in the Kanazawa Bunko includes the name Nichiren among those given Shingon ordination. Ōno Tatsunosuke, *Nichiren* (Tokyo: Yoshikawa Kōbunkan, 1958), pp. 30–31.

     The activities of the various sects in Kyōto surely left their mark on Nichiren during his years of study. The phenomenal growth of the worship of Amida, attested by numerous reprintings of Amidist works, and the corresponding increase of anti-Amidist sentiment; the growth of Zen under Dōgen, of whom Nichiren does not seem to have heard, and under Rankei Dōryū and Enni, to whom he refers in his letters; conflicts between and within the established sects over the *nenbutsu;* the revival of the Ritsu (Vinaya) school under Eizon and his disciple Ninshō; the sermons of the Agui school of popularizers of Buddhism; and the activities of pilgrims and preachers surrounded him during the 1240s. Takagi, *Nichiren: sono kōdō to shisō,* pp. 26–29.

27.   Takagi, *Nichiren: Sono kōdō to shisō,* pp. 31–33.

28.   Copies of the Lotus Sutra and various other scriptures in Nichiren's hand are kept at Hokekyōji, a temple established after Nichiren's death in the home of Toki Tsunenobu, a lay disciple in Nakayama. The number of his letters which request copies of various books or lament the losses incurred in his peripatetic life indicate the effort Nichiren put into keeping his library at hand, and the sheer number of historical writings and anecdotes as well as sutras and religious commentaries Nichiren cited in later writings testifies to his wide reading.

29.   *Hōonshō, STH,* pp. 1193–1194.

30.   This sutra presents the doctrine that the *dharmakāya,* the absolute principle, is everlasting and that all beings possess the Buddha-nature. The Tendai sect regards both the Lotus Sutra and the *Nehangyō* as the final and ultimate teaching of the Buddha.

31.   The *Muryōgikyō* and *Kanfugenkyō* have long been considered the introduction

and conclusion to the Lotus Sutra. The translation is from Katō Bunnō et al., trans., *The Threefold Lotus Sutra* (New York: Weatherhill, 1975), p. 14; T9, p. 386b.

32. *Kiyozumidera daishūchū*[t], *STH*, p. 1134.

33. *Myōmitsu shōnin goshōsoku*[u], *STH*, p. 1165.

34. *Kiyozumidera daishūchū*, *STH*, p. 1135.

35. *Ōshajō*[v], *STH*, p. 915. According to this letter, Nichiren's parents "wrung their hands and admonished," while his teacher repudiated him (p. 917).

36. *Honzon mondōshō*, *STH*, p. 1585.

37. See *Musashi dono goshōsoku*[w], *STH*, p. 87, for some of Nichiren's activities during this period.

38. *Ōshajō*, *STH*, p. 917.

39. When Buddhism was first introduced into Japan in the sixth century, the number of priests was controlled by the government so as not to undermine the economy. One became a priest or nun by taking vows at the designated ordination hall *(kaidan)*, the first of which was established in 754 at the Tōdaiji. The vows and ceremony differed from sect to sect, but all made the taking of vows a prerequisite for becoming a priest and for salvation. As the governmental control of religion eased, it became easier to take the vows, although the established sects still maintained *kaidan*.

40. This phrase of Nichiren's brought him into conflict particularly with Ninshō (1217–1303), a disciple of Eizon (1201–1290), who was working to revive the *vinaya* as the foundation for the religious life.

41. Takagi Yutaka devotes a chapter of *Nichiren to sono montei* (pp. 45–81) to a detailed account of Nichiren's lay followers. The first is believed to have been the samurai Toki Tsunenobu. One hundred sixty-two lay followers, among them forty-nine women, can be identified by name from Nichiren's writings.

42. Lotus Sutra, chapter 13, "Fortitude." The *mappō* is a period of degeneracy when there is no practice of Buddhism and no enlightenment. See chapter 2 for a discussion of Nichiren's beliefs about the stages of the Dharma.

43. Ōno, *Nichiren*, p. 50. Chih-i (538–597) is considered the founder of the T'ien-t'ai sect in China. Miao-lo (Chan-jan, 711–782) was the ninth patriarch of the sect. Saichō (747–822) was the founder of Tendai in Japan.

44. Chapter 21, "Supernatural Powers of the Tathāgata," T9, p. 52b. See Appendix E herein for a list of chapters of the Lotus Sutra.

45. Chapter 15, "Welling up out of the Earth," T9, p. 42a.

46. The *Azuma kagami* records this series of disasters:
"1254-1-10:   West wind fierce; several hundreds of houses between the harbor and Nagoe were destroyed by fire.
    6-16:   Eclipse of the moon.
    7-1:   The worst winds and rain in twenty years.
    9-4:   Terrible destruction caused by continuing rain; rites held to stop torrents.
"1256-2-29:   Hard rain, floods, lightning and thunder.
    3-6:   Great fire.
    6-7:   Heavy rain.
    6-14:   In midmorning a bright light about five feet in diameter appeared in the sky.
    6-26:   The *bakufu* ordered rites performed, fearful of the numerous mysterious astronomical occurrences.

8-6:   Violent winds, floods, landslides. Many killed. Great destruction of crops. Many suffering from inflamed pustules.

9-1:   Shōgun beset by inflamed lesions. Disease spreading like an explosion. Reading and lectures on the *Ninnōkyō* performed at each temple to control the plague. High officials in the *bakufu* all ill.

10-5:   Era name changed from Kenchō to Kōgen in an attempt to control the calamitous events.

11-22:   Tokiyori handed over office of regent to Nagatoki.

11-23:   Tokiyori took orders at Saimyōji at age twenty-nine.

12-11:   Fierce winds from north. Several temples in Kamakura burn to the ground.

"1257-3-14:   Era name changed from Kōgen to Shōka.

5-18:   Earthquake around midnight.

8-23:   Earthquake around 8 P.M. No shrine or temple left standing in Kamakura. Landslides, houses collapsed, the earth opened and water gushed out or flames burned up with a blue glow.

8-25:   Five or six small tremors. Rites held.

9-4:   Earthquake at about 4 P.M. In the twenty-three days since the main quake tremors have not ceased.

10-13:   Thunder and lightning at night, continuing all night.

10-15:   Heavy rain and thunder during the night. Earthquake around 2 A.M.

11-22:   Wakanomiya, the main street of Kamakura, destroyed by fire.

"1258-1-17:   Mansions burn in Kamakura. Fanned by fierce winds, the flames spread through the city into the mountains behind, destroying the Jūfukuji. Much of the population burned to death.

8-1:   Fierce wind and rain destroyed fields and paddies.

8-28:   Shooting star of about four feet in length appeared.

9-2:   Heavy rain and wind all day.

10-16:   Great rains, floods.

"1259:   Famine, plague, death. Change of era name.

"1260-3-14:   Red sun during the day.

3-15:   Red sun.

3-25:   Strong earthquake at dawn.

4-29:   Great fire in Kamakura soon after midnight.

6-1:   Typhoon, driving rain, floods. All the houses along the river washed away. Many killed in landslides.

6-5:   Rain. Prayers to end rains."

Cited in Nakajima Shōshi, *Nichiren* (Tokyo: San'ichi shobō, 1970), pp. 64–65, and Kino Kazuyoshi and Umehara Takeshi, *Eien no inochi* (Tokyo: Kadokawa shoten, 1969), pp. 35–38.

47.   In *Shugo kokka ron*[z], *STH*, p. 89, Nichiren wrote: "Anyone who practices Buddhism and believes in the salvation promised by the Lotus Sutra should not seek rebirth in other places. Wherever there lives a person who practices the Lotus Sutra, that place is paradise." Tendai doctrine emphasizes the idea of mutual identification of all dharmas. When this is applied to the religious life, the everyday life of the layman is the life of the Buddha.

48.   *Ankokuron gokan yurai*[aa], *STH*, pp. 421–422.

49.   *Risshō ankokuron*[ab], *STH*, p. 209.

50.   Ninshō had come to Kamakura in 1252.

51.   The *Konkōmyōkyō* promises the protection of the four heavenly kings to the

nation which reveres it. Nichiren often cited the passage of this sutra which describes the divine protection accorded the ruler who achieves his position as karmic reward for converting to the true Dharma and the disasters that befall the ruler who does not believe. Readings from another *chingo kokka kyō*, the *Ninnōkyō*, were held as rites for peace and security as early as the Nara period. This sutra and the *Yakushikyō* describe seven types of disasters which befall nonbelieving countries. The Lotus Sutra was especially revered, and, because it was ranked first in the Tendai classification, became even more valued after Saichō founded his monastery on Mount Hiei. See the translation of *Risshō ankokuron* in Part II for Nichiren's citations from these sutras.

52. Miyazaki Eishū and Motai Kyōkō, eds., *Nichiren shōnin kenkyū* (Kyoto: Heirakuji shoten, 1972), p. 119.

53. *Kaimokushō*[ac], *STH*, p. 535.

54. *STH*, p. 209.

55. Takagi, *Nichiren: Sono kōdō to shisō*, p. 73.

56. It is interesting to note in passing that one of the sentences often cited by twentieth-century nationalists who viewed Nichiren as a precursor, "First we must pray for the nation and then establish the Buddha Dharma," is spoken by the visitor whose view Nichiren is correcting. It inverts Nichiren's goals; he sought to establish the Buddha Dharma and believed peace would follow.

57. Tokiyori (1227–1263) became *shikken* in 1246. Under his leadership the regency became the most powerful office in the *bakufu*, combining political power with the private authority of the head of the extensive Hōjō clan. Practically all *bakufu* offices were held by Hōjō family. As informal meetings of the Hōjō absorbed the decision-making functions of the government from the Council of State, the Hōjō control became increasingly authoritarian. In 1256 Tokiyori resigned his office in the first systematic transfer of that post. His young son, Tokimune, became regent, and Hōjō Nagatoki was made his guardian. Tokiyori, however, retained control of the *bakufu* until his death in 1263.

58. *Risshō ankokuron, STH*, p. 209.

59. *Gezan goshōsoku*[ad], *STH*, p. 1330.

60. Dōa Dōkyō of the Shinzenkōji was a disciple of Kakumyō, a disciple of Hōnen. He and Nōan of the Chōanji, of whom nothing more is known, led the Jōdo movement in Kamakura.

61. *Rodan tekitai gosho*[ae], *STH*, p. 274.

62. *Gezan goshōsoku, STH*, p. 1330.

63. *Hōonshō, STH*, p. 1192, and *Ichinotani nyūdō gosho*[af], *STH*, p. 989, describe Nichiren's arrest and banishment. It is unclear whether the date, 5/12, given in *Rondan tekitai gosho* is the date of arrest, banishment, embarkation, or debarkation.

64. Shigetoki (1198–1261) had retired from his post as *rensho*, or deputy to the *shikken*, in 1256. At his temple-villa, the Gokurakuji, located on the outskirts of Kamakura, he gave political counsel and listened to priestly advice on how to attain salvation. He did not recite the *nenbutsu* as a "sole practice" as some priests were recommending but seems to have had eclectic religious interests. His son Nagatoki was coregent in 1261. See Carl Steenstrup, "The Gokurakuji Letter," *Monumenta Nipponica* 32 (Spring, 1977):5.

   In *Myōhō bikuni gohenji, STH*, p. 1559, Nichiren wrote: "The *nenbutsu* believers, hearing my words, plotted to kill me. When that failed, Shigetoki of the Gokurakuji influenced his son Nagatoki to exile me to Izu." Several modern Nichiren scholars surmise that it was Nichiren's threats of invasion and rebellion that decided the *bakufu* to remove him. He was an agitator, and the *bakufu*'s role was that of peace-keeper. See Takagi, *Nichiren: Sono kōdō to shisō,* pp. 77–79, for a discussion.

65.   *Funamori no Misaburōgari gosho*[ag], *STH,* p. 229.

66.   Chapter 10, "Preachers of Dharma," T9, p. 31b.

67.   Chapter 13, "Fortitude," T9, p. 36bc.

68.   *Shionshō*[ah], *STH,* pp. 246–247.

69.   *Rakan nado o yaburu gosho, STH,* p. 1286.

70.   Ibid., p. 1286.

71.   *Kōnichibō gosho*[ai], *STH,* p. 1152.

72.   Lotus Sutra, chapter 16, "Life-span of the Tathāgata," contains a parable in which a father resorts to apparent deceit to induce his sons to take the medicine which will save their lives. Nichiren refers to this healing in *Kaen jōgō gosho*[aj], *STH,* p. 861, translated in Part II, herein.

73.   *Nanjō Hyōeshichirō dono gosho*[ak], *STH,* p. 326.

74.   Toki and other lay supporters, Ōta, Sōya, Shijō, Nanjō, and Hakii, a group of middle-rank samurai who lived in these provinces, formed the nucleus of Nichiren's lay following. When Nanjō Hyōeshichirō died around 1265, Nichiren visited his widow and young son, Tokimitsu, in Ueno, Fuji district of Suruga province, securing some of the staunchest converts of his later years. The disciple Nikkō, who founded Taisekiji, was attracted to Nichiren during this visit. Part II includes letters to Toki *(Teradomari gosho, Sado gosho,* and *Toki dono gosho)* and his family *(Kaen jōgō sho* and *Toki amagozen gosho);* Shijō's wife *(Shijō Kingo dono nyōbō gohenji);* Nanjō's family *(Ueno dono no haha amagozen gohenji* and *Ueno amagozen gohenji);* and Hakii *(Hakii dono gohō).*

75.   *Nanjō Hyōeshichirō dono gosho, STH,* p. 327.

76.   In *Hokke daimoku shō*[al], *STH,* p. 391, written at Kiyozumidera in 1266, Nichiren advises a woman correspondent to recite the title of the Lotus Sutra even if only between recitations of the *nenbutsu.* The practice of reciting the *nenbutsu* was spreading rapidly; there is no doubt that Nichiren urged the *daimoku* as a substitute phrase for recitation and meditation. This is his first statement that the title of the Lotus Sutra is the sum of all Buddhist teaching, the repository of the Dharma, and that recitation and meditation on it can lead to enlightenment. See my translation of *Hokke daimoku shō* in Part II, herein.

77.   Lotus Sutra, chapter 23, "The Story of Bhaiṣajyarāja," Hurvitz, p. 298, and T9, p. 54a.

78.   Quoted in Kawazoe Shōji, *Nichiren* (Tokyo: Shimizu Shoin, 1971), p. 53.

79.   Yoritsuna was a vassal of the Hōjō who headed both the *samuraidokoro* (retainers' bureau) and the Hōjō household office. During the time of the Mongol threat he and his rival Adachi Yasumori exerted major governmental power. See Hori Kyotsu, "The Economic and Political Effects of the Mongol Wars," in John W. Hall and Jeffrey P. Mass, eds., *Medieval Japan* (New Haven, Connecticut: Yale University Press, 1974), p. 196.

80.   *Ankokuron okugaki*[am], *STH,* p. 443.

81.   *Zenmui sanzō sho, STH,* p. 473. Nichiren's combativeness was engendered by the sense of urgency the Mongol threat lent his teachings, but he found scriptural support in the *Nehangyō* in particular. See Nichiren's quotations from the *Nehangyō* urging punishment of enemies of Buddhism in *Risshō ankokuron,* translated in Part II, herein.

82.   Ninshō (1217–1303) was a disciple of Eizon (1201–1290). In 1262, while Nichiren
       was banished to Izu, Eizon had been invited to Kamakura by Kanezawa Sane-
       toki. His renewed emphasis on monastic disciplines and stress on philanthropic
       activities soon attracted a following, and Kamakura became the headquarters of
       their Shingon-Ritsu movement. See Joseph M. Kitagawa, *Religion in Japanese
       History* (New York: Columbia University Press, 1966), p. 105, and Takagi,
       Nichiren: sono kōdō to shisō, p. 79.
83.   *Gezan goshōsoku, STH,* p. 1322.
84.   *Gyōbin gohenji*[an], *STH,* p. 496, is evidently part of an ongoing correspondence
       between Nichiren and a group of other Kamakura priests.
85.   *Gyōbin sojō goetsū*[ao], *STH,* p. 497, is Nichiren's brief as defendant.
86.   Takagi, *Nichiren: Sono kōdō to shisō,* p. 105. Another letter from the Mongols
       arrived 1271/9/2. On 9/2 readings of the *Ninnōkyō* and divination ceremonies
       were ordered by the imperial court. On 9/13 all samurai with lands in Kyūshū
       and the Kantō area were mobilized and ordered to quiet unruly elements on their
       estates.
87.   *Jinkokuō gosho*[ap], *STH,* p. 892.
88.   *Senjishō*[aq], *STH,* p. 1053.
89.   In the light of day on 9/14, Nichiren was able to describe his situation calmly in a
       letter to Toki: "About six in the evening I was sentenced. In custody of the Gov-
       ernor of Musashi, I left Kamakura around two in the morning on the thirteenth.
       I had been exiled to Sado, but was to go first to the home of the man called Hon-
       ma in Echi, under the guard of the deputy of Lord Rokurō Saemonnojō,
       Umatarō." *Toki dono gohenji*[ar], *STH,* p. 503.
90.   "They said I was to be exiled, but secretly they intended to behead me." *Gezan
       goshōsoku*[as], *STH,* p. 1323.
91.   From Sado he wrote: "The man called Nichiren was decapitated last year on the
       twelfth of the ninth month. His ghost has come here to Sado to live." *Kaimoku-
       shō,* STH, p. 535.
92.   A number of disciples were jailed. (See *Tsuchirō gosho*[at], *STH,* p. 509,
       translation in Part II.) Others who were retainers of *bakufu* samurai had
       stipends, lands, or offices revoked.
93.   *Ben dono amagozen gosho*[au], *STH,* p. 752.
94.   *Ueno dono gohenji*[av], *STH,* p. 1309.
95.   *Niiama gozen gohenji, STH,* p. 864.
96.   *Toki dono gohenji, STH,* p. 503. Behind the self-confidence displayed in this
       letter, Nichiren himself knew doubts. The years of exile on Sado gave him time
       for introspection and examination of his beliefs. *Kaimokushō* and *Kanjin hon-
       zon shō*[aw], *STH,* p. 702, two long essays composed in 1272 and 1273, show Ni-
       chiren grappling with the questions his followers too were asking: Why, if I live
       the Lotus Sutra, have I not been protected by the gods, and what benefit is there
       in condemning the Amidists and Zen Buddhists and making enemies of them?
97.   At least one disciple, Sammibō, was exiled to Sado (*Yorimoto chinjo*[ax], *STH,* p.
       1346), and Nichiren was worried that "the food I received from my keepers was
       limited, and there were many disciples with me." *Ichinotani nyūdō gosho, STH,*
       p. 989.
98.   *Toki nyūdō dono gohenji*[ay], *STH,* p. 516.
99.   *Nichimyō shōnin gosho*[az], *STH,* p. 647.
100.   *Sado gosho, STH,* p. 616.
101.   Among them was a retired gentleman farmer who had taken lay vows to follow a

religious life worshipping Amida. Abutsubō and his wife Sennichini managed to bring supplies to Nichiren at night during several months when food was scarce. "The *jitō*'s men and the Amidists lay watch and prevented anyone from visiting my hut, but you loaded provisions on Abutsubō's back and sent him time and again during the night. My loving mother must surely have been reborn here on Sado." (*Sennichini gohenji*[ba], *STH*, p. 1759.) Abutsubō continued to make pilgrimages to visit Nichiren at Mount Minobu until he was in his eighties.

    Converts on Sado included priests as well as lay persons. Sairenbō, who became Nichiren's disciple in a ceremony held in 1272/2, returned to Kamakura with Nichiren. Gakujōbō, Bungōbō, and Yamabushibō took over leadership of the congregation on Sado. See Takagi, *Nichiren: Sono kōdō to shisō,* pp. 181–182.

102.   *Myōhō bikuni gohenji, STH,* p. 1562.

103.   Nichiren felt that his suffering was purging him of evil karma from past lives in which he had slandered the Lotus Sutra and was necessary before he could achieve his own salvation or his goal of converting others.

104.   Takagi, *Nichiren: Sono kōdō to shisō,* p. 180, lists these visitors.

105.   In *Sennichi amagozen gohenji*[bb] (*STH,* p. 1545), Nichiren recalled "Ryōkan [Ninshō] of the Gokurakuji preached to the former Governor of Musashi about my teachings and made him his disciple. I wonder that my life was spared."

106.   *Migenta dono gohenji*[bc], *STH,* p. 805.

107.   *Kōnichibō gosho,* p. 1152.

108.   "It had become apparent that I had committed no crime and that my words were not empty; so, although most of the Hōjō did not approve, Tokimune pardoned me at last and I returned to Kamakura." *Nakaoki nyūdō goshōsoku, STH,* p. 1715.

109.   *Senjishō, STH,* p. 1053.

110.   *Gezan goshōsoku, STH,* p. 1322.

111.   Ibid., *STH,* p. 1322.

112.   "If the sage admonishes the ruler three times unheeded, he withdraws to the mountains and forests." *Hōonshō, STH,* p. 1219. Nichiren had submitted the *Risshō ankokuron* in 1260 and 1271. He counted the audience of 1274 his third attempt to lead the government to the true religion. For an analysis of Confucian elements in Nichiren's secular morality, see Tokoro Shigemoto, *Nichiren no shisō to Kamakura bukkyō* (Tokyo: Fuzanbō, 1965), pp. 179–309.

113.   *Toki dono gosho*[bd], *STH,* p. 809. See translation in Part II, herein.

114.   Ibid., p. 809.

115.   *Hyōeshichirō dono gohenji, STH,* p. 1605. The Nanjō family lived nearby at Ueno in the Fuji district, and one of Nichiren's most zealous disciples, Nikkō, had been working in this area since the late 1260s (see Takagi, *Nichiren: Sono kōdō to shisō,* pp. 197–198). Perhaps this is one reason Nichiren settled at Minobu.

116.   Nichiren first mentions the invasion in a letter dated 11/11 (*Ueno dono gohenji*[be], *STH,* p. 835), surprisingly soon after the battle. Evidently his samurai followers kept him posted as the news was rushed to Kamakura.

117.   "The heavens have arranged that the saints from neighboring countries should punish this one." *Senjishō, STH,* p. 1053.

118.   *Oto gozen goshōsoku*[bf], *STH,* p. 1099.

    The suffering of the islanders of Iki and Tsushima shocked Nichiren, and again he tried to convey his sense of the urgent need to convert Japan to the true religion. Again and again he lamented that "among the farmers, every man was slain or taken prisoner and every woman captured and tied to the ships by ropes passed through the palms of her hands. No one escaped." *Ichinotani nyūdō gosho, STH,* p. 989.

Other descriptions of the destruction of the battle are found in *Kyōdaishō*[bg], *STH,* p. 918 (translation in Part II, herein); *Oto gozen goshōsoku, STH,* p. 1095; and *Myōshinni gozen gohenji*[bh], *STH,* p. 1102.

Nichiren also reminded his followers frequently of the pain of parting with loved ones in wartime: "At the time of the rape of Iki and Tsushima and of Dazaifu, being in Kamakura was like being in heaven; but for those who were sent to Kyūshū, for the women who stayed behind and for the men who departed, parting was like having the skin stripped from the body. They pressed their faces together and their tears mingled on their cheeks." (*Toki amagozen gosho*[bi], *STH,* p. 1148.)

There is no mention in Nichiren's writings of the typhoon, the *kamikaze.* His faith did not falter; rather, he felt grateful for another reprieve during which to try to save Japan from self-destruction.

119. See *Kyōdaishō, STH,* p. 918, and *Hyōe sakan dono gohenji, STH,* p. 1401, translations in Part II, herein.

120. *Shijō Kingo dono gosho*[bj], *STH,* p. 1436.

121. The incident which precipitated this decision occurred on 1277/6/9. Yorimoto and the priest Sammibō stopped to listen to the Tendai priest Ryūshō at Kuwagayatsu in Kamakura, and Sammibō began a debate. Yorimoto's fellow retainers complained to Mitsutoki that he had gone armed to listen to the sermon, that he had criticized the priests Ninshō and Ryūshō, whom Mitsutoki revered, and that he was disloyal to Mitsutoki in putting his religious beliefs above his feudal ties. Yorimoto was ordered to sign a vow of fealty to Mitsutoki and adopt Mitsutoki's belief in the efficacy of keeping the precepts. Instead, he sent a promise of faith to Nichiren and planned to leave Mitsutoki. *Yorimoto chinjō, STH,* p. 1346.

122. "If Yorimoto becomes a Buddha, he will save his lord, too," Nichiren wrote. Therefore, true loyalty to Ema consisted in Yorimoto's following his conscience in religious matters. *Shijō Kingo dono gohenji, STH,* p. 1665.

123. All three of these temples were in Fuji district, Suruga province, home of the Nanjō family and the disciple Nikkō. Nanjō Tokimitsu and Nikkō were working together to draw a congregation from among the local farmers and artisans, Nanjō providing material support and example and Nikkō acting as Nichiren's representative at services and lectures. See *Ueno amagozen gohenji, STH,* p. 1894, for examples of their activities.

124. For example, the abbot *(inzudai)* of the Ryūsenji, a Tendai Amidist named Gyōchi, had in 1276 forbidden the priests of his temple to recite the Lotus Sutra and ordered them to recite instead the Amida sutras and the *nenbutsu.* Confronted with a choice between agreeing to these conditions and leaving the temple, one gave in, one left, and two refused to be bullied. Support from the other priests and the Nanjō family gave them victory in this opening skirmish between the Nichiren and Amidist factions.

125. A second fight took place in 1279 when the priests of Jissōji petitioned the *jitō* to remove the appointed abbot, an Amidist. Fifty-one offenses ranging from lack of order in the temple to threats against priests, servants, and farmers were listed. The petition was authored by Nikkō. Hyōchi and the Amidists presented a counterpetition, charging Nichiren's followers with violence and bloodshed at a

local festival. In the eighth month a farmer was beheaded for his part in the violence.

The Atsuhara *hōnan* took place in the following two months. Gyōchi accused Nichiren's followers of heresy, of forcing their way into his quarters armed with bows and arrows, and of harvesting fields not theirs. Twenty farmers were arrested, and several were executed.

Nichiren's followers accused Gyōchi of lying and of cutting their fields, of using temple thatch for his own dwelling, of having the lay believer put to death on false charges, of leading his own army of peasants, and of trespassing to hunt. Probably the trespassing was mutual.

126. *Ueno dono gohenji, STH,* p. 1767.
127. *Ueno dono haha amagozen gohenji*[bk], *STH,* p. 1896–1897.
128. *Hakii dono gohō*[bl], *STH,* p. 1924. (See translation in Part II, herein.)

[a] 佐渡御勘気鈔		[ag] 般守彌三郎許御書
[b] 佐渡御書		[ah] 四恩鈔
[c] 本尊問答抄		[ai] 光日房御書
[d] 中興入道御消息		[aj] 可延定業御書
[e] 日蓮上人註画讃		[ak] 南條兵衛七郎殿御書
[f] 本化別頭仏祖統記		[al] 法華題目鈔
[g] 新尼御前御返事		[am] 安国論奥書
[h] 報恩抄		[an] 行敏御返事
[i] 授決圓多羅義集唐決		[ao] 行敏訴状御會通
[j] 善無畏三蔵鈔		[ap] 神国王御書
[k] 華果成就御書		[aq] 撰時抄
[l] 妙法尼御前御返事		[ar] 土木殿御返事
[m] 是聖房蓮長		[as] 下山御消息
[n] 南條兵衛七郎殿御返事		[at] 土籠御書
[o] 妙法比丘尼御返事		[au] 弁殿尼御前御書
[p] 破良觀等御書		[av] 上野殿御返事
[q] 戒体即身成仏義		[aw] 観心本尊抄
[r] 五輪九字秘釈		[ax] 頼基陳状
[s] 理性院血脈		[ay] 富木入道殿返事
[t] 清澄寺大衆中		[az] 日妙聖人御書
[u] 妙密上人御消息		[ba] 千日尼御返事
[v] 王舎城		[bb] 千日尼御前御返事
[w] 武蔵殿御消息		[bc] 彌源太殿御返事
[x] 蓮		[bd] 富木殿御書
[y] 日		[be] 上野殿御返事
[z] 守護国家論		[bf] 乙御前御消息
[aa] 安国論御勘由来		[bg] 兄弟鈔
[ab] 立正安国論		[bh] 妙心尼御前御返事
[ac] 開目抄		[bi] 富木尼御前御書
[ad] 下山御消息		[bj] 四條金吾殿御書
[ae] 論談敵対御書		[bk] 上野殿母尼御前御返事
[af] 一谷入道御書		[bl] 波木井殿御報

CHAPTER 2

The Teaching

Nichiren considered himself a revivalist and spoke of a return to the Tendai teachings brought to Japan by Saichō in the ninth century; in fact, he molded a highly syncretic doctrine and practice. He was but one of many priests in medieval Japan who carried Buddhism out of the monasteries to the people, but he was outstandingly effective in his letters, and no doubt in his sermons, in adapting his understanding of Buddhism to his audience. His success was due to his unflagging efforts to nurture the seed of his ideas among his followers by letters and personal contact, and to his selection of elements of Buddhist thought and practice which were well suited to the situation of the social class which provided his audience. If he had a gift, it was for teaching: he was able to convey his ideas to each person in a cogent manner.

The belief Nichiren acquired as a young man changed little during his lifetime: his fundamental faith in the Lotus Sutra as the vehicle for the highest teaching of the Buddha was constant. What did change was Nichiren's understanding of the best way to express faith in the sutra and to achieve the salvation it promises.

Worship of the Lotus Sutra was not new in Japan; it had been the most popular sutra since the introduction of Buddhism in the sixth century and was widely believed to have magic powers to break the karmic chain of cause and effect.[1] Nichiren achieved his success by combining elements of various Buddhist schools of thought and practice including Lotus worship, esoteric symbolism, Amidism, and *mappō* consciousness.

Various schools of Buddhism competing for followers in Nichiren's time offered basically similar methods of practice and teachings to converts. All, of course, set enlightenment as the ultimate goal, and all shared in the Mahāyāna philosophy, so that their explanations of the nature of the universe and of nirvana were, at least to the layman, quite similar. It was less with philosophy, than with methods of religious practice, that the schools attracted the faithful. This is the reason competition was so severe and the reason Nichiren felt obliged to attack other teachings so vociferously. The very similarities between the schools made it necessary for adherents to stress their differences and uniqueness. Nichiren made his teaching stand out by successful presentation, easy and attractive methods of practice, and the promise of salvation.

THE TENDAI TEACHING

Kiyozumidera, the country temple where Nichiren began his Buddhist training, belonged to the Tendai sect. This sect is based on a system enunciated by the Chinese founder, Chih-i (531–597), by which the contradictions in Buddhist teachings are explained as a pedagogical method created by the Buddha Śākyamuni. Chih-i suggested that Śākyamuni, realizing that most beings were incapable of understanding difficult philosophy or undertaking strict religious training, devised a series of accommodations or partial truths to lead his audience gradually toward the Absolute Truth. Inventing a chronological order for the scriptures, Chih-i announced that Śākyamuni had revealed the Absolute Truth in the last two sutras he preached before his nirvana, the Lotus Sutra and the *Nehangyō*.[2]

The Tendai sect became a great eclectic school embracing all forms of Buddhism. Tendai scholars held all scriptures to be the word of Buddha: although the essence of the Buddha's teachings is contained in the Lotus Sutra, other scriptures are of value and have a place in Buddhist study and practice because they are suited to the differences in the abilities and experiences of those who practice Buddhism. Therefore, at the Enryakuji monastery, headquarters of the Tendai sect in Japan, scholars studied all Buddhist scriptures. This breadth of doctrine encouraged disparate factions within the sect, some stressing esoteric philosophy and practice, others emphasizing worship of the Buddha Amida or other buddhas and bodhisattvas, recitation of certain sutras or parts of sutras, meditation, or monastic discipline. From these factions developed the medieval Japanese Buddhist schools, including Zen, Jōdo, and Nichiren Lotus.[3]

The Tendai priests at Kiyozumidera taught Nichiren both the open practice of Amida worship and the secret esoteric practices. Conflict between faith in the Lotus Sutra and worship of Amida led Nichiren to abandon his prayers to Amida during his first years of study in Kamakura. The influence of esoteric ideas and practices, however, dominated his personal syncretization of Tendai philosophy and determined the method of worship Nichiren advocated to his followers.[4]

Saichō (766–822), the founder of the Japanese Tendai sect, brought Chih-i's teachings from China in the ninth century. He also brought a method of mystic contemplation as a means for experiencing the truth of the Lotus Sutra and established a Lotus Contemplation Chapel at Enryakuji for its performance.[5] This interest in esoteric disciplines balanced his concern for the exoteric teachings and led him to establish the selection each year of two gifted young priests to undertake a twelve-year course of study. One of the young men would concentrate on exoteric literature; the other would devote himself to the *Dainichikyō* and esoteric Buddhism.

Saichō's younger contemporary, Kūkai (774–835), visited China slightly later and became a master of the flourishing combination of mysticism and the occult known as Tantrayāna. Kūkai, who founded the Shingon sect based on these principles, taught only the esoteric practices and focused worship upon the Buddha Dainichi and the *Dainichikyō*. Two of Saichō's successors at Enryakuji, Ennin and Enchin, also studied in China and became imbued with the esoteric practices. They in turn introduced more esoteric practices into Saichō's teachings.[6] As a result both Tendai and Shingon became known as esoteric or *mikkyō* sects. Both prospered through the support of the court and aristocracy and performed rites and prayers in return.[7]

Initiates considered esoteric Buddhist practices superior to the exoteric as a means to enlightenment. Nichiren, too, in his early writings, described *mikkyō* as the epitome of the Buddhist teachings,[8] and, while he later attacked the Shingon sect for luring people from faith in the Lotus Sutra and criticized Ennin and Enchin for eclipsing the exoteric with the esoteric, he never repudiated the efficacy of the symbolic *mikkyō* practices. His criticism was reserved for those who set as a goal for their practice comprehension of the doctrine of some sutra other than the Lotus.

In pursuit of his goal, the spread of worship and practice of the Lotus Sutra, Nichiren adapted and modified the practices of other Buddhist schools of thought and joined esoteric Buddhism to Lotus worship, introducing a Lotus mantra *(daimoku)* and Lotus mandala *(honzon)*.[9] He rejected other scriptures but maintained the emphasis on esoteric practices as a means to understand the Dharma, and "shared with the Shingon school the use of the mandala and the belief in *sokushin jōbutsu* (becoming a Buddha with one's body during one's earthly existence)."[10]

LOTUS SUTRA

The Lotus Sutra, which Nichiren revered and which Chih-i had considered the epitome of the Buddha's teachings, is one of the most widely known of Mahāyāna scriptures.[11] It consists of a series of sermons preached to a host of bodhisattvas, arhats, and supernatural beings by the Buddha Śākyamuni on earth and in an other-worldly setting called Vulture Peak.

There are two essential points in the Lotus sermons. The first is that the Buddha is not just a man but is a manifestation of an eternal, all-pervading Buddha-nature. Śākyamuni had originally presented himself as but one of a series of buddhas who were born into the world as men, were enlightened after a series of ascetic and meditative practices, and were extinguished in a nirvana which was believed to be death followed by no reincarnation. In the Lotus, Śākyamuni reveals that he himself has appeared in the world many times in the past and will appear in the future. His semblances of nirvana were only a device to awaken a feeling of urgency in his contemporaries.

The second teaching of the Lotus and its particular attraction for Nichiren, who sought universal salvation, derives from the concept of the Buddha-nature as eternal and all-pervading. Since the Buddha-nature is not limited by time or space, it exists equally within all beings and Buddhahood is possible for all.

Mahāyāna Buddhists had envisioned three types of saints: the bodhisattva, whose goal is the salvation of self and others; the *pratyekabuddha,* whose goal is personal salvation through his own effort; and the *śrāvaka,* whose goal is personal salvation through listening to a buddha. The Lotus Sutra denies that there are three paths. In fact, there is only one goal, Buddhahood, and one path, the *ekayāna.* The other goals were presented only as devices to lead beings far enough toward understanding that they would be able to accept the truth.

This doctrine of merciful devices gave the Buddhist philosophers a way to explain the diversity that exists within Buddhism and encouraged Buddhist priests to modify their doctrine to take their audience into account. In the Lotus, preachers could study such teaching devices as dramatic presentation, simplification, similes, metaphors, analogies, parables, and tales.

The first half of the Lotus Sutra contains several famous parables which explain the principles of unity of the path, the eternal, all-encompassing Buddha-nature, and universal salvation. The parable of the burning house, for example, compares the merciful half-truths about the paths to salvation preached by the Buddha to the promise by a father to his children of varied types of chariots if only they will leave their toys in the burning house and come out to safety. Another parable compares the teachings of the Buddha to rain which falls equally on all the plants on earth but nourishes them differently.

In his sermons Nichiren told these parables from the Lotus, made up original stories, or adapted historical anecdotes and traditional tales to convey the teachings of the Lotus and the promise of salvation to any who would worship and practice the Lotus Sutra. Having learned his pedagogy through the Lotus Sutra, he used illustrative stories, modified his teachings for the individual, and contrived to lead each of his followers to practice the Lotus.

PERIODS OF THE LAW

The most rapidly growing school of Buddhism in Nichiren's day was the Jōdo or Pure Land school, which encouraged devotees to recite a brief expression of faith, the *nenbutsu,* to the Buddha Amida in hope of rebirth in his Pure Land paradise. The Amidists believed that the final period of the Law had arrived and personal effort could no longer bring enlightenment. They substituted faith in the saving grace of Amida for individual effort to understand Buddhist philosophy. The Amidists did not deny the truth of the Lotus Sutra, but they rejected it as being too difficult for the degenerate beings of the last period of the law *(mappō),* for whom easy practices, simple teachings, and outside assistance were needed. Recitation of the *nenbutsu* and dependence on Amida answered that need.

The Amidists based their teachings on the theory of the three periods of the law. According to this theory, history is cyclical. After a buddha is born and preaches there is a period of true law, *shōbō,* in which the Buddhist doctrine, practice, and enlightenment all exist and are accessible. As time passes, the number of people able to understand the teaching of the Buddha diminishes. This marks the beginning of the age of imitation law, *zōbō,* in which the doctrine and practice exist but enlightenment is no longer possible. The third period is a period of degeneracy, the *mappō,* in which the doctrine alone remains, while a corrupt people no longer practice it and no longer achieve enlightenment. At the end of the *mappō* a new buddha appears and the cycle begins again.

Most Japanese believed, as did Nichiren, that the *mappō* had begun in 1051. The date was derived from assumptions about the dates of the Buddha's life and the length of the three periods.[12] The calculations were buttressed by external evidence: Japan was in turmoil as old institutions broke down and new ones evolved. The rule of the imperial court had been supplanted by military rule, the older religious orders were quarreling among themselves, and militant monks had often left their monasteries to impose their will by force. It was apparent the age of corruption had begun.

The Amidists urged faith in Amida based on his vows to save all sentient beings. In an age when individual effort could not bring salvation, appeal to Amida seemed the only answer. These arguments were widely accepted, and Nichiren needed an equally strong explanation for the efficacy of the Lotus Sutra in the *mappō* and an equally simple method of religious practice to draw people away from practices he considered heretical.

Based on the vows of the bodhisattvas in the Lotus Sutra to appear in the world "after the Buddha's passage into extinction, in a frightful and evil age" to "propagate this scripture broadly,"[13] Nichiren evolved a theory that the Lotus Sutra was the one scripture designed specifically to save those who live in the *mappō*.

Most Tendai scholars had considered the diverse teachings of the Buddha to be accommodations for individual beings at different stages of personal understanding. Nichiren came to place greater emphasis on the historical context than on individual progress toward enlightenment. He believed Buddha's mercy increases in proportion to the need of mankind. Thus Śākyamuni's highest and most complete doctrine was reserved for the most needy age, the *mappō*.

FAITH AND WITNESS

Having determined that beings in the *mappō* must rely on the Lotus Sutra for salvation, Nichiren faced the choice of the appropriate religious practices and expressions of faith. He turned to the scripture for models of the religious life and absorbed two lessons from the examples he found: any who accept the scripture must preach it, and suffering is a concomitant of the missionary life.

In the Lotus Sutra, after Śākyamuni assures his audience that they will all become buddhas, he tells them their religious practice should include "keeping, holding, reading, and reciting" the sutra and preaching its truth to others. Many of the listeners step forward and vow to preach after Śākyamuni's nirvana; the earth ruptures and multitudes of bodhisattvas, led by the bodhisattva Jōgyō (Viśistacāritra), emerge to worship the Buddha and to promise to proselytize in the "latter age"; and gods and demons vow to protect any being who preaches the Lotus.[14]

From this Nichiren deduced that it is the duty of one who accepts the Lotus Sutra as the Truth to preach it to others. Rather than term himself and his followers *jikyōsha,* signifying one who has accepted and vowed to keep the sutra, Nichiren preferred the term *gyōja,* one who lives the events of the sutra in his own life, for he felt faith without practice was insufficient for salvation.

Nichiren set out to follow the examples of the bodhisattvas whose stories are told in the scripture. He emulated Jōgyō, the leader of the bodhisattvas who emerged from the earth to preach during the *mappō,* and identified with Jōfukyō (Sadāparibhūta), the bodhisattva Never Disparaging, who bowed to all he saw because he knew everyone eventually would become a buddha. Jōfukyō was ridiculed and reviled for presuming to prophesy. Whenever he spoke "some in the multitude would set upon him with sticks and staves, with tiles and stones," but he was able to bear this with equanimity because of the reward that would be his: "When his penalty had been paid, and he faced the end of his life, he was able to hear this scripture."[15]

Nichiren did not expect the life of the *gyōja* to be easy, for Śākyamuni had warned:

> This scripture has many enemies even now when the Tathāgata is present. How many more there will be after his nirvana!"[16]

Any who undertake to proselytize must bear persecution both to fulfill the prophecy of the Buddha and to expiate sins they themselves committed in past lives. Nichiren took to heart the vows of the bodhisattvas in the chapter "Fortitude," reminding himself and his followers again and again that they must live by those vows to achieve salvation:

> We beg you not to be concerned, for after the Buddha's passage into extinction in a frightful and evil age, we will broadly preach. Those ignorant men, whoever they may be, that revile us with foul mouths or attack us with knives and staves, we will all endure. The bhikṣus [monks] in an evil age, men of twisted wisdom, their hearts sycophantic and crooked, say they already have attained what in fact they have not yet attained, their hearts being full of pride. Or there are āraṇyakas [forest-dwelling hermits], clothed in patched rags and living in the wilderness, who say of themselves that they are treading the True Path, holding mankind cheaply. Because they covet profit and nourishment, they preach Dharma to white-robed laymen and are held in humble reverence by the world, as though they were arhants of the six penetrations. These men, harboring evil thoughts, constantly mindful of the affairs of the world, borrow the name of āraṇyakas because they love to display our faults. Then they make such talk as this: "These bhikṣus, out of greed for profit and nourishment, preach the arguments of external paths. Having themselves created this scriptural canon to deceive worldlings and lead them astray, in the quest for name and renown they preach this scripture with much discrimination." Since within the great multitude they ever wish to ruin us, turning to kings and great ministers, to Brahmans and householders, and to multitudes of other bhikṣus, they slanderously speak evil of us, saying, "These fellows of wrong views preach arguments of external paths." Out of veneration for the Buddha, we will endure all these evils. By them we shall be addressed with derision, "You fellows are all Buddhas!" Such words of derision as these we will all endure with patience. In a muddied kalpa, in an evil age, many shall be the fright-

ful evil demons that enter their bodies to malign and disgrace us. We, venerating and believing the Buddha, will don the armor of forbearance and, to preach this scripture, will endure these troubles. We do not covet bodily life, we do but regret the Unexcelled Path. In an age to come, we will guard and keep what the Buddha has assigned. The World-Honored One himself must know that in the muddied age the evil monks shall not know the Buddha's expedient devices, the Dharma he preaches in accord with what is appropriate. Foul language and wry faces, repeated banishment [from the order], separation from stūpas and monasteries—such shall the many evils be; but, mindful of the Buddha's commands, we will all endure these things. In villages, cities, and towns, if there is a person who seeks Dharma, we will all go to that place to preach the Dharma assigned by the Buddha. We are the messengers of the World-Honored One, dwelling in the multitude without fear. Well will we preach the Dharma: We beg the Buddha to remain tranquil. In the presence of the World-Honored One, to the Buddhas who have arrived from the ten quarters we utter such an oath as this, and the Buddha himself knows our thoughts.[17]

Nichiren saw this passage realized in his life; preaching, persecution by heretics, slander, and forbearance had all been foretold. When they were attacked, he and his followers consoled themselves with the thought that they were "emissaries" of the Buddha and so destined to be exalted. Śākyamuni had promised:

If this good man or good woman, after my passage into extinction, can secretly for a single person preach so much as a single phrase of the Scripture of the Dharma Blossom, be it known that that person is an emissary of the [Tathāgata], sent by the [Tathāgata], doing the [Tathāgata's] business.[18]

By preaching and suffering persecution, they were fulfilling the predictions of the Buddha for the *mappō* and serving as his messengers.

HERESY

In the Lotus Sutra Śākyamuni threatens dire retribution for anyone who persecutes or maligns the preachers of the Lotus:

If there is a man who utters words of disparagement: "You are nothing but a madman! In vain are you performing these practices! You shall never get anything for them!"; the retribution for sins such as this shall be that from age to age he shall have no eyes. If there is anyone who makes offerings and gives praise, in this very age he shall get his present reward. If, again, one sees a person receiving and holding this scripture, then utters its faults and its evils, be they fact or not fact, that person in the present age shall get white leprosy. If anyone makes light of it or laughs at it, from age to age his teeth shall be far apart and decayed, he shall have ugly lips and a flat nose, his arms and legs shall be crooked, his eyes shall be pointed and the pupils out of symmetry, his body shall stink, he shall have sores running pus and blood, his belly shall be watery and his breath short: in brief, he shall have all manner of evil and grave ailments.[19]

Nichiren believed that "uttering words of disparagement," denying the truth of the Lotus Sutra, was the most serious of sins. He called it *hōbō,* "slander of the Dharma," and warned that perpetrators would suffer in the deepest hell. Because the Lotus promises salvation to beings in the "latter, evil age," Nichiren taught that any in the *mappō* who trusted in Amida or other buddhas or turned to other scriptures were slandering the Dharma and were destined for hell. He begged all who would listen to give up the *nenbutsu* and turn to Śākyamuni and his truth:

> The karmic retribution of the Jōdo sect is rebirth in the deepest hell. The Lotus Sutra is the correct path to Buddhahood. Forthwith quit the Jōdo sect and accept the Lotus Sutra; leave the cycle of births and deaths and obtain enlightenment. In the chapter called "Parable" in the Lotus Sutra, it is written: "If someone does not believe this sutra and slanders it, he kills his seeds of Buddhahood in this life. When his life is over, he will be reborn in the deepest hell. After a *kalpa* he will be born again in hell, and this cycle will continue for countless *kalpas*." According to the sutra, if someone believes in the preliminary teaching of the *nenbutsu* and does not believe the true Lotus, he will fall into hell. The *nenbutsu* faithful reply: "We are not able to understand the Lotus Sutra and so we do not believe. Disbelief is not slander. For what sin will we fall into hell?" But the Lotus says that disbelief *is* not following the teaching. What is called slander of the sutra is nothing other than disbelief.[20]

Nichiren taught his followers that they must fight the heresies of the other sects and eradicate them to make possible the universal enlightenment promised by the Lotus.

DAIMOKU

Responding to requests by his converts and to the challenge of his competitors, Nichiren invented some specific practices for the worship of the Lotus Sutra. In so doing he drew on several traditions. He combined the Amidist invocation, the tradition of reading and reciting the Lotus, and the symbolic chants and diagrams of the esoteric schools.

Among the practices of the Tendai monks was recitation of the name of a buddha or a portion of a scripture as an aid to meditation, enabling the devotee to focus the mind. Recitation of the name of Amida had begun in China and became widely popular there. Genshin (942–1017) was the first in Japan to take the practice of recitation of the name out of the monasteries and meditation halls and make it accessible to lay devotees.

Many were attracted by the idea that salvation is attainable for the spiritually weak through faith and invocation of the Buddha's name.[21] Hōnen (1133–1212) built upon Genshin's concept of the *nenbutsu* as an aid to meditation and expression of faith and asserted that the recitation of the name was the one practice given to beings to make salvation possible in the *mappō* and that it was thus the only practice men should perform.

Faith in the Lotus Sutra and belief in the efficacy of reading or reciting the whole or parts of the sutra also had a long history. The practice was based on these passages from the Lotus:

> If again there is a man who offers a thousand-millionfold world full of the seven jewels to Buddhas, great bodhisattvas, pratyekabuddhas, and arhants, the merit gained by him shall not match that of one who holds of this Scripture of the Dharma Blossom, so much as a single four-foot gāthā, for the latter's merit shall be the greatest.[22]
>
> If any like these in the Buddha's presence hears a single gāthā or a single phrase of the Scripture of the Blossom of the Fine Dharma, or devotes to it a single moment of rejoicing, I hereby confer on him a prophecy that he shall attain [supreme perfect enlightenment] . . . . Again, if there is a man who shall receive and keep, read and recite, explain, or copy in writing a single gāthā of the Scripture of the Blossom of the Fine Dharma, or who shall look with veneration on a roll of this scripture as if it were the Buddha himself, or who shall make to it sundry offerings of flower perfume, necklaces, powdered incense, perfumed paste, burnt incense, silk canopies and banners, garments, or music, or who shall even join palms in reverent worship of it, O Medicine King, be it known that this man or any other like him shall have already made offerings to ten myriads of millions of Buddhas in former time, and in those Buddhas' presence taken a great vow.[23]

The Lotus Sutra had early become the object of popular devotion, and the merits accruing to those who worshipped it were a common subject of popular stories. Certain chapters, such as "The Life-span of the Tathāgata," which reveals the eternal Buddha-nature; or verses, such as the "I, myself" *(jiga)* verse,[24] in which the Buddha tells of the incalculable ages that have passed since he achieved Buddhahood, were commonly chosen for recitation and meditation.

Nichiren countered the Amidist "sole practice" of the *nenbutsu* with a sole practice of his own: he urged his followers to recite "Namu Myōhō-rengekyō," "Homage to the Sutra of the Lotus of the Wonderful Law," instead of "Namu Amida Butsu," "Homage to the Buddha Amida." The practice was similar, but the theory behind the recitation was different. Whereas the *nenbutsu* was an appeal to a humanized buddha, Nichiren's *daimoku* served as a mantra, or symbolic magical chant.[25]

Recitation of the *daimoku* was Nichiren's answer to the attraction of the *nenbutsu:* it required no study or difficult religious training, and it was available to everyone. Nichiren advocated the *daimoku* as a combination of witness and meditation. Like the *nenbutsu,* the *daimoku* was a simplified practice and a way to achieve enlightenment without long years of study of Buddhist philosophy.

HONZON

To help his followers understand the abstract object of their worship—the Dharma or nature of the universe as explained in the Lotus Sutra—Nichiren devised a concrete representation of those principles. He designed a mandala, or symbolic representation of the cosmos, another feature of esoteric Buddhism. Nichiren's mandala, which he called the *honzon,* or "chief object of worship," was a scroll bearing the names of representative beings arranged to illustrate their places in the universe. At the center Nichiren inscribed the title of the Lotus Sutra as a symbol of the Dharma. This was flanked by the names of the buddhas Śākyamuni and Tahō (Prabhūtaratna), who play a major role in the Lotus Sutra and represent the Buddha-nature. Surrounding these are the names of various bodhisattvas, gods, and men, illustrating that all share in the Buddha nature.[26]

The *honzon* answered the need of Nichiren's lay followers for a concrete object of worship. Devotees of the Lotus needed an image to place upon their altars, a substitute for the images of buddhas or bodhisattvas which Nichiren deemed too particularized to represent the eternal Dharma. Many devotees requested copies of the Lotus Sutra to keep and worship, but Nichiren could hardly fill all such requests. The *honzon* mandala was a satisfactory solution.

KAIDAN

The act of presenting a follower with the *honzon* as a symbol of the teaching was in itself a symbol of their entry into a new religious life and provided the opportunity for a ceremony to mark the occasion. The older sects in Japan had established ordination halls *(kaidan)* where aspirants could be consecrated to the religious life. Nichiren taught that no such structure was necessary. The ordination hall is a state of mind, just as salvation depends solely on the mental state of the religious practitioner.[27] All were ordained who accepted the Lotus Sutra as a guide by which to live and vowed to proclaim its teaching to others as the bodhisattvas in the sutra had done.

APOCALYPTIC VISION

Nichiren shared with the Jōdo school a concern with the means to salvation most suited for the weak and ignorant beings of the *mappō*. For some time his solution to the problem was to urge faith in the Lotus and to promise that such faith would transform the surroundings of the believer into a superior world.[28] This idea is founded in the Tendai teaching of interpenetration of dharmas. In brief, each of the ten worlds from hell to the Buddha paradise contains each of the other worlds. The world which the individual being perceives depends on his own state of enlightment. Thus the least enlightened perceive hell, while the most enlightened perceive the Buddha world. Nichiren's hope was to bring all the Japanese to a state of enlightenment that would transform the entire country into a Buddha world or paradise.

The obstacle to Nichiren's goal was named in the sutras: a country in which heresy was rife would lose the protection of the gods and gradually lose all hope of enlightenment. Nichiren viewed the natural disasters of the mid-thirteenth century as well as the warfare of the previous century as signs that the gods had abandoned Japan. To effect their return, the only hope was to eliminate heresy, if necessary by eliminating heretics.

As years passed with no sign that his program of eradication of heresy would be undertaken by the *bakufu* while the Mongol threat grew more imminent, Nichiren's sense of urgency increased. His first reaction was to encourage his followers to attack heresy vigorously and directly. His disciples staged public debates with priests of other sects and warned the common people of the consequences of giving alms to heretics.

Still there seemed no hope for a general conversion, and Nichiren gradually focused his concern on the next life. He adapted the Jōdo promise of rebirth, for the faithful, in paradise, where the religious life would be easier to maintain. Instead of the Pure Land paradise of Amida, Nichiren told of the Vulture Peak paradise of Śākyamuni.[29] His scriptural source was again the Lotus Sutra. Śākyamuni promised: "These beings, having heard the Dharma, in the present age are tranquil and are later born in a good place."[30]

The promise of a tranquil life and good rebirth became a catch phrase for Nichiren in his later years. He himself was aging, ill, and less optimistic about achieving his goal of converting all Japan. Many followers, too, were growing old and losing loved ones to death or to duty on the battle lines in Kyūshū. Many were facing religious persecution. Instead of reiterating the possibility of salvation in this life, Nichiren began to use the image of Vulture Peak as a counter to the Pure Land paradise promised to Jōdo believers. As Vulture Peak is the place where Śākyamuni preached the Lotus, Nichiren was assuring his believers that they would hear the Lotus in the next life and thus be assured salvation then.

NOTES

1. Many Buddhist tales tell of miracles achieved by prayers to the Lotus Sutra. The earliest Japanese collection, the ninth-century *Nihon ryōiki,* relates how worship of the Lotus caused a trunk to expand (II, 6) and obtained an explanation of the rebirth of the worshipper's mother (II, 15), among other miracles, and how speaking ill of a devotee of the sutra brought the penalties of a twisted mouth and sudden death (II, 18). An eleventh-century collection, *Dainihonkoku Hokkegenki* [Tales of miracles through the Lotus Sutra], attests the continuing popularity of the sutra. The cult of the Lotus Sutra was gradually overshadowed by the Amida cult in China, but, due largely to Nichiren's efforts, managed to hold its own in Japan.

2. According to Chih-i, Śākyamuni revealed the Dharma in five stages during the fifty years of his life. The stages are named after scriptures representative of each period. Kegon, with which Śākyamuni began, proved too difficult for his audience. Therefore, the Buddha began again with less profound teachings and worked from Agon, or Hīnayāna doctrine, through the Mahāyāna doctrines in the Hōdō and Hannya scriptures, to gradually lead his audience to the full truth of the Lotus Sutra. Chih-i assigned the *Nehangyō* to the same chronological period as the Lotus and considered it to have equal religious value but a different function. The essential message was contained in the Lotus, while the *Nehangyō* served to convert those the Lotus had not reached.

3. Most of the Buddhist leaders of the thirteenth century, including Hōnen of the Jōdo sect, Shinran of the True Jōdo sect, Ippen of the Ji sect, Ryōnin of the Yūzu-nenbutsu sect, Eisai of the Rinzai Zen sect, Dōgen of the Soto Zen sect, and Nichiren, had studied at Mount Hiei and many were ordained in the Tendai sect.

4. Esoteric Buddhism, or Tantrayāna, was the final stage in the evolution of Indian Buddhism. Emphasis was given to meditational methods and disciplines, "psycho-experimental practices" as Agehananda Bharati terms them (*The Tantric Tradition* [New York: Doubleday & Company, 1970]), rather than to speculative philosophy. Often the methods or the symbolic meaning of the practices were kept secret from noninitiates. Nichiren based his theory of the *daimoku* on the practice of meditation on a mantra.

5. Joseph M. Kitagawa, *Religion in Japanese History* (New York: Columbia University Press, 1966), p. 74.

6. Nichiren singled out Ennin (794–864) and Enchin (814–891) for criticism for their roles in introducing esoteric practices. For example, in *Hōonshō, STH,* p. 1230, he wrote: "But with the third chief priest, Ennin, and with the fifth, Enchin, Tendai slid irretrievably toward the esotericism of Shingon," and, "the whole of Japan has turned to Shingon; Tendai no longer has a single adept."

   Ennin is also credited with bringing the practice of invoking the name of Amida from China. It was during Enchin's tenure as chief priest of the sect that the split into the Sanmon and Jimon branches took place. Ecclesiastical disputes led to armed battles between these two camps, beginning in the tenth century, and contributed to a gradual loss of prestige for the Buddhist establishment.

7. Kitagawa, op. cit., p. 65.

8. For example, in *Kaitai sokushin jōbutsugi, STH,* p. 1.

9. In *Teradomari gosho, STH,* p. 512, translation in Part II, herein, Nichiren goes so far as to state that the Lotus Sutra as it existed in India actually contained mudras and mantras which were omitted by the Chinese translators.

10.   Kitagawa, *op. cit.,* pp. 120–121.

11.   It has been particularly popular in China and Japan in the artistic and readable Chinese version of Kumārajīva, the *Myōhōrengekyō,* completed in 406. This is the version generally cited by Nichiren. Of five other Chinese translations, two survive and were consulted by Nichiren: These are the *Shō Hokekyō* translated by Dharmarakṣa in 286 and the *Tenbon Myōhōrengekyō* translated by Jñānagupta and Dharmagupta in 601. All three versions of the Lotus were introduced to Japan before the Nara period.

12.   They set the date of the nirvana as 949 B.C. and believed the *shōbō* and *zōbō* each lasted a thousand years.

13.   Chapter 13, "Fortitude," T9, p. 36b; Chapter 14, "Comfortable Conduct," consists of advice for those who wish to preach in the "latter evil age."

14.   Chapter 15, T9, pp. 39c–40a.

15.   Chapter 20, "Sadāparibhūta," T9, p. 51b.

16.   Chapter 10, "Preachers of Dharma," T9, p. 31b.

17.   Chapter 13. Hurvitz, pp. 204–207; T9, p. 36bc.

18.   Chapter 10. Hurvitz, p. 175; T9, p. 30c.

19.   Chapter 28, "The Encouragements of Samantabhādra." Hurvitz, pp. 336–337; T9, p. 61c.

20.   *Nenbutsu mugen jigoku shō*[a], *STH,* p. 34.

21.   Alfred Bloom, *Shinran's Gospel of Pure Grace* (Tucson, Arizona: The University of Arizona Press, 1965), p. 18.

22.   Chapter 23. Hurvitz, p. 298; T9, p. 54a.

23.   Chapter 10. Hurvitz, p. 174; T9, p. 30c.

24.   Chapter 16, "The Life-span of the Tathāgata," contains the verse: "Since I, myself, attained Buddhahood, throughout the incalculable hundred thousands of myriads of kalpas that have passed, ever have I been preaching Dharma, teaching, and converting." T9, p. 43b.

25.   The esoteric practices include a variety of symbolic means to invoke gods and demons which represent various aspects of the universe. Among the symbolic esoteric practices is the recitation of mantras, mystic syllables or formulas which "are said to be the epitome of the sutras and the short cut to enlightenment." (Kenneth Ch'en, *Buddhism in China* [Princeton, N.J.: Princeton University Press, 1972], p. 327.) Mantras are believed to have magic powers to break the chain of karma and cause miracles of rebirth or deliverance. Nichiren's *daimoku* was such a symbolic vocalization, not intended as an appeal to Śākyamuni in the way the *nenbutsu* was an appeal to Amida, but as a magic force which would awaken the saving powers inherent in the Lotus Sutra.

     Chih-i had prepared the way for Nichiren's use of the title by professing "to find in the title intimations as to the significance of the total scripture." (Hurvitz, *Chih-i,* p. 206.) His title commentary, found in *Fa hua hsuan i,* was often cited by Nichiren.

26.   The ontological view illustrated by the *honzon* is that of the Tendai sect. The ideas Nichiren most often attempted to convey to his followers were "mutual identification" or "interpretation of dharmas" as summed up in the slogan "three thousand worlds in one thought"; the resultant notion of the possibility of enlightenment and Buddhahood in this very body; and the lack of dichotomy between the absolute and the temporary.

27.   The difference between the world of common experience and the absolute is subjective: the enlightened being perceives the latter; the ignorant, the former.

28.   The doctrine Nichiren preached was that of the Tendai sect as expounded by

Chih-i. Letters to lay believers, such as those translated in Part II, illustrate his method of explaining the difficult philosophical system to the uneducated.

For a more detailed explanation of Chih-i's teachings and the doctrine of the Tendai sect see Ch'en, pp. 303–313; Hurvitz, *Chih-i;* and Andō Toshio, *Tendai-gaku* (Kyoto: Heirakuji shoten, 1968).

29. Nichiren's conception of Vulture Peak paradise was probably influenced by the description of nirvana and paradise in the *Nehangyō*. That sutra, contradicting the view of nirvana as devoid of attributes, attributes positive characteristics to nirvana, declaring it to be "permanent, pleasant, personal, and pure." This view had reinforced early Chinese views that *samsara*, "if one could but see it in a different light, is in and of itself the realm of release" (Hurvitz, *Chih-i,* p. 194), and encouraged an equation of nirvana and paradise in the uneducated mind.

30. Lotus Sutra, chapter 5, "Parable of the Medicinal Herbs," T9, p. 19b.

a 念仏無間地獄鈔

CHAPTER 3

Nichiren and Setsuwa

Among Nichiren's writings are complex doctrinal essays written for himself and for those disciples who were educated in Buddhist philosophy. But Nichiren's originality and genius are evident in the letters to lay followers in which his gift for pedagogy shines. These letters, most of which were written during the periods of exile and retirement on Sado and Mount Minobu, are of two broad types: there are those using tales with morals and those closer to *zuihitsu,* or lyrical personal essays.

Nichiren ranged widely in his search for tales, using jataka and other tales from the Buddhist canon, miracle tales from the Chinese and Japanese storytelling traditions, historical anecdotes, and secular stories. Clearly he recognized, as most preachers do, the value of narrative interest and drama in proselytization.

The *zuihitsu* are attractive because of the polished language and the revelation of the personality of the author. The anxieties and search for answers of another human being have a universal fascination; the problems and solutions of another, particularly such an articulate other as Nichiren, are difficult to resist.

A majority of Nichiren's letters were written to individuals; these became family treasures, preserved for generations.[1] The lives of several of the recipients are revealed in the series of letters they received from Nichiren, making the letters even more valuable as illustrations of the technique of adapting the message to the hearer.[2]

Nichiren used a blend of Chinese and Japanese *(wakankonkōbun)* in doctrinal essays and in letters to educated disciples. The language in the rest of his writings is much closer to the contemporary colloquial Japanese. The vivid and powerful style of his letters probably echoes the style with which he won numerous debates and numerous converts.

SHŌDŌ

Nichiren was but one of a growing class of nonmonastic preachers who carried Buddhism throughout Japanese society in the late Heian and Kamakura periods. *Shōdō,* or the art of persuasive preaching, had a long history in Japan, and in China as well, where popular recitation of Buddhist stories by monk preachers had developed by the end of the seventh century. When Ennin visited Ch'ang-an in the ninth century, he attended some recitations and noted that the most famous preacher, Wen-hsu, was noted for noncanonical Buddhist tales.[3]

Such preaching was transmitted to Japan, where at first the audience was limited. The monasteries had official patronage and received rent from their estates, or *shōen,* and therefore could afford to concentrate on internal affairs and religious study rather than proselytization. As rents declined, temples turned actively to converting the aristocracy and inviting their patronage. Sermons on the miracles brought about by prayer and austerities and the virtues of reading the sutras and listening to them multiplied. Staging of memorial services and canvassing for funds for temple buildings and images also increased. Many priests made reputations as orators and storytellers, and religious lectures became social events.[4] Temple lecturers *(kōshi)* were no longer scholars who led daily study meetings, but performers who had to attract crowds.

Outside the monasteries holy men began to preach to the masses in return for alms. These individuals, known over the centuries as *shidosō, hijiri,* and *inja,* among other names, were wandering mendicants. To attract an audience they included music and dance in their programs, illustrated their lectures with pictures, and related stories.[5]

As the established schools of Buddhism began to compete for followers among the commoners in the twelfth and thirteenth centuries, their sermons became less structured.[6] The Agui school of Tendai preachers became particularly well known, and source books of tales classified by type were compiled for the use of its members. Preachers chose material from the books to suit the audience.[7]

Even services and ceremonies at the temples acquired a new character. The atmosphere at such services was "that of a carnival, with all manner of means employed to appeal to and sway the minds of the congregation."[8] Plays, music, and vaudevillelike programs—festivities which evolved into the Nō drama—enlivened the proceedings. An essential part of such entertainments was storytelling, and secular tales as well as religious ones had their place.[9]

Nichiren was one of those seeking followers among the peasants, fishermen, and warriors who had been largely excluded in the early, aristocratic days of Japanese Buddhism. He and the other traveling priests preached to the illiterate and poor as well as to the rich and educated, in temples when they were invited, or in homes and on the streets. Their sermons became individual efforts to persuade the hearers to faith and to teach elementary points of doctrine.

Although there exist a few collections believed to be notes for use by preachers or notes taken during sermons,[10] these are fragmentary. Nichiren's letters provide one of the best illustrations of what *shōdō* was like in the thirteenth century. His letters are unique in that they are written in colloquial Japanese, they are addressed to identifiable individuals, and they are written substitutes for oral sermons.

Nichiren used several hundred different anecdotes and tales in his letters. Some appear to be original, but many others are found in one or more of the collections of tales produced during the centuries of Buddhism in Japan or have their source in the Lotus Sutra. Buddhist tales and tales from Chinese history illustrating Confucian virtues, which Nichiren promoted as a basis for secular morality, are the most common.[11]

NICHIREN AND THE TALE-CENTERED SERMON

A fairly short letter, "Ueno ama gozen gohenji," [Reply to my lady the nun Ueno],[12] sent to a woman believer after she had sent alms on the anniversary of the death of her father, illustrates how Nichiren used tales. He tells the story of the salvation of Wu-lung, a famous Chinese calligrapher and enemy of Buddhism. This story appears in the T'ang collection, *Fu hua ch'uan chi.*[13] It is found in two Japanese collections: in the *Shishū hyakuinnenshu* in the mixed Chinese and Japanese *wakankonkōbun;* and in the *Jikkinshō* in Japanese. Both these collections appeared around the middle of the thirteenth century when Nichiren was preaching.

The *Jikkinshō* version is spare:

The man named Wu-lung did not believe in Buddhism. Although he wrote about many things he did not write one single character about Buddhism. His son I-lung inherited his talent, and he too became a marvelous calligrapher. When Wu-lung was dying, he told his son, "You must follow my example and never write a character of anything that advocates Buddhism." Since he was an evil man, he fell into the evil destinies and suffered terribly. I-lung, in accordance with his late father's wishes, became an unshakable enemy of Buddhism. He was commanded by the king to write the eight characters of the title of the Lotus Sutra on the outside covering of each of the eight scrolls of the sutra. In a dream I-lung saw these characters become sixty-four buddhas and descend to the hell to which Wu-lung had fallen. There they relieved his suffering and Wu-lung was enlightened.

When we think about this we realize that even if one does not believe and is not pure of heart, if he writes but one character of the Sutra, there need be no doubts about the next life (*Jikkinshō* 6-27).

Written in Japanese, Nichiren's letter is straightforward, easily understood and suited to Nichiren's personality and the simplicity of the teaching conveyed. It opens with a word of thanks for a gift of rice and potatoes. Then, after an extended introductory series of analogies explaining how the Lotus Sutra brings instantaneous enlightenment "just as the reflection of the moon floats upon the water the moment the moon rises from east of the mountains and just as the sound and echo ring out simultaneously," Nichiren launches into his version of the story of the calligrapher and his son, implicitly comparing Ueno Ama Gozen and her memorial offerings for her nonbelieving father to I-lung's salvation of his father.

Nichiren's version is more than five times as long as the *Jikkinshō* version, amplified by fuller narrative technique; more vivid detail; human touches, such as description of feelings, designed to draw sympathy to the characters and make them more real; and dialogue.

With his opening description of the setting, Nichiren engages his reader's attention:

If you cross the great sea to the southwest of Japan, you will come to the country called China. In that country there were men who believed in Buddha but not the gods, and there were men who believed in the gods but not the Buddha. In the beginning it was the same in Japan, too.

The story may take place in China, but Nichiren has placed it within the experience of his reader and within the scope of the nun's imagination. Using comparisons again, he introduces the main character:

In China there was a man named Wu-lung who was the greatest calligrapher in the country. He was as famous as Michikaze or Yukinari in Japan. This man hated Buddhism and vowed that never in his life would he copy a sutra.

In dialogue Nichiren introduces the vow that gives rise to the conflict portrayed in the story: Should the young man keep his vow to his dying father never to write the sutras, or should he break it and obey the command of his lord?

The king, barely mentioned in the *Jikkinshō,* plays a major role in Nichiren's version. He is a "great admirer of Buddhism with a special faith in the Lotus Sutra." Wishing a copy of the Lotus to worship, he summons I-lung, "the best calligrapher in the country." At first he accepts I-lung's refusal, but, dissatisfied with the copy made by another calligrapher—a character added by Nichiren for dramatic tension—he again summons I-lung.

> You say you cannot copy the sutra because of your dying father's wish. So I order you to copy just the *daimoku* on the eight volumes of the sutra.

Again I-lung refuses and the king is enraged.

> Your father was my retainer. How can you fear to break your vow to your father, and yet refuse to obey your lord's command, a far worse sin?

By this time Nichiren's readers would be as torn as I-lung. Which comes first, loyalty to parent or loyalty to lord? Carefully, Nichiren balances forward movement and pauses in the action to build the tension that leads to the climax. At last I-lung gives in and writes the title, but he rushes immediately to his father's grave, "weeping tears of blood."

> There was no apology he could make for his disobedience. Three days he stood by the grave, refusing all food and bewailing his unfilial conduct. Around five on the morning of the third day, he fell to the ground as if dead. In a vision he saw a god up in the sky. The god looked like pictures of Indra. His retinue surrounded him.

In the ensuing conversation, I-lung discovers that the god is his father, who explains in great detail how he had suffered in hell for his sins against the Buddhist teachings and how he was finally rescued by the personified characters of the title of the Lotus Sutra which I-lung had written. At length I-lung inquires:

> "How could the titles which I wrote have saved you, for I wrote the characters without faith?" "Your hand is my hand," his father explained. "Your body is my body. The characters you wrote were characters written by me. You did not believe in the Lotus Sutra, but you saved me by writing the title. This is like a child who, playing with fire, burns something by accident. Faith in the Lotus Sutra is the same. You can have faith without realizing it and still be saved."

The liberal use of simile and metaphor, common to all Nichiren's writing, and the dialogue, add sparkle to an explanation that is best characterized by a Japanese word, *setsumeiteki* (explanatory). After this lecture in dialogue, there is a rapid conclusion—

> I-lung was favored by the king and soon the entire country had come to believe in the Lotus Sutra.

and a succinct moral—

Now the late lord Goro and the *nyūdō* were your father and son. You are the daughter of the *nyūdō*. Your faith in the Lotus Sutra has undoubtedly already guided your father and child to the palace of the Tusita heaven.

NICHIREN AND THE ZUIHITSU-CENTERED SERMON

The *zuihitsu* is closely related to the journal *(nikki)* in Japanese letters: both contain a loose, quixotically ordered collection of personal comments on events, conversations, fruits of contemplation, nature, or whatever interests the author. Shaping of the material is informal, reflecting the personality and sensitivities of the writer. It is this personal revelation that is most attractive in sermons which follow this style, and Nichiren was a master of it. His religious meditations speak to a wide audience. These letters, often lyrical, reflect the charismatic aspect of Nichiren's proselytization. In them he describes his surroundings, muses on his life and role, explores his doubts and joys, and expresses his love for his followers.

"Niiama gozen gohenji" [Reply to my lady Niiama],[14] is addressed to a young woman of the manorial family in Tōjō district, Awa province, where Nichiren grew up. She had requested a *honzon,* a mandala designed by Nichiren as a concrete object of worship, for her mother-in-law, known to us as Ōama.

The letter combines Nichiren's reminiscences about his childhood home, his expression of love for Niiama and her family, a simple discussion of the meaning of the *honzon,* and a description of Mount Minobu and Nichiren's sense of isolation there.

Opening Niiama's gift, a packet of dried seaweed, Nichiren grows nostalgic and compares the beauties of the gentle seacoast he has not seen in a decade to his hermitage in the mountains of Minobu. Wistful idealization of his boyhood home transforms the rolling mountains of Minobu into a rugged and dangerous landscape.

The Ukishima Plain of Suruga stretches more than two hundred fifty miles from the seacoast to Mount Minobu here in the Hakii district in Kai. A hundred leagues over this road are more difficult to travel than a thousand on any other. Here the swiftest river in Japan, the Fuji, plunges from north to south. On either side rise towering mountains. The valleys are deep, bordered by huge boulders aligned like folding screens. The water rushes past like an arrow shot from a tube by a stalwart warrior. At times the water is so swift and the rocks are so numerous that boats following along the banks or crossing the river are smashed to bits. Beyond these rapids stands the peak called Minobu. To the east is Tenshi Peak; to the south is Mount Takatori; to the west is Mount Shichimen; and to the north, Minobu. These mountains encircle the valley like folding screens. When I climb the mountain to look around, the forest is dark and dense. Descending into the valleys, I find fallen boulders ranked in rows.

Nichiren's reader senses his love of Awa and those who live there, banished as he was to the lonely forest where "the howls of wolves fill the mountains, while monkeys' screams echo in the valleys, and cries of deer longing for their loved ones touch the heart over the clamorous shrilling of the cicadas." His visitors are rare: a peasant gathering wood, or an old friend and fellow believer.

Dreaming of home, Nichiren superimposes the landscape of Awa upon that of Minobu:

> When I clamber eagerly up the mountain, thinking I have seen *wakame* growing, it is only bracken that grows there, row upon row. When I climb down to the valleys thinking I have seen *nori* growing, again I am mistaken: it is only parsley that sprawls in thick clumps. I had long forgotten my native village, but the *nori* you sent brought sad memories rushing over me.

Tōjō district had the added virtue in Nichiren's eyes of having been chosen by Amaterasu as her home:

> Although the Tōjō district of Awa is remote, it may be thought of as the center of Japan. This is because the great goddess, Amaterasu, appeared there. Long ago she manifested herself in Ise province, but the ruler's deepest devotion was turned to the Hachiman and Kamo shrines, and his devotion to Amaterasu was shallow. At that time, when Amaterasu was angered, there lived a man called Minamoto Yoritomo, General of the Right. He wrote a pledge of faith in Amaterasu and presented it to a priest, Ōka Kodayū, who secreted it in the Outer Shrine at Ise. It is because this pleased Amaterasu that Yoritomo became the general who took all Japan into his grasp. Did this great goddess leave Ise to settle in Tōjō of Awa when he decided on that district as her dwelling?

The sad memories inevitably include Nichiren's parents, who died two decades or so before this letter was written; thoughts of them bring him back to the problem at hand: Ōama's faith and the question of a *honzon* for her. Nichiren's father had probably been a manorial functionary. He had sided with Ōama's family in its quarrels with the *jitō* Kagenobu, as he, like the other *jitō* of the time, attempted to extend his administrative rights and his lands. In turn, Nichiren's family had been aided by the manorial family over the years, and Nichiren felt a debt of gratitude to them.

However, the problem of faith overrides all Nichiren's personal attachments to Ōama: she and her family were "given to foolish lies, sometimes believing me, sometimes attacking me—thoroughly inconstant."

Nichiren's *honzon* was a symbol of confirmation given only to those he deemed ready to practice their faith and to lead others to salvation.

Nichiren reminds Niiama of the uniqueness of his *honzon:*

> This *honzon* I worship is not mentioned in the writings of any of the many monks who traveled from India to China, nor is it mentioned by the Chinese scholars who traveled to India. If you look into such books as *Journey to the West,* the *Tz'u en ch'uan,* or the *Ch'uan teng lu,* there is mention of the *honzon* of every temple in each of the five regions of India. There are also the *honzon* of the many temples described by the saints who crossed from China to Japan and the wise men who left Japan to go to China. Because all the temples of Japan, beginning with the oldest, Gangōji and Shitennōji, have appeared in the various books written since the time of the *Annals of Japan,* surely no *honzon* has been omitted. Among them all, there is no *honzon* such as this.

He explains that the Lotus Sutra promises salvation for beings in *mappō:*

> This doctrine must not by any means be propagated during the thousand years of the True Law after my death, nor during the thousand years of the Imitation Law. At the beginning of the Latter Days when heretics fill the land, all the heavens will be angered, comets will shoot across the sky, and the earth will rumble like waves crashing onshore. Such terrible disasters as droughts, fires, floods, high winds, epidemics, plagues, famines, and armed riots will occur without number. At that time when every man will wear armor and carry a sword; when all buddhas, bodhisattvas, and good gods of heaven will have exhausted their powers; when the bodies of men falling into the deepest hell will be thick as falling rain; if you gird your body with this five-word mandala and lodge it in your heart, all rulers will be able to aid their countries and the people will escape tribulation. Moreover, in future lives they will escape the great fires of hell.

As the apostle of the Buddha sent to prepare the way for the bodhisattvas who will preach the Dharma, Nichiren has suffered exile and slander as predicted in the Lotus Sutra. The unique *honzon,* symbol of faith and practice and presented by the apostle of the Buddha, cannot be disseminated indiscriminately. Nichiren refuses, with an apology, to send a *honzon* to Ōama:

> Let me make my reasoning a little more clear. When I was in disfavor in Kamakura, 999 out of 1,000 followers lost faith, but now that the persecutions have lessened, these people have come back in repentance. Of course, your mother-in-law means more to me than these, but, while I am very sorry, I cannot return flesh to the bones. I shall forever say that one must not turn one's back on the Lotus Sutra.

The beauty of this letter lies in the smooth combination of the disparate elements. The opening nature description has Chinese overtones: the balanced prose, allusions to Chinese hermits, images from Chinese literature, and the craggy landscape reminiscent of a Chinese painting all combine to make the reader feel Nichiren's distance from home. The landscape becomes Japanese as Nichiren envisions *wakame* and *nori* growing there, and then the people of Nichiren's childhood appear in the scene.

In quest of the *honzon* Nichiren retraces this imaginary journey from India and China, where no hint of his *honzon* appeared, to earliest Japan, where again there was no such object of worship, to the Japan of his day and particularly to Tōjō in Awa, site of the revelation of the true teaching for the *mappō*. This double journey emphasizes both Nichiren's isolation and the miracle of the revelation of the *honzon* in Tōjō of all places in the wide world and in history.

Reflecting on his own role in the propagation of the teaching, Nichiren reviews the persecution he has suffered at the hands of various enemies. His reflections return to Awa as he recalls Kagenobu, his enemy and enemy of the manorial family.

The final paragraphs trace the relationship of the manorial family of Tōjō district, the "center of Japan," and the Lotus Sutra; Nichiren concludes that he cannot send a *honzon* to one whose faith has faltered, no matter how dearly he loves her.

NOTES

1. Nearly one hundred letters still exist in Nichiren's hand. *STH* includes 434 writings believed to be authentic. These, including the autographs, are scattered among numerous temples concentrated in the vicinities of Nichiren's various dwelling places: Sado, Kyōto, and the Kantō area.

2. About one hundred of Nichiren's followers can be identified by name. Of these, several are recipients of from five to twenty letters apiece. This makes it possible to trace their conversion, their doubts and fears, and Nichiren's persuasion and reassurances. Answers to their questions, suggestions for solving personal problems, and explications of doctrine enlivened by anecdotes chosen for the individual fill these letters.

3. *Ennin's Diary: The Record of a Pilgrimage to China in Search of the Law,* trans. E. O. Reischauer (New York: Ronald Press, 1955), pp. 298–299.

4. Kadokawa Motoyoshi and Sugiyama Hiroshi, *"Ai to mujō no bungei"* in *Nihon bungaku no rekishi,* volume 5 (Tokyo: Kadokawa shoten, 1967), pp. 165–166.

5. Such mendicant preachers were known as *shidosō* in the Nara period, *hijiri* in the Heian period, and *inja* in the Kamakura period. All were independent of the great monasteries and supported themselves by preaching and holding religious services. Kadokawa and Sugiyama, pp. 164, 309.

6. Kikuchi Ryōichi discusses the changes in the nature of the sermon in Japan in *Chūsei no shōdō bungei* (Tokyo: Kōshōbo, 1968).

7. Takahashi Mitsugu, *Chūko setsuwa bungaku kenkyū josetsu* (Tokyo: Ōbūsha, 1974), p. 196. Among the Agui texts are *Gonsenshū, Tenbōrinshō, Sōanshū, Hyōbyakushū,* and *Chōken sakumonshū.* Kadokawa and Sugiyama, p. 173.

8. D. E. Mills, *A Collection of Tales from Uji* (Cambridge: Cambridge University Press, 1970), p. 35.

9. The preface to the *Shasekishū* justifies the use of secular tales for religious purposes: "There is not just one gate to enter the path. There are many karmic connections that lead to enlightenment. Broadly speaking, the doctrines of the various sects do not differ. If you cultivate the way, all practices are alike. Therefore, from gossip come lessons on the Law; from jokes come enlightenment." Cited in Kubota Jun, *Chūsei bungaku no sekai* (Tokyo: Tokyo University Press, 1972), p. 124.

10. *Hokke hyakuza, Uchigikishū,* and *Kanazawa bunko-bon bukkyō setsuwashū* are believed to be sermon notes because they contain passages on doctrine and interpretation of sutras as well as plots of parables and reflective passages like those in most *setsuwa* collections.

11. Takagi Yutaka lists tales cited and related in Nichiren's letters in charts on pages 109–110, 122–123, and 141 of *Nichiren to sono montei.*

12. *STH,* pp. 1890–1894; translation in Part II of this book.

13. Takagi, *Nichiren to sono montei,* p. 114.

14. *STH,* pp. 864–870; translation in Part II, herein.

Part II
SELECTED TRANSLATIONS

Treatise on the Establishment of the Orthodox Teaching and the Peace of the Nation[1]

I. On the Cause of Natural Disasters

A visitor came and lamented: "During recent years cosmic cataclysms, natural disasters, famines, and epidemics have filled the world. Oxen and horses collapse at the crossroads; skeletons fill the lanes. Already more than half the population has died; no one is free from affliction."

In such times, some think the words "The efficacious sword is none other [than Amida's name]" are applicable, and they intone the name of the Buddha of the Western Land.[2] Others believe in the promise to eradicate all illness and recite the sutra of Yakushi, Buddha of the East.[3] Some trust in the words, "Sickness will disappear and there will be no old age, no death," and they revere the Lotus Sutra.[4] Others believe that "the seven troubles will disappear; the seven fortunes arise," and they hold the ceremony of one hundred recitations in one hundred sittings.[5] Others fill the five vessels with water according to the secret Shingon teachings.[6] Others perform *zazen* and light the moon of the vision of emptiness, or write the names of the seven guardian genies and paste them up on one thousand gates, or hang pictures of the five bodhisattvas of great power over ten thousand doors,[7] or worship the gods of heaven and of earth and hold services for them in the four quarters,[8] or govern the people with sympathy and benevolence.[9] But while we rack our minds and bodies, famine and plague grow more menacing. Everywhere we see beggars; our eyes cannot escape the sight of death. Bodies are piled as high as watchtowers, and lined up side by side like bridge planks.

The sun and moon and stars of the zodiac continue to shine in the heavens, the Three Treasures endure unchanging,[10] and the imperial line continues uninterrupted. Why then is the world crumbling so fast and the

Buddha Law decaying? What curse is this? From what fault issue such ills?

The master replied: I have sorrowed over these things, my heart filled with anger and distress. You have come to me with familiar worries. Let us talk awhile.

Those who become monks and set out on the Path hope to become buddhas through the Teaching. However, today the powers of the gods are insufficient and there are no indications of the might of the Buddha. Seeing the state of the world, men realize their own inability and have doubts about the life to come. Therefore, they look to heaven and swallow their reproaches and scrupulously bow to the earth. Knowing their limitations, they try, nevertheless, to read just a little of the scriptures, but they all turn their backs on the Truth and return to evil ways. For this reason the good gods have left the country[11]; and the sages have departed.[12] The evil spirits and demons rush in; troubles arrive, and calamities spring up. I must tell of this; I must speak forthrightly.

II. SCRIPTURAL TESTIMONY TO THE CAUSE OF NATURAL DISASTERS

The visitor said: I see that I am not alone in deploring the calamities which afflict the world and the sufferings which overwhelm the country; everyone is tormented. I have come today to your abode, in which the orchid of wisdom blooms, and for the first time I have heard that the gods and wise men have abandoned the country and disaster and calamity follow in their wake. Pray, in which sutra is this explained? Please give me evidence.

The master replied: The texts are many and evidence is plentiful. It is said in the *Konkōmyōkyō*[13]:

In that country this sutra exists, but it has not been widely taught. The people abandon the Buddha's Teachings and do not wish to hear them. No one worships or esteems them or sings praises. Even those who have entered one of the four Buddhist lives[14] and accepted the sutras[15] neither revere the sutra nor celebrate services in its honor. Finally, we four Heavenly Kings and the myriad other gods have become unable to hear the profound and marvelous Teaching. Separated from the taste of its sweet dew and from the stream of the Dharma, our majesty and strength ebb. The evil realms grow while the human and heavenly realms diminish. We have tumbled into the river of transmigration and left the path to nirvana.

Ah, World-Revered, we Heavenly Kings and all our tribe and the *yakṣas*[16] see the state of this country and renounce it, having lost all desire to protect it. We are not the only ones to abandon this realm, for the innumerable good gods who protected it go with us. When we are all gone there will be all manner of calamities and this will be the ruin of the country. There will be not one virtuous person. The people, enchained by their passions, will fight and kill. They will vilify each other, perverting the truth to slander even the innocent. Plague and disease will ravage the land; comets will cross the sky repeatedly. Two suns will shine at once. Eclipses will be irregular. Rainbows of black and white will appear as evil omens. Shooting stars will cross the sky, and the earth will shake as strange rumblings resound in the depths of wells. Violent rains and cruel winds will blow in and out of season. There will be continuous famine and plants will bear no fruit. Brigands will invade the country again and again. Every sort of misery will beset the people, and no place in the country will be happy.

The *Daishukkyō* tells us[17]:

The treasure of the Buddhist Law having disappeared, the hair, beard, and nails of priests will be allowed to grow, for monastic discipline will be lost. A loud voice will resound from high above and the earth will shake. All beings will tumble to the ground like the slats of a waterwheel. Castle walls will crumble and collapse, roofs and eaves will break and fall. Roots, branches, petals, leaves, and fruit will yield no more medicine. In all the realms below the heavens of purity,[18] the seven flavors and three vitalities[19] will fade. All good teachings which lead to deliverance will come to an end at once. The flavor of the few fruits borne will be unsavory. Every well, spring, and pond will dry up. The earth will become salt waste and erode into ridges and ravines. The mountains will parch; no rain will fall. Seedlings will wither and all life will come to an end. No more grasses will spring up. All will be dark, for dust storms will hide the moon and sun. Drought will occur everywhere. Sinister omens will recur. The ten sins and covetousness, anger, and stupidity will double. People will have no more feeling for their parents than do the animals. Short will be the lives of all beings; ugly their form. They will be weakened, and their honor and happiness will fade. All will fall into the evil destinies. By their evil acts bad rulers and monks will destroy my True Teaching, and the heavenly realms will diminish. All the good heavenly kings, those who pity living beings, will desert this impure land and turn in other directions.

We read in the *Ninnōkyō*[20]:

When a country is disturbed, the demons become restless and demoralize the people. Invaders terrorize the country and slay the people. Lords, vassals, princes, and officials quarrel. There are strange signs in heaven and on earth. The twenty-eight constellations, the stars, and the sun and moon lose their regular rhythm and stray from their courses. Outlaws appear.

The *Ninnōkyō* also says[21]:

With my five kinds of vision[22] I now see clearly all the three ages.[23] Monarchs have become rulers because they served the five hundred buddhas in the world of the past. Because of this past service, sages and arhats are born in their countries and profit it. If a ruler's good karma should be exhausted the saints will abandon the country and then the seven calamities will occur.

The *Yakushikyō* says[24]:

When these warriors and kings suffer the calamities, there will be: pestilence among the people, foreign invasion, civil revolt, stars wandering from their heavenly positions, eclipses of the sun and moon, typhoons out of season, prolonged drought.

The *Ninnōkyō* says[25]:

Oh great king! In the place where I now appear there are ten thousand million Mount Sumerus[26] and ten thousand million suns and moons. On each Mount Sumeru there are four worlds. In Jambudvīpa there are sixteen large countries, five hundred medium-sized countries, and ten thousand small countries. In each of those countries there will be seven dreadful calamities brought about by the rulers of the countries. What are those calamities? The sun and moon will stray from their paths; the seasons will come out of order; a red sun or a black sun will appear; two, three, four, or five suns will appear at once; the sun's light will be eclipsed; two, three, four, or five rings will appear around the sun. This is the first calamity.

The twenty-eight constellations will stray, and all the stars will change. This is the second calamity.

Enormous fires will sear the country. All the population will be consumed by fires caused by demons, by dragons, by the heavens, by mountain divinities, by men, by vegetation, or by brigands. Such catastrophes make up the third calamity.

Great floods will drown the people. The seasons will be reversed, with rain in winter and snow in summer. Winter will bring thunder and lightning, while June brings ice, frost, and hail. Red, black, or green rain will fall, along with mountains of earth and rocks, sand, and pebbles. Rivers will reverse their courses, carrying off mountains and boulders. Such phenomena are the fourth calamity.

Terrible winds will blow death upon the people. In an instant all the land —mountains, rivers, and forests—will be destroyed. There will be tempests out of season; black, red, and green winds; winds from the sky; winds from the earth; winds of fire and winds of water. These are the fifth calamity.

There will be drought on earth and in heaven. Flames will burst from the ground. Green plants will dry out; the five grains will not ripen. The earth will burn and the people be destroyed. These catastrophes are the sixth calamity.

Brigands will approach from all directions and invade the country. At the same time there will be rebels within the country. There will be brigands of fire, brigands of water, brigands of wind, and demon brigands. The populace will be terror-stricken and there will be fighting. Such extraordinary events are the seventh calamity.

In the *Daishukkyō* we read[27]:

> Even if a ruler in innumerable previous lives has given alms, kept the commandments, and sought wisdom, if he does not protect the Teaching when he sees it being destroyed but abandons it, the fruit of his innumerable good works will be lost and his country will be visited by three omens. These are famine, war, and epidemic. If all the good gods abandon the country, the ruler commands in vain, for the people will not obey him. Neighboring countries will invade. Fierce fires will rage uncontrolled, violent storms scourge the populace, and floods swell and submerge them. Relative will fight relative. The king will fall prey to serious illness and be reborn in the deepest hell. His wife, the crown prince, the nobles, the village chiefs, military chiefs, local rulers, and all functionaries will suffer the same fate.

The meaning of these four sutras is clear. Who in this world could doubt them? Nevertheless, these blind and deaf men, these men who have strayed, recklessly put their faith in false theories and do not recognize the correct doctrine. That is why all the Buddhas intend to abandon us and no longer want to protect us, the good gods and the sages leave the country, and demons and heretics cause trouble and give rise to disasters.

III. ASPECTS OF THE SLANDER OF THE TRUE TEACHING

The visitor replied angrily: Emperor Ming of the Latter Han dreamed of a golden man. He understood and accepted the teaching the white horse carried.[28] Prince Shōtoku punished Moriya for his treason and built a temple.[29] After their example, everyone, from sovereign to subjects, revered the images of Buddha and gave themselves to the study of the scriptures. Thus the temples of Eizan, Nanto, Onjō, and Tōji were built,[30] and now in the five central provinces and seven regions of the land copies of the sutras are scattered like stars and temples cluster thick as clouds. Wise men like Śāriputra meditate on the moon of Vulture Peak; those who follow Padmaratna follow the breezes of Mount Kukkutapada.[31] Who then scorns the teaching of Śākyamuni? Who is abandoning the Three Treasures of the Dharma? If there is proof, give it to me in detail.

The master presented these examples: The temples and sutra libraries are lined up eave to eave. Monks are countless as stalks of bamboo or reeds, lay believers as numerous as rice or hemp plants. The religious have been respected for many years, and they are honored more each

day. However, these monks deform the Teaching and lead the congregation astray. The rulers are unenlightened and do not perceive the heresy.
   In the *Ninnōkyō* it is written[32]:

There are many bad monks who seek fame and profit. To the sovereign, the crown prince, and the imperial family they preach teachings that will destroy the Law of the country. The rulers do not discern this, and, believing what they are told, they write laws arbitrarily, with no regard for the Buddhist prohibitions. This is the cause of the destruction of the Law and of the realm.

In the *Nehangyō* we read[33]:

A bodhisattva does not fear a mad elephant, but in the presence of an evil learned man, he is afraid. If one is killed by a mad elephant, one is not reborn in the three evil destinies,[34] but if one dies because of an evil friend, one will inexorably fall into those evil destinies.

In the Lotus Sutra we read[35]:

The monks of the evil world will have heterodox understanding and seek to curry favor. They will believe they have achieved enlightenment when they have not, and they will be filled with pride. Some will live in the forests, or dress in rags as hermits, and, believing they are on the True Path, they will disdain the rest of society. Because they still covet profit, they will preach to laymen and be honored like arhats of the six supernatural powers. Others constantly will go among the people and slander those who practice the Lotus Sutra. To kings and ministers and Brahmans and householders and to multitudes of other monks they will speak evil of us and say we have heretical views and preach non-Buddhist teachings.
   In an impure age and an evil world there will be much to fear. Demons will enter human bodies to malign and harm and disgrace us. The evil monks of the impure world will not know that Buddha preaches according to the audience and the time, as is appropriate. We will suffer abusive language and disgusted looks and repeated banishments from our monasteries.

The *Nehangyō* says[36]:

In the course of the centuries after my entry into nirvana, all the saints of the four paths will also enter nirvana. After the True Law is gone, in the age of the Imitation Law, there will be monks, but they will observe the discipline in appearance only. They will read the sutras but superficially. They will covet food and drink and will take great care of their persons. They will wear monks' robes, but this will be a ruse, as a hunter stalks prey or cats stalk mice. They will constantly announce that they have attained enlightenment. They will look like good and virtuous men, but they will harbor greed and jealousy. They will look like Brahmans practicing the vow of silence, but in reality they will not be true monks: They will preach wrong views vociferously and discredit the True Teaching.

Looking at the world with these scriptures in mind, we see that these things have come to pass. We must correct these bad monks to restore the good.

IV. ON THE JŌDO NENBUTSU

More angered, the visitor declared: The enlightened rulers govern by the natural laws of heaven and earth; the sages examine what is right and wrong. The monks today have converted the people of the world. If they were evil monks, the rulers would not believe them. If they were not saints, the wise men and sages would not revere them. When we see that the saints and sages honor them, we cannot belittle these great priests. Why do you spit out such lies and vilify these priests? Which of these monks is evil? Tell me precisely.

The master replied: During the reign of former Emperor Gotoba,[37] there lived a man named Hōnen who wrote the *Senjakushū*.[38] This book destroys the sacred teachings preached by Śākyamuni during his life on earth and induces all living beings to err.

In the *Senjakushū* Hōnen wrote:

The meditation master Tao-ch'o[39] established that there are two gates, that of the saints and that of the Pure Land. He rejected the way of saints and said we must return to the Pure Land. According to him, in the beginning the path of saints was divided into two: the esoteric Mahāyāna teaching and the revealed Mahāyāna teaching. But the present-day Shingon, Zen, Tendai, Kegon, Sanron, Hossō, Jiron, and Shōron teachings belong to the way of the saints.[40]

In the *Wang sheng lun chu* T'an-luan wrote[41]: "Studying the *Commentary on the Ten Stages* of Vasubandhu respectfully,[42] one reads that there are two paths for bodhisattvas who aspire to nonregression. One is the way of difficult practices; the other, the way of easy practices. The way of difficult practices is the way of the saints; that of easy practices is the way of the Pure Land. Scholars of the Pure Land sect must understand this point. Even a man who has studied the saintly way must reject it and give himself entirely to the way of the Pure Land if he intends to embrace the doctrine of easy practices."

T'an-luan also said: "The master Shan-tao[43] distinguished two types of practice, the correct and the diverse. He rejected the diverse practices and turned to the correct practice. The first of the diverse practices was the fervent reading of any of the sutras, Hīnayāna or Mahāyāna, esoteric or revealed, with the exception of the three sutras of Amida. The third of the diverse practices was the adoration of any buddha or bodhisattva or divinity, with the exception of Amida."

When one ponders this text, one must give up the diverse practices and devote oneself solely to the correct practice taught by Amida. Why reject the correct practice, which assures that of one hundred people one hundred will be reborn in paradise, and cling to the diverse practices by which only one in a thousand will be saved? You who practice, reflect on this.

Hōnen also wrote:

In the catalogue compiled in the Cheng-yuan era,[44] from the six hundred volumes of the *Daihanyakyō* to the *Hōjōjukyō,* there are 637 works of Mahāyāna esoteric and revealed scripture in 2,883 volumes. All of these must be read and understood. Know this: when the Buddha adapted his teachings to his audience's abilities, he opened two gates, one for those who could concentrate and one for those who are distracted, but when he stopped considering the abilities of beings, he stopped adapting his teachings and the separate gates of concentration and distraction were closed. The one gate which once opened will not be closed is the gate of the *nenbutsu.*

He also wrote:

In the *Kanmuryōjukyō* we read that those who practice the *nenbutsu* must be gifted with the three minds.[45] And in the commentary on this sutra,[46] we read the question: "If explications and practices differ and there are those who believe the false or diverse teachings, how can we avoid false and perverse views? Beset by false views and practices, we are like men who set out upon the road but are immediately dragged back by highwaymen." All that which is called false teaching and diverse practice and mistaken knowledge and understanding is none other than the way of saints.

At the end Hōnen wrote:

If one wishes to separate oneself from the suffering of the cycle of life and death, one must close the gate of the saintly path and choose to enter the gate of the Pure Land. If one chooses to enter the gate of the Pure Land, one must reject the diverse practices and choose to devote oneself to the correct practice.

Reading this we see that Hōnen has differentiated between the saintly path and Jōdo and between difficult practice and easy practice by citing the false explications of T'an-luan, Tao-ch'o, and Shan-tao. He has combined the Lotus teachings with Shingon and all the 2,883 scrolls of the 637 scriptures preached by Śākyamuni and all the buddhas and the bodhisattvas and heavenly beings of all the three thousand myriad worlds. He has called them "the saintly way," and "difficult practices," and "diverse practices," and has said to "reject, combat, rebuff, and cast them aside." With these four exhortations he has led many people astray and he has slandered all the saints of India, China, and Japan as well as all the disciples of the buddhas of the ten directions: he calls them highwaymen.

Moreover, he has misread the very sutra he cites, in which is found

Amida's vow to save all sentient beings, "always excepting those who break the five commandments and those who slander the True Teaching."[47] Nor did he understand the warning in the second book of the Lotus Sutra, the sutra which is central to all the teachings of the five periods of Śākyamuni's life: "If men do not believe this sutra and so treat it with disdain . . . when they die they will be reborn in the deepest hell."[48]

We have now entered the *mappō* and there are no saints, for all have set out on wrong and obscure paths and have forgotten the correct path. Is it not sad that their eyes are blind and cannot see? How pitiful that they cling to false beliefs! From ruler to people, all accept no sutras but the Amida sutras, think of no buddha but Amida with his attendants Kannon and Seishi. Dengyō, Gishin, Jikaku, Chishō,[49] and other high priests of Tendai crossed the broad seas and brought the sacred texts to Japan. Searching the mountains and rivers, they found revered Buddhist images, and they built temples on mountain summits to enshrine them and chapels in deep valleys to enthrone them.

Śākyamuni and Yakushi together distribute their power and light in the present and the future worlds.[50] The bodhisattvas Kokūzō and Jizō refuse Buddhahood for the sake of the beings of this and future worlds.[51] The sovereign and local lords donate fields and paddies throughout the country to keep the torch of the Law ablaze.

However, because of Hōnen's *Senjakushū*, Śākyamuni is forgotten and the Lord of the Western Pure Land revered. Worship of Yakushi, to whom Saichō built an altar, is rejected, and people cling only to the four schools of the three Amida sutras, while throwing away all the other sutras preached by Śākyamuni during the five periods of his life.

No one makes offerings or worships in any temple unless it is dedicated to Amida, and no one thinks of giving alms to a monk who does not practice the *nenbutsu*. Temples fall to ruin and moss covers their roofs. No one walks in the compounds where wild grasses grow. Yet there is no one who is sorry and no one who wishes to rebuild. Since the monks have gone, the gods who protect the temples have left as well. All of this is because of Hōnen's *Senjakushū*.

How sad that in a few decades hundreds and thousands have been fascinated by this devil and so have lost the Buddhist path. They anger the good gods by loving the false teaching and forgetting the True. They reject the perfect teaching and adore the imperfect. Is this not the work of evil demons? Rather than hold rites and services, would it not be better to outlaw this one false teaching?

V. The Cause of Calamity and Disaster

The visitor's face turned purple and he argued: After our teacher Śākyamuni preached the three Pure Land sutras, the Master T'an-luan abandoned the teachings found in the four commentaries,[52] and fervently longed for the Pure Land; Tao-ch'o gave up the study of the *Nehangyō* and taught only practices leading to the Western Pure Land; Shan-tao rejected the diverse practices and established the sect which practices only the *nenbutsu;* Genshin[53] extracted the essence of all the sutras and wrote the *Ōjōyōshū,* honoring the sole practice of the *nenbutsu*. In truth, it was thus that devotion to Amida was born.

Are there not many who achieved rebirth in paradise through this teaching? Among them is Hōnen, who climbed Mount Hiei as a youth and at seventeen was versed in the Lotus Sutra and the sixty scrolls of commentary by Chih-i. He had a thorough knowledge of the doctrines of the eight sects. He had read all of the sutras and *śastras* seven times; there was not a commentary or biography he had not examined. His wisdom was bright as the sun and moon; his virtue surpassed that of masters of old.

However, he could not find the path that leads from the cycle of births and deaths, and he could not divine the meaning of nirvana. He searched everywhere, reflected profoundly and extensively, and finally gave up all the sutras for the sole practice of the *nenbutsu*. Then he was favored with a dream in which Shan-tao appeared to him, and he propagated the *nenbutsu* everywhere among those whom he loved as well as among those who were unknown to him to the borders of the country. Thus, some call him an incarnation of Seishi (Mahāsthāmaprāpta), and others regard him as a reincarnation of Shan-tao. Everywhere the humble and the grand bowed their heads before him, and men and women throughout the country flocked to him. Since that time many springs and autumns have passed and the bright stars and frosts of winter have returned again and again.

Now, without regard for the teachings of the venerated Śākyamuni, you willfully denigrate the sutras of Amida. Why do you blame the recent calamities on earlier innocent times, malign former teachers, and calumniate the saints? If you blow the hair aside, you will find scratches; if you cut the skin, you will make blood flow.[54] Never have I heard such outrageous arguments. You should be ashamed and humbled. Your sin is grave. How can you escape its consequences? To sit here face to face with you frightens me. I want to take up my staff and leave.

The master repressed a smile as he spoke: People get used to the taste of nettles and forget the stench of latrines.[55] Hearing good, they think it is bad. They point to liars and say they are saints. They doubt the teachers of the Truth and call them heretics. Truly these are profound errors, grave sins. Hear how this came about. I will explain it with care.

The Venerable Śākyamuni, in presenting his teaching in the course of the five periods of his life, distinguished between early and later teachings, and provisional and True teachings. T'an-luan, Tao-ch'o, and Shan-tao clung to the provisional teachings and forgot the True ones; they trusted in the early teachings and rejected the later ones. They did not explore the great depths of Buddhism. Hōnen delved into their teachings, but did not explore their sources. Therefore, when he said to reject, combat, rebuff, and cast aside the 2,883 scrolls of the 637 Mahāyāna scriptures and all the buddhas, bodhisattvas, and divinities of the world, he damned all living beings.

He spread his own perverse beliefs and did not reflect on the scriptures. His were the worst of lies, wicked speech which has no equal and which cannot be sufficiently condemned. All the world believes his lies and all the world reveres the *Senjakushū*. They honor the three Amida sutras and reject all other sutras, worship the Buddha of the Pure Land and forget all others. Truly this man was an enemy of all the buddhas and all the scriptures, a foe of the saintly monks and of humanity.

These perverse teachings have spread through the world; they circulate everywhere. Therefore people fear to attribute the calamities of recent years to these past errors. I will give you some illustrations to dispel your illusions.

In the *Mo ho chih kuan,*[56] Chih-i cites the *Shi chi*[57]: "At the end of the Chou period, there were men who went about with hair disheveled, unclothed, ignoring the rules of etiquette." In the *Hung chüeh*[58] commentary on this passage, we read the following quotation from the *Tso chuan*[59]: "When the Emperor P'ing was moving the capital to the east, they saw, at the I River, men with disheveled hair performing religious rites in the fields. A wise man said, 'Not one hundred years will pass before etiquette dies'." He meant by this that such signs were a portent of calamities in the future.

In the *Mo ho chih kuan* we also read:

> Yuan-chi,[60] an eminent sage, was an eccentric who went about with hair disheveled and sash unfastened. Later the children of the nobility copied his behavior. They said that hurling insults in rude language testified to their naturalness and that those who were concerned with manners deserved to be called peasants. This was an omen of the fall of the Ssu-ma family.

In *Travels in China* by Jikaku,[61] we read that in 841 the Emperor Wu-tsung ordered the monk Ching-shuang of the Chang-ching Temple to propagate the invocation to Amida in all the temples. At each temple he preached for three days. In 842 the Uigur troops breached the frontiers, and in 843 the military governor of Hopei revolted. After that, Tibet refused tribute, and the Uigurs grasped more and more territory. The warfare recalled that of the time of Hsiang-yu.[62] Fire destroyed villages and cities. There was a repression of Buddhism, and many temples and pagodas were leveled. Unable to master the disorder, Wu-tsung died insane.

Reflect on this then. Hōnen lived under former Emperor Gotoba in the Kennin era, and what happened to Gotoba we have seen with our own eyes. Such evidence is found in both China and Japan. Have no further doubts, no uncertainty. Chase away the evil and return to the good. Block evil at its source. Cut it off at the roots.

VI. Precedents for Condemnation of Heretics

The visitor, somewhat reassured, said: I am beginning to understand where you are leading. However, from Kyōto to Kamakura there are many eminent monks who are pivots and pillars of the Law. Not one of these men has advanced such reflections or addressed them to the authorities. You are but a humble man, yet you give out such obloquy. This is really unjustifiable.

The master replied: I myself have little weight, but I have studied the Mahāyāna with gratitude. If a fly rides on the tail of a good horse, it can travel ten thousand leagues. Ivy can climb a thousand feet if it clings to the branches of a pine. I was born a child of the Buddha and I serve the Lotus, king of the sutras. How could I not feel desolate at the spectacle of the decay of the Buddha's teachings?

Moreover, the *Nehangyō says:*

> If a good monk, knowing that someone attacks the Law, lets him do it and does not attack him or pursue him or condemn him, know well that that monk is an enemy of the Buddha Law. If he chases the evildoer and punishes him and condemns him, that monk is my disciple and hears my teaching.

I am not a "good monk," but to avoid being punished as an enemy of the Law, I must preach the essence of the Buddha's teaching.

In the Gennin era,[64] at the instigation of Enryakuji and Kōfukuji, which had addressed frequent requests to the government, an imperial edict and a shogunal order were sent out to assemble at the Daikōdō the printing blocks of the *Senjakushū* of Hōnen and to burn them to attain thereby the grace of the Buddha in the three worlds. The shrine servants of the Kanjin'in were to destroy Hōnen's tomb. His disciples, Ryūkan, Shōkō, Jōkaku, Sasshō, and the rest, were exiled to distant provinces and have not been pardoned. How can you say that critical memorials have not been addressed to the authorities?

VII. Countering the Calamities

The visitor, almost convinced, replied: The debasement of the sutras and calumnies against monks are hard for me to judge myself. Hōnen did say to reject, combat, rebuff, and cast aside all the 2,883 scrolls of the 637 Mahāyāna scriptures as well as all the buddhas, the bodhisattvas, and gods of the three thousand myriad worlds. There is no denying this, the texts are clear.

But you say that this is erroneous and slanderous to the Law. It is difficult to know if Hōnen was wrong or right, whether he spoke from ignorance or sagacity. However, it is widely rumored that the *Senjakushū* is the cause of the recent calamities; many people give this explanation.

And, after all, peace in the world and tranquility in the country are desired by sovereign and subjects alike. Countries flourish because of the Law, and the Law is revered by the people. If the country disappears and the people die, who will worship the Buddha and who will believe the Law? One must pray for the country, and then the Buddhist Law can be established. If there is a way to end these calamities, I want to know it.

The master said: I am stubborn and pigheaded. I do not believe myself a superior man. But I am going to tell you what I think about the sutras. There are so many texts, both Buddhist and non-Buddhist, which tell how to avoid calamities that it is impossible to peruse them all. However, if one takes the Buddhist Path and meditates, one realizes that if one opposes those who speak ill of the Law and honors those who keep to the Correct Path, the country will be tranquil and the world will be at peace.

For it is written in the *Nehangyō*[65]:

The Buddha said: It is praiseworthy to give alms, but there is one category to whom you should not give. Cunda asked: Who are these men who are excepted? The Buddha replied: Those whom this sutra shows to violate the prohibitions. Cunda spoke again: Still I do not understand. Will you explain this to me? The Buddha spoke these words: The violators of the prohibitions are *icchantika*.[66] To give alms to anyone else is praiseworthy and brings great rewards. Cunda again asked: What does this word *icchantika* mean? Buddha replied: Oh, Cunda. If a monk or a nun, a layman or laywoman, uses abusive language to outrage the True Law, if in committing this heavy sin he has no remorse and no regret in his heart, such a person has taken the path of the *icchantika*. If he commits the four sins or breaks the five prohibitions, and, knowing his grave sin, has no fear or remorse and refuses to confess; if he has no thought of protecting the Law to make it prosper, but violates it and degrades it; if his words are sinful and untruthful, such a man or woman is said to take the path of the *icchantika*. Excepting such *icchantika,* it is praiseworthy to give alms to all.

It is also written[67]:

I remember long ago I was king of a great country in this world and my name was Hsien-yu. I loved the Mahāyāna scriptures and venerated them. My heart was pure and good, without coarseness, jealousy, or avarice. Oh excellent man! At that time I honored the Mahāyāna, and when I heard the

Brahmans speak ill of the Mahāyāna teachings I cut short their lives immediately. Oh excellent man! Though I committed such acts, I have never
fallen into hell.

It is also written[68]:

Long ago, when the Tathāgata was king and practiced the way of the
bodhisattva, he killed some Brahmans of that country.

It also is written[69]:

There are three types of murder, called minor, middle, and major. The
killing of any animal down to an ant is a minor murder. Only an instance
where a bodhisattva has assumed animal form to effect a salvation is excepted. In consequence of a minor murder, one falls into the realms of hell,
of animals, or of hungry ghosts, and suffers minor torment. Why? It is
because there exist among the animals some seeds of good and their
murderer must receive some punishment for his fault.

A middle murder is the killing of beings ranging from ordinary men to
anagāmin.[70] In consequence of a middle murder, one falls into the realms
of hell, of animals, or of hungry ghosts, and suffers middle torment.

Killing beings ranging from one's father and mother to *pratyekabud-
dhas*[71] or bodhisattvas[72] leads to the deepest hell.

Oh excellent man! If one should kill an *icchantika,* his action does not fit
into any of these types of murder. Excellent man, the Brahmans of whom I
spoke were all *icchantika.*

In the *Ninnōkyō* we read[73]:

The Buddha said to King Prasenajit: It is for this reason that the Teaching depends on kings and not on monks and nuns. Monks and nuns do not
have the same power as a king.

In the *Nehangyō* we read[74]:

Now the prosperity of the Correct Teaching, which is without superior,
depends on kings, nobles, ministers, and the faithful of the four categories.
If someone tries to malign the Teaching, the ministers and the faithful
should apply themselves to countering this.

We also read in the *Nehangyō*[75]:

Kāśyapa attained the indestructible body of a Buddha by protecting the
True Teaching. O excellent man! Those who protect the True Teaching are
exempt from the five prohibitions and need not keep the monastic rules.
They may carry swords, and bows and arrows, and pikes.

We also read[76]:

If there is a man who accepts the five prohibitions, he cannot be called a
man of the Mahāyāna. If he protects the true teaching, even without accept-

ing the five prohibitions, he is called a man of the Mahāyāna. A man who protects the true teaching must carry swords and weapons. Though he bears sword and staff, I say this shall be called keeping the prohibitions.

We also read[77]:

Oh excellent man! In a past world there appeared in Kōshinajō a buddha called the Tathāgata Kangizō. After this buddha entered nirvana, the reign of the True Law lasted for countless kalpas. Forty years after the end of this period, when the reign of the True Law was over, there was a monk who observed the prohibitions. He was called Kakutoku. At that time there were also many monks who violated the prohibitions. Hearing Kakutoku preach the Law, evil intentions came to them and they took arms and attacked him. The king, Utoku, wishing to protect the Law, went to the preacher and fought resolutely against all the monks who transgressed the prohibitions. The preacher thus escaped harm, but the king was wounded by sword and arrow and lance. Not an area the size of a poppy seed was uninjured. At that time Kakutoku praised the king: "This is good. This is good. Oh King, you have truly protected the Teaching. In a future life you will become an immeasurable receptacle of the Buddha's Teachings."

The king, having been able to hear the Teaching, felt great joy, and, when he died, he was reborn in the land of the Buddha Ashuku and became his first disciple. After their deaths the generals and soldiers, the people and household of the king, all those who had fought and who felt great joy, conceived the unchanging idea of attaining Buddhahood and all were reborn in the country of the Buddha Ashuku. The monk Kakutoku was also reborn in the country of Ashuku and became the second disciple among all those who heard this buddha.

If there comes a time when men want to bring an end to the Teaching, it will be necessary to protect it and to defend it. Oh Kāśyapa. That king was me. And the monk who taught the Law was the Buddha Kāśyapa. Oh Kāśyapa. Those who protect the Teaching gather immeasurable rewards comparable to these. Thanks to this causal chain I am today endowed with all manner of signs which are my ornament, and I have attained the indestructible body of the Dharma.

Continuing to instruct Kāśyapa, the Buddha said:

Thus it is that the laymen who guard the Teaching should take up swords and staves to protect it. Oh excellent man! After my nirvana, the world will be impure and the country troubled. Men will rob each other and people will starve. Many will become monks because of hunger. Such people will be called the shaven-heads. When this band of shaven-heads see monks defend the Law, they will pursue them and kill them or injure them. Therefore I permit those who observe the prohibitions to arm laymen and keep them as bodyguards. Even though they have arms, they will not kill.

The Lotus Sutra says[78]:

> If men do not believe this sutra and so treat it with disdain, all seeds of
> Buddhahood will disappear from this world . . . . Moreover, after they die
> these men will fall into the deepest hell.

The texts are clear. What can my words add? According to the Lotus
Sutra, those who denigrate the scriptures of the Mahāyāna commit a sin
far worse than the five immeasurable sins, and they will fall into the
deepest hell from which they will not escape through all eternity. According to the *Nehangyō,* one may give alms to those who have committed
the five immeasurable sins, but it is forbidden to give to those who denigrate the Law.

Those who kill even an ant fall into the three evil realms, but those
who prevent slander of the Teaching will achieve the stage from which
there is no backsliding. He who was called Kakutoku was the Buddha
Kāśyapa. King Utoku was Śākyamuni. The teachings of the Lotus Sutra
and the *Nehangyō* are the most important of all the teachings of the five
periods of Śākyamuni's life. To obstruct their distribution is extremely
grave. Who could turn from them and disbelieve?

Nevertheless, that rabble who slander the Law forget those who follow
the Correct Path and are led to even darker ignorance by the *Senjakushū*
of Hōnen. Some revere his mortal body and carve statues of wood or
paint his image; others believe his lies and engrave the *Senjakushū* on
wood, carrying it through the country and making it known to all the
people. People revere Hōnen's teaching and give alms to his followers.
Some cut the hands from statues of Śākyamuni and substitute hands in
the mudra of Amida. Others transform the temples of Yakushi, enshrin-
ing statues of Amida there, and some stop copying the Lotus Sutra,
which has been a tradition for four hundred years, and copy instead the
three Amida sutras. Still others substitute lectures commemorating Shan-
tao for those held in memory of Chih-i. In truth, it is difficult to describe
all such instances.

Is this not destroying the Buddha? destroying the Law? destroying the
Community of Monks? These heretical beliefs are due to the *Senjakushū.* How sad to see people turning from the true admonitions of the
Buddha! How lamentable to see people follow the perverse teachings of
an ignorant man! If one wishes to return peace to the world, it is necessary to stop the spread of heresy.

VIII. Outlawing Heresy

The visitor spoke: Must one kill, as in the sutra, to suppress those who
desecrate the Law and eliminate those who do not observe the Buddha's
prohibitions? That will just add to the killing, and sins will multiply.

The *Daishukkyō* says[79]:

> When a man has shaved his head and put on the robes of a monk,
> whether he observes or despises the prohibitions, the gods and men must
> make offerings to him, for it is to me that those offerings are addressed.
> That man is my child, and if someone strikes him, it is my son he strikes. If
> someone insults him, it is my son he insults.

We know by this that we must give alms whether a monk be good or
bad, worthy or unworthy. To strike and insult the child is to attack the
father. Those pagans armed with bamboo staves who murdered the venerated Maudgalyāyana sank to the depths of the deepest hell. Devadatta
killed the nun Utpalavarṇa and suffered the flames of the deepest hell.
This testimony is clear, and generations to come will fear it. Punishing
those who despise the Law is prohibited by Buddha. How can I believe it
is right? How may I understand this?

The master replied: You have heard the sutras and still you speak so!
Have I not touched your heart, not made you understand? I have not
forbidden alms to all monks, for monks are the children of the Buddha,
but only to those who slander the Teaching. In the ages before Śākyamuni, those who sinned were put to death, but Śākyamuni taught us to
cease to make offerings to them. If all four categories of Buddhists in
every country of the world stop giving alms to sinful monks and return to
the True Teaching, what kind of calamities can occur, what evils can appear?

IX. The Visitor's Understanding and Discussion of the True Buddhist Country

The visitor knelt on the floor and adjusted his robe: The teachings of
Buddha are varied and it is difficult to discover their import. Incertitudes
abound and my comprehension is hazy. However, the errors of Hōnen
are evident. He wrote that all the buddhas, all sutras, all bodhisattvas,
and all gods should be rejected, combated, rebuffed, cast aside: the texts
are clear. The consequence is that the saints leave the country, the good
gods renounce it, hunger and thirst reign throughout the land, and the
world is prey to epidemics. Master, you have quoted widely from the
scriptures and made the meaning clear. My blind attachments are loos-
ened; my eyes and ears have seen and heard clearly. In sum, everyone
from ruler to peasants loves and demands peace and tranquility in the
country and the world. If we stop giving alms to *icchantika* and make offerings to monks and nuns, if we clear the pirates from the ocean of Buddhism and slay the robbers in the mountains of the Law, the idyllic world
of emperors Hsi and Nung will return and there will be peace as in the
time of T'ang and Yu. Having judged the depth of the teachings of the
Buddha, people will revere that teaching which is the pillar of the house
of Buddhism.

The master joyfully answered: As the pigeon changes into a hawk and the sparrow becomes a clam to live through the winter,[80] so you have changed. How happy I am that, like the creeping artemesia which grows upright in hemp fields, you have changed in my company. In truth, if people reflect on the calamities of recent years and believe my words, the wind will calm, the waves will quiet, and soon there will be only years of abundance.

However, people's hearts vary with the times and the nature of objects changes with the milieu, just as the moon shifts as it is reflected in the waves and the tide of battle sways toward the stronger camp. For the moment you have faith, but later you will forget. If you seek present and future peace for the country, you must not hesitate to take measures against false ideas.

For what reason, you ask. Of the seven calamities described in the *Yakushikyō*,[81] five have occurred. Only two remain: invasion from abroad and internal fighting. Of the three disasters foretold in the *Daishukkyō*,[82] two have occurred and only one, warfare, has not. The various troubles and unhappinesses described in the *Konkōmyōkyō*[83] have all occurred one after the other except invasion by pillagers from another land. Of the seven calamities foretold in the *Ninnōkyō*,[84] six have wreaked their havoc and only one has not yet happened: again it is the arrival of brigands to violate the country. The *Ninnōkyō* also says that such suffering is caused by the unleashing of the evil demons and when the demons are active the people are prey to troubles. It is predicted that one hundred demons will become active, and many people will be killed.

The calamities of the past are well known to us all. Why doubt those which are to come? If all the remaining disasters befall us at once because of the spread of heresy, what will be our fate?

The foundation of an emperor's rule is his country; the people cultivate the fields and maintain the nation. Should there be a foreign invasion or internal rebellion, the country will be in turmoil and confusion. When one's house is in ruins, when one has lost his country, where can one flee? If you wish tranquility for yourself, you must pray for the peace of the world. Men in this world fear for the future and put their faith in false teachings or revere those who slander the True Teaching. Each is afraid of choosing the wrong path and finds it hard to give himself up to the Law of Buddha. Why put the effort of faith into lies and heresy? If you do not reverse your attachments and give up your mistaken ideas, you will soon leave this inconstant world and fall into the deepest hell.

The reason for this is found in the *Daishukkyō*[85]:

Even when in innumerable former lives a king has given alms, observed the prohibitions, and worked for wisdom, if he does not protect my Law but abandons it when he sees it being destroyed, the innumerable seeds of good that he planted will be annihilated. The king will soon fall ill, and after his death he will be reborn in the deepest hell. His wife, the crown prince, the nobles, the village chiefs, the military chiefs, the local ruler, and the officials all will suffer the same fate.

The *Ninnōkyō* says[86]:

If the Buddhist teaching is destroyed, there will be no more filial piety, no more peaceful relationships; the gods will no longer give aid; daily the world will be beset by epidemics and evil demons; unnatural phenomena will assail us and disasters spread far and near. At their death men will go to hell or to the realms of the hungry ghosts or animals. If they should be reborn as men, they will be fighting slaves, as surely as an echo follows sound or a shadow chases its object. If a man is writing at night and the light is extinguished, the characters continue to exist. Just so the retribution of rebirth in these three realms persists.

We read in the second roll of the Lotus Sutra[87]: "If a man does not believe in this sutra and speaks ill of it, that man will go to the deepest hell after death." In the seventh roll, Jōfukyō chapter,[88] we read: "For one thousand kalpas, they suffered terrible torments in the deepest hell." The *Nehangyō* says[89]: "If a man leaves his good companions and does not listen to the True Teaching but believes the false teachings, he will sink to the deepest hell and his body will be stretched 840,000 kalpas in every direction."

Having widely examined the sutras, we find that the denigration of the Law is the heaviest of sins. How sad that all the world has left the gate of the True Law and entered that passageway to hell which is the false teaching. How stupidly each is caught up in the nets of evil teachings, tangled in the snares of slander of the True Law forever. This fog of errors will lead to the flames of hell. Is this not sad? Is it not pitiful?

Hurry to modify your faith and return quickly to the good, true vehicle. These three realms will become the unchanging realm of Buddha. The whole world will become a jeweled land, a land which will last forever. The country will never decline, never collapse; men will live in security and serenity. Believe and trust these words.

X. Promise of Conversion

The visitor said: Who in this world and in the world to come will not respect and fear your words? Having now opened the sutras and understood the meaning of the Buddha's words, I know that slandering the Teaching is a grave sin and disgracing the Law a serious crime. I had faith in one Buddha and rejected all others, revering three sutras and casting the rest aside, but I was following the teachings of others and not my own ideas. The other men of this world do the same. We make ourselves suffer in this life and cause ourselves to fall into hell in the next. The texts show this clearly; there is no doubt. More and more I respect your loving teaching, and my stubborn heart opens to the truth. May people promptly take action against the propagation of errors! May they soon pacify the land! In this life we will know peace and in the next we will be saved. May I be not alone to believe and may the errors of others be corrected!

NOTES

1.   *STH*, pp. 209–227. This essay was composed in 1260 as a memorial to the shogunate. The divisions and titles are those supplied in *Shinranshū Nichiren-shū*, NKBT 82, pp. 292–318.

2.   A phrase from *Pan chou san mei tsan* by Shan-tao (613–681). This Amidist work begins: "The efficacious sword is none other than Amida's name. If you once call on his name, all your sins will be cancelled." T47, p. 448c. This plaint by the visitor introduces the inefficacy of Jōdo, Tendai, Shingon, Shintō, and divination in dealing with the current calamities and the desperate search for a religious solution to problems of a troubled age.

3.   This is the seventh of the twelve vows made by Yakushi when he became a bodhisattva, as recorded in the *Yakushi nyōrai hongankyō*. T14, p. 405a.

4.   Lotus Sutra, chapter 23, T9, p. 54c.

5.   T8, p. 832b. The *Ninnōkyō*, by virtue of a story it contains in which a king defeats another by having the sutra read one hundred times by one hundred priests, was considered one of the "nation-protecting sutras."

6.   One type of ritual worship service performed by Shingon priests involves pouring water into five different-colored flasks arranged on an altar.

7.   The *Ninnōkyō* promises that these gods will protect both the country and its people. T8, p. 833a.

8.   Shintō propitiatory rites were held in the northeast, northwest, southeast, and southwest quarters.

9.   This is the Confucian program for keeping a country happy and peaceful.

10.   The Three Treasures of Buddhism: Buddha, the Law, and the Community of Monks.

11.   Indian and Japanese gods adopted by Buddhism were considered protectors of the people and the Buddhist teachings.

12.   Men of superior understanding recognize the degeneracy of the times and abandon the country to its decline.

13.   T16, pp. 429c–430a.

14.   Ordained priests and nuns and lay men and women, the "four categories of believers."

15.   *Jikyōsha.*

16.   Originally Hindu gods, adopted into Buddhism as protectors and defenders of

believers under the command of one of the four Heavenly Kings, Bishamonten (Vaiśravaṇa).

17. T13, p. 379b.
18. The dwelling place of those who will not return to the world of desire.
19. Sweet, sour, bitter, salt, vinegar, astringent, and light tastes and vitalities of the earth, of laws, and of mankind.
20. T8, p. 830a.
21. T8, p. 833a.
22. Human, deva, Hīnayāna wisdom, bodhisattva, and Buddha-vision.
23. Past, present, and future.
24. T14, p. 407c.
25. T8, p. 832bc.
26. The central mountain of the universe in Indian cosmology. At each cardinal point is a continent. Jambudvīpa, the continent to the south of Mount Sumeru, comprises the world known to the early Indians. To the east is Pūrva-videha; to the west, Apara-godānīya; to the north, Uttara-kuru.
27. T13, p. 173a.
28. Emperor Ming (reign, A.D. 58–75) helped propagate Buddhism in China. According to legend, an enormous golden man appeared to him in a dream. Understanding that this was the Buddha, he sent a mission to India. The mission returned with missionaries traveling with a statue of Buddha and a white horse.
29. Shōtoku Taishi (571–631) was important in the early acceptance of Buddhism in Japan. He founded Shitennōji, among other temples. Mononobe Moriya was an adversary who opposed Buddhism and supported a rival candidate to the throne.
30. Enryakuji, the Nara temples, Onjōji near Ōtsu, and Tōji in Kyōto.
31. Śāriputra, wisest of the Buddha's disciples, meditated on the Buddha's teachings and attained enlightenment through knowledge. Padmaratna is the twenty-third Indian patriarch of the Zen sect, and Mount Kukkuṭapāda is the site of the nirvana of Kāśyapa, the disciple to whom the Buddha is said to have imparted the tradition of Zen.
32. T8, p. 833c.
33. T12, p. 401c.
34. The hells, life as an animal, and the condition of a hungry ghost.
35. T9, p. 36bc.
36. T12, p. 386b.
37. Gotoba reigned from 1183–1198. He died in 1239 after years of intrigue, including the Jōkyū War of 1221 for which he was exiled. Nichiren often reminded his followers that Gotoba had relied on Shingon rituals and prayers to support his causes.
38. Hōnen (1133–1212) founded the Jōdo sect. He wrote the *Senjakushū* in 1198.
39. 562–645. Second of the five Chinese patriarchs of the Pure Land sect.
40. Jiron is a school which studied commentary on the *Daśabhūmika* by Vasubandhu. The Shōron school studied the *Mahayana saṁparigraha-śāstra* attributed to Asaṅga of the Yogācāra school.
41. 476–542. Founder of the Pure Land sect in China.
42. *Daśabhūmi vibhāṣa śāstra.*
43. 613–681.
44. The *Cheng yuan hsin ting shih chiao mu lu,* compiled in 800, by Yuan-chao.
45. Three assured ways of reaching the Pure Land: by perfect sincerity, profound resolve, and profound determination to distribute one's merits to others.

46. *Kuan ching shu* by Shan-tao.
47. T12, p. 268a.
48. Chapter 3; T9, p. 15b.
49. Dengyō Daishi, or Saichō (767–822), was the founder of the Tendai sect in Japan. Gishin, Jikaku (Ennin), and Chishō (Enchin) were later superiors at Enryakuji.
50. Images of Śākyamuni and Yakushi are enshrined at Enryakuji.
51. These bodhisattvas are also enshrined at Enryakuji.
52. The three texts studied by the San-lun (Sanron) school, the *Mādhyamika śāstra* of Nāgārjuna, the *Śata śāstra* of Āryadeva, and the *Dvadaśanikāya śāstra* of Nāgārjuna, plus the *Ta chih tu lun* of Nāgārjuna.
53. 942–1017. A Tendai priest who was a great exponent of the cult of Amida, author of the *Ōjōyōshū,* an Amidist classic.
54. When you look for trouble, you will find it.
55. People become accustomed to even the worst things.
56. Lectures by Chih-i (538–597), founder of T'ien-t'ai.
57. The *Historical Records,* by Ssu-ma Ch'ien (145–86 B.C.?).
58. *Mo ho chih kuan fu hsing chuan hung chüeh* by Miao-lo (711–782).
59. A commentary on *The Spring and Autumn Annals,* one of the classical Chinese histories.
60. 210–263. One of the Seven Sages of the Bamboo Grove.
61. Jikaku (794–864) is better known in the West as Ennin. The record of his journey to China has been translated by E. O. Reischauer as *Ennin's Diary* (New York: Ronald Press Company, 1955).
62. 233–202 B.C. King of the Chou who spent his whole life at war.
63. T12, p. 381a.
64. 1224–1225.
65. T12, p. 425a.
66. "A sentient being who, being inherently unreceptive to the teachings of the Buddha, will never attain enlightenment," *Japanese-English Buddhist Dictionary,* p. 132.
67. In the *Nehangyō,* T12, p. 434c.
68. T12, p. 459a.
69. T12, p. 460b.
70. One who has become exempt from transmigration and will not be reborn into the world of desire.
71. One who attains enlightenment alone and has as object only his own nirvana.
72. One who has vowed not to enter nirvana but to work for the salvation of sentient beings.
73. T8, p. 832c.
74. T12, p. 381a.
75. T12, p. 383b.
76. T12, p. 384a.
77. T12, pp. 383c–384b.
78. Chapter 3; T9, p. 15b.
79. T13, p. 379c.
80. A traditional explanation of hibernation and migration. NKBT, p. 315, n. 27.
81. See *Risshō Ankokuron,* part II, note 24.
82. See *Risshō Ankokuron,* part II, note 27.
83. See *Risshō Ankokuron,* part II.

84.   See *Risshō Ankokuron,* part II, note 20.
85.   T13, p. 173a.
86.   T8, p. 833c.
87.   Chapter 3, "Parable"; T9, p. 15b.
88.   Chapter 20, "Sadāparibhūta"; T9, p. 51a.
89.   T12, p. 575a.

Treatise on the Recitation of the Title of the Lotus Sutra[1]

WRITTEN BY NICHIREN,
DISCIPLE OF KONPON DAISHI

Namu Myōhōrengekyō

Question: If someone did not know the real meaning of the Lotus Sutra and did not understand its import, but merely recited the words "Namu Myōhōrengekyō" once a day or once a month or once a year or once in ten years or once in a lifetime, without being tempted by evil deeds, great or small, would that person not only avoid the four evil realms but also achieve that stage from which there is no return?

Answer: He would.

Question: Fire does not burn unless you touch it. Water does not quench thirst unless you drink it. How can recitation of the *daimoku,* "Namu Myōhōrengekyō," without understanding exempt you from the evil destinies?

Answer: If you pluck a lute string made from the sinews of a lion, all other strings are silenced.[2] If you hear of the refreshing fruit of the plum, saliva moistens your mouth. These are mysteries of the world. How much more mysterious the Flower of the Law! The parrot which chirped the four noble truths was reborn in heaven.[3] Those who remembered the Three Treasures escaped the whale.[4] How much more miraculous is the Title of the Lotus Sutra, the essence of the eighty thousand holy teachings, the eye of all the buddhas! In the Lotus Sutra, where the Buddha dispenses with expedient devices,[5] are these words: "By faith you can enter."[6] The *Nehangyō,* the last sutra preached in the grove of *śāla* trees, says: "Enlightenment has many causes, but all are united in a faithful heart."

Faith is the basis for entering the Buddha Way. The fifty-two stages to enlightenment are founded on the ten stages of faith.[7] The first of the ten stages of faith is a faithful heart. He who has a faithful heart, though he be unenlightened, is a wise man despite his ignorance. He who lacks faith, though he be enlightened, slanders the Teachings and is an *icchantika*. The monk Sunakṣatra[8] kept the two hundred fifty rules of discipline, performed the four meditations, and recited the twelve types of scripture; and Devadatta memorized the sixty thousand non-Buddhist and the eighty thousand Buddhist scriptures and mastered the eighteen supernatural powers; but both these men had knowledge without faith. We hear that they are still in the deepest hell.

The most foolish disciple, Kṣudrapanthaka, had no wisdom and no enlightenment. But he believed with all his heart and he became the Tathāgata Fumyō.[9] Maudgalyāyana and Śāriputra too were without enlightenment but full of faith. The Buddha promised they would become the tathāgatas Kekō and Kōmyō.[10]

The Buddha said: "He who begins to doubt and does not have faith will fall into the evil destinies."[11] This is his statement that those who are enlightened but have no faith will all fall into the evil destinies. However, scholars today insist no one can escape the evil destinies by reciting "Namu Myōhōrengekyō" with faith but without understanding. As predicted in the scripture, these scholars will be unable to avoid the deepest hell. Even if you are not enlightened, you will escape the evil destinies if you recite "Namu Myōhōrengekyō."

The lotus blossom turns to face the sun though it has no mind. The banana tree grows when it thunders though it has no ears.[12] We are like the lotus blossom and the banana tree, and the Title of the Lotus Sutra is like the sun and thunder. If you hold the horn of a rhinoceros, the waters will part for you to pass.[13] A leaf of sandalwood will mask the smell of the pungent *erāvana*.[14] Our evil karma is like the *erāvana* and the water. The Title of the Lotus Sutra is like the horn of the rhinoceros or the leaf of sandalwood. The diamond is so hard it cuts anything but the horns of a sheep or the shell of a tortoise.[15] The branches of the *ni-chu-lei* tree never break under the weight of the largest bird, but the *chiao-liao*, which can nest on the eyelash of a mosquito, breaks those branches.[16] Our bad karma is like the diamond or the *ni-chu-lei*. The Title of the Lotus Sutra is like the horn of the sheep or the *chiao-liao*. Amber attracts dust; magnets draw iron. Our bad karma is like dust or iron, and the Title of the Lotus Sutra is like a magnet or amber. Think of this and continuously recite "Namu Myōhōrengekyō."

In roll one of the Lotus Sutra,[17] we read: "It is difficult to hear this Dharma during innumerable, countless *kalpas*." Roll five says[18]: "In in-

numerable realms, not even the Title of this Lotus Sutra can be heard."
To hear even faintly the Title of the Lotus Sutra will be gratifying. Thus,
the buddhas Shusenta and Tahō appeared in the world, but did not
preach even the Title of the Lotus Sutra.[19] Śākyamuni came into the
world for the sake of the Lotus Sutra, but for more than forty years he
kept the Title secret and did not speak. When the Buddha was, it is said,
seventy-two years old, he first preached the Lotus Sutra.

However, the people of the border countries, great China and Japan,
did not hear the Title until more than 1,350 years after Buddha's nirvana. It is as difficult to come across this scripture as for a man to discover the *udumbara* flower which blooms once in three thousand years
or for a one-eyed tortoise to find a hole in a floating piece of wood during innumerable, countless *kalpas*.[20] It is more difficult to come across
the Title of the Lotus Sutra than to impale a poppy tossed from Brahmā's heaven upon an awl set upright on the earth. It is more difficult to
come across the Title than for a sun-thread blown from Mount Sumeru
by a great wind to pass through the eye of a needle. Those who recite the
Title of this scripture should remember this. Regard it more joyfully than
the first sight of mother and father by a blind man whose sight has been
restored. Cherish it more than a prisoner cherishes his wife and children
after he is released by his enemies.

Question: Is there scriptural support for reciting only the *daimoku*?
Answer: Roll eight of the Lotus Sutra[21] tells us if anyone accepts and
keeps the name of the Lotus Sutra, that person shall have incalculable
happiness. The *Shōhokekyō* contains these words[22]: "If any hear this
scripture and keep and proclaim the Title, their virtue is incalculable."
The *Tenbon Hokekyō* tells us[23]: "If anyone accepts and keeps the name
of the Lotus Sutra, that person shall have incalculable happiness." We
see from these passages that the happiness derived from reciting merely
the Title is incalculable. Receiving, keeping, reading, reciting, adoring,
and protecting the entire twenty-eight chapters in eight rolls[24] is the
broad practice. Receiving, keeping, reading, reciting, adoring, and protecting the chapters "Expedient Devices" and "Life-span of the Tathāgata"[25] is the curtailed practice. Reciting, protecting, and keeping just
one four-line verse or even the Title alone is the essential practice.
Among the broad, curtailed, and essential practices, the *daimoku* is the
essence of the essence.

Question: How much virtue is contained in the words "Myōhōrengekyō"?
Answer: The sea enfolds the currents of the rivers. The earth holds

both the animate and the inanimate. The magic gem[26] rains ten thousand treasures. Brahmā rules the three realms.[27] The words "Myōhōrenge-kyō" are like these things: they include all the beings of the nine worlds and of the Buddha world. Since they include the ten worlds, they include all the conditions one may be born into in the ten worlds.[28] If the words "Myōhōrengekyō" include all dharmas, one word of the scripture is lord of all scriptures. It embodies all scriptures.

The Buddha appeared in this world and for more than fifty years preached eighty thousand holy teachings. In an age when the life-span of humans was one hundred years, he entered nirvana at midnight on the fifteenth day of the second month of the ninth year of the cycle. Then from the eighth day of the fourth month to the fifteenth day of the seventh month, during the ninety days of summer,[29] one thousand arhats gathered to transcribe the teachings.[30]

During the thousand years of the True Law, the canon spread throughout the five regions of India, but it did not reach China. After the period of Imitation Law had begun, one thousand fifteen years after the Buddha's nirvana, in the tenth year of Yung-p'ing,[31] in the reign of Emperor Hsiao-ming of the Latter Han, the scriptures first were brought to China. By the eighteenth year of K'ai-yüan[32] in the reign of Emperor Hsüan-tsung of T'ang, 176 translators had come, and the sutras, *vinaya,* and *śāstras* they brought numbered 1,076 works in 5,048 rolls, 480 boxes. All of these scriptures are included in one word of the Lotus Sutra.

Among the sutras preached by the Buddha during the more than forty years before he revealed the Lotus Sutra is the *Daihōkōbutsu kegonkyō.* The three books of this sutra were hidden in the dragon king's palace. The first book contains chapters the number of the dust motes of thirteen worlds; the second consists of twelve hundred chapters in 498,800 verses; the third contains 100,000 verses in forty-eight chapters. There are forty or sixty or eighty chapters in translation in China and Japan.

The next sutras preached were the Hīnayāna *Agonkyō,* all the Hōdō and *Hannya* Mahāyāna sutras,[33] and the *Dainichikyō* which contains thirty-five hundred verses propagating the five Sanskrit syllables, A-va-ra-ha-kha[34] alone. How many more verses it must contain on the other revered seed letters, honored images, and emblems of the vows![35] Nevertheless, the *Dainichikyō* brought to China consists of only six or seven rolls.[36] The *Nehangyō,* the last sermon preached by the Buddha in the *śāla* grove, consists of forty rolls in Chinese, but this, too, is much longer in Sanskrit.

All these scriptures are included in the Lotus Sutra preached by the Tathāgata Śākyamuni. The scriptures preached by the seven buddhas of the past, the thousand buddhas of this *kalpa,* the buddhas of eternity, and the buddhas of the ten directions of the present are also all included in a single word of the Lotus Sutra.

In the chapter "Bhaiṣajyarāja," the Buddha said to the Bodhisattva Shukuōke that the Lotus Sutra surpasses all others just as the ocean surpasses all rivers and streams, just as Mount Sumeru towers over all other mountains, just as the moon outshines all the stars.[37] In the commentary of Miao-lo,[38] we read, "This teaching is superior to all former teachings." In one word of this sutra are all the scriptures of the dharma worlds of the ten directions. In the same way, the magic gem contains all treasures, and *śūnyatā*[39] includes all phenomena. Because one word of the Lotus Sutra is superior to all other scriptures preached by the Buddha during his lifetime, the words "Sutra of the Lotus of the Marvelous Law" are superior to all the eighty thousand scriptures.

About the word "marvelous" the Lotus Sutra says, "Open the gate of expedient devices and disclose the truth."[40] Chih-i commented, "This sutra divulges the secret storehouse of the teaching and so it is called 'marvelous.' "[41] Miao-lo commented, "To divulge is to open."[42] What is called wonderful is this opening.

If a storehouse in which treasure is amassed has no key, it cannot be opened. If it is unopened the treasure cannot be seen. The Buddha preached the *Kegonkyō*, but he did not disclose the key to that sutra as he spoke. For more than forty years the Buddha preached such sutras as the *Agon, Hōdō,* and *Hannya,* and the *Kankyō,* but he did not disclose the heart of these sutras. Because the gate was closed, no one was enlightened by these scriptures. Any who believed themselves enlightened were mistaken.

But the Buddha opened the doors to all the treasure-houses of the scriptures when he preached the Lotus Sutra, and after more than forty years the living beings of the nine worlds saw the treasure inside those storehouses. On earth there are men and animals, trees and grasses, but if there is no sun or moon, even beings with eyes cannot discern the colors and shapes of the men, animals, trees, and grasses. When the sun and moon appear, these can be seen. The anterior sutras are like the darkness of a long night. The *shakumon* and the *honmon* of the Lotus Sutra are like the sun and moon.

The two eyes of the bodhisattva, the narrowed eyes of the followers of the two vehicles, the unseeing eyes of common men, the *icchantika*'s eyes blind from birth could never discern the colors and shapes in the anterior sutras. When the Buddha preached the Lotus Sutra, he revealed the moon of the *shakumon,* and the two eyes of the bodhisattvas could see. Then the narrowed eyes of the followers of the two vehicles opened; then the unseeing eyes of common men; and at last a karmic bond was tied which will open the born-blind eyes of the *icchantikas*. This is the virtue of the word "wonderful."

There are the wonderful *shakumon* and the wonderful *honmon*. This makes two "wonderfuls." Together the ten "wonderfuls" of the *shakumon* and the ten "wonderfuls" of the *honmon* equal twenty. The thirty "wonderfuls" of the *shakumon* and the thirty of the *honmon* make sixty. The forty of the *shakumon* and forty of the *honmon* added to the forty "wonderfuls" of the meditating mind equal one hundred twenty.[43] Beneath each of the 69,384 words there is a "wonderful." In India the word for "wonderful" is *sat;* in China they say *miao.* "Wonderful" is the complete meaning. "Complete" means "perfect." Each word of the Lotus Sutra contains all the other 69,384 words, just as a drop of the ocean contains all rivers, and the magic gem holds all treasures.

The withered grasses and trees of autumn and winter put forth new twigs, leaves, flowers, and blades when spring and summer come. The living beings of the nine worlds during the time of the anterior sutras were like the grasses and trees of autumn and winter. When it feels the warm sun of the word "wonderful" of the Lotus Sutra, the flower of enlightenment will bloom and fruit of Buddhahood will set. Nāgārjuna wrote in the *Great Treatise on the Perfection of Wisdom*[44]: "This is like the great bodhisattva Yakuo taking poison and making medicine."[45] This passage is a comment on the virtue of the "wonderful" of the Lotus Sutra. Miao-lo commented: "It cures those who are difficult to cure. Thus it is called 'wonderful.' "[46]

There are four kinds of people who have difficulty achieving Buddhahood. First are those followers of the two vehicles whose status is innately set,[47] second are the *icchantika,* third are the empty-headed, fourth are the transgressors. According to the Lotus Sutra these too attain Buddhahood; therefore, it is called "wonderful."

Devadatta was a crown prince, son of King Droṇodana, raised by Śuddhodana, elder brother of Ānanda,[48] cousin of the Teacher Śākyamuni, a not unimportant man on earth. He left the secular life under the tutelage of the monk Śūdra, and learned the eighteen transformations from Ānanda.[49] In his mind were the sixty thousand non-Buddhist scriptures and the eighty thousand Buddhist scriptures. He practiced the five ascetic rules and looked almost more reverent than the Buddha. He called himself Buddha, and built an ordination platform on Gayāśīrsa to stir up dissension among the monks.

He said to Prince Ajātaśatru: "I shall kill the Buddha and become the new Buddha. You must kill your father and become king." When the prince had murdered his father, Devadatta spied out the Buddha, sent blood flowing from his body with a great stone and murdered the nun

Utpalavarna who was an arhat. Thus he committed three of the five transgressions.[50]

He led Kokālika[51] to become his own disciple and attracted King Ajātaśatru's patronage. All those in the sixteen great countries of India and the five hundred middle countries who have committed one, two, or three of the transgressions are members of Devadatta's assemblage just as the great sea unites all the rivers, and innumerable plants cluster in the mountains. Those with wisdom assemble around Śāriputra; those with supernatural powers follow Maudgalyāyana; the evil are won by Devadatta.

The earth, which is 168,000 *yojanas* thick, has already split open as far as the diamond wind-circle,[52] and living beings are falling into the palace of the deepest hell. Kokālika, the first of Devadatta's disciples, has fallen, as have Cinca-mānavikā, King Virūdaka, and the monk Sunakṣatra.[53] Everyone in the ten thousand small, fifty-five medium, and sixteen large countries of the five regions of India has seen the bodies of these transgressors fall. The beings in the *devalokas*, the four *dhyāna* heavens, the *rūpadhātu*, and the *arūpadhātu*,[54] Brahmā, Indra, King Māra of the sixth heaven of desire, and King Yāma have all seen this. All the living beings of the three thousand myriad worlds and the realms of the ten directions have heard of this. Though *kalpas* exceeding the number of dust motes of the earth pass, they will be unable to leave the deepest hell. Though the *kalpa* stone be worn thin, the sufferings of hell will not end.[55]

Pondering this we realize how marvelous it is that Devadatta was the teacher of our teacher Śākyamuni in the past and that he will become the Buddha Tennō in the future, as recorded in the "Devadatta" chapter of the Lotus Sutra. If the anterior sutras are true, the Lotus Sutra is a huge lie; if the Lotus Sutra is true, the anterior sutras are great sins of falsehood. Devadatta committed three of the five transgressions as well as innumerable heavy sins, yet he became the Tathāgata Tennō. Can there be any doubt that those many sinners who commit but one or two transgressions can achieve enlightenment? This is as certain as that when the earth revolves the grasses and trees turn with it, as certain as that a strong man who can smash stone can crush a blade of grass. Therefore this scripture is called "wonderful."

In Buddhist and non-Buddhist writings women are disparaged. In the books of the Three Emperors and Five Rulers,[56] they are judged obsequious and fawning. It is said that disasters were caused by three women,[57] and at the root of the destruction of nations and the ruin of men there is always a woman.

In the *Kegonkyō,* the first sutra the Buddha preached, we read:

"Women are messengers of hell. They cut off the seeds of Buddhahood. They have the faces of bodhisattvas, but their hearts are like *yakṣas*."[58] In the last sutra Śākyamuni preached in the grove of *śāla* trees, the *Nehangyō,* we read: "The course of a river and a woman's mind both wander." This scripture also says: "The passions of all the men of the three thousand words and the hindrances to the salvation of one woman are comparably immeasurable."[59]

The phrase, "they cut off the seeds of Buddhahood," in the *Kegonkyō* means that women can no more attain Buddhahood than can a dried-up seed sprout. At a time of terrible drought an enormous cloud appeared in the sky and rain fell on the earth so that the wilted grasses, trees, and flowers bloomed and bore fruit. However, the dried-up seeds did not grow, and finally they decayed. The Buddha is like the cloud. His teachings are like the rain. The wilted plants represent living beings. Moistened by the rain of Buddhism, they produce the blossoms and fruit of the ten good deeds, meditation, and observance of the five prohibitions. The dried-up seeds do not grow but rot in the rain. They are like women who discover the teaching of Buddha and do not leave the cycle of life and death, but rather lose the teaching and fall into the evil destinies. This is called "cutting off the seeds of Buddhahood."

The *Nehangyō* tells us women's minds wander like rivers: since water is malleable, it turns here and there when rocks and mountains block its path. Women are like this. They are inconstant as water. Although they know what is right, when they run into the strong will of a man, they are checked and turn in bad directions. The right fades like a line drawn on the water. Women's nature is unsteady: though they see what they should be, they soon become what they should not be. Buddhahood is founded on integrity. Therefore, women, who are easily swayed, cannot become Buddhas. Women have the "five obstacles" and "three followings."[60] Thus in one sutra it is written: "Even should the eyes of all the buddhas of the three worlds fall to the earth, women cannot become Buddha."[61] Another text says: "Even if you can capture the clear wind, you can never capture the mind of a woman."[62]

The bodhisattva Monjushiri (Mañjuśrī) preached only the word "wonderful," and women, despised in earlier scriptures, were able to attain Buddhahood.[63] In disbelief the bodhisattva Chishaku, who was the foremost disciple of the Buddha Tahō of the realm Hōjō, and the revered Śāriputra, who was the wisest of the disciples of the Tathāgata Śākyamuni, argued that, according to the scriptures of the Hīnayāna and Mahāyāna preached by the Buddha for more than forty years, the daughter of the *nāgas* could not attain Buddhahood. They were proved wrong, as she became a buddha.

The words "they cut off the seeds of Buddhahood" and "rivers wander" from the first and last sutras preached in the *śāla* grove were disproved. The *Konjikinyokyō* and the *Ta lun,* too, were shown to be empty. Chishaku and Śāriputra rolled their tongues and closed their mouths, and the great assembly of men and gods were overjoyed and clasped their hands in obeisance. All this is the virtue of the word "wonderful."

In southern Jambudvīpa there are two thousand five hundred rivers. Each of them wanders, just as the women of Jambudvīpa waver. But there is one river called the River of Sahā; straight as a stretched rope it runs into the western Sea. Women who believe in the Lotus Sutra are like this river and will enter straight into the western Paradise.[64] This is the virtue of the word "wonderful."

"Wonderful" has the meaning "to resurrect." "To resurrect" means "to recall to life." When the child of the crane was dying, the mother cried out, "Shian," and the baby returned to life. When the *chen* bird enters the water, fish and shellfish die. If any are touched by the horns of the rhinoceros, they revive.[65]

In just this way followers of the two vehicles, *icchantikas,* and women, whose seeds of Buddhahood have been dried up by the anterior sutras, may attain Buddhahood by keeping the word "wonderful," which brings the seeds back to life. Chih-i said: "*Icchantika* have minds and can still attain Buddhahood. The wisdom of the followers of the two vehicles is gone and their thoughts of enlightenment are dead, but the power of the word 'wonderful' of the Lotus Sutra will cure them."[66] Miao-lo said: "Other sutras are called 'great' but not 'wonderful.' These sutras can easily cure those who have thought, but only the Lotus Sutra can cure those without thought, and thus it is called 'wonderful.' "[67]

The essence of these passages is that the titles of the *Daihōkōbutsu kegonkyō, Daishukkyō, Daihannyakyō,* and *Dainehangyō* all contain the word "great," but none contains the word "wonderful." These sutras cure those who are living, but do not resurrect the dead. Because the Lotus Sutra resurrects the dead, it is called "wonderful." Those who may be expected to attain Buddhahood cannot do so by virtue of these other sutras, but even those for whom the path to Buddhahood is difficult will attain Buddhahood by virtue of the Lotus Sutra. Not only those who are expected to attain Buddhahood, but *all* beings, will turn away from the other scriptures after the Lotus Sutra is proclaimed.

Now that the two thousand years of the True Law and Imitation Law have passed and the *mappō* has begun, it is a thousand, million, trillion times more difficult for the beings of this world to be reborn as Buddhas than it was for the followers of the two vehicles and the *icchantikas* of the Buddha's lifetime. How can beginners today escape the cycle of births and deaths if they rely on the sutras which the *Kankyō* tells us were preached "in forty years and more"? Insubstantial! Undependable!

If a woman gives up the Lotus Sutra for any of the other scriptures of the Buddha's lifetime or of the periods of the True Law, Imitation Law, or *mappō,* she can never achieve Buddhahood.[68] The Man of Wisdom, the Great Teacher Chih-i, who was awakened at the seminary to his own presence at the sermon on Vulture Peak,[69] determined: "Other sutras are written for men only. This sutra is for everyone."[70]

The Tathāgata Śākyamuni preached the Lotus Sutra for eight years, before the Buddha Tahō and all the buddhas of the ten directions, at a place called Vulture Peak, northeast of the palace of the king of Magadha. Chih-i, the Man of Wisdom, heard this sutra on Vulture Peak. During the fifty years of his life on earth the Buddha preached the holy scriptures for the benefit of all living beings. The scriptures taught for the first forty years indicated that women could not achieve Buddhahood. In the Lotus Sutra for the first time the Buddha revealed that women could attain Buddhahood. Fifteen hundred years after the Buddha's nirvana, this scripture was carried eighteen thousand leagues over mountains and seas to China. A messenger of the Buddha named Chih-i concluded that women could attain Buddhahood only through the Lotus Sutra.

More than three thousand leagues to the east of China is another country. This country is called Japan. Some two hundred years after the death of the Great Teacher of Tendai, a man named Dengyō was born.[71] In *Shūku,*[72] he confirmed that the *nāga* girl had become Buddha, and that "neither she, who achieved Buddhahood through ability, nor those who achieved Buddhahood as her disciples, practiced for countless *kalpas.* By the strength of the Wonderful Lotus Sutra, they achieved Buddhahood in this very body."

There is no doubt that women in this world should pray to the Lotus Sutra for Buddhahood in this very body. Enlightenment will be swifter than the great rivers, faster than the rain falling from the sky. Nevertheless, the women of Japan do not recite "Namu Myōhōrengekyō," but rely on the *Sōkangyō*[73] which will not lead them to rebirth in paradise. They chant the name of Amida ten thousand or sixty thousand times a day, which would seem to be a good practice since it is the name of a Buddha, but, in fact, they are depending on the teachings of sutras that do not lead to Buddhahood or rebirth in paradise. This is like uselessly counting someone else's fortune. Such people have been completely taken in by heretical teachings. The worst enemies of Japanese women, worse than tigers or wolves, worse than bandits or pirates, worse than the enemies of their fathers and mothers, are those who do not teach the

Lotus Sutra but lead women to repeat the *nenbutsu*. If you recite "Namu Myōhōrengekyō" ten thousand, sixty thousand, a million times a day, and have some free time, you may occasionally say the name of Amida to rest your mouth and still be a devotee of the Lotus Sutra. If a woman recites the name of Amida incessantly all her life, with never a pause, and never chants the Lotus Sutra, there can be no memorial service for her. However, if she has a practitioner of the Lotus Sutra read the sutra for her even briefly, even if she regards the *nenbutsu* believers as her own family and regards the practitioner lightly as a retainer or servant, this woman will be known as a devotee of the Lotus Sutra.

Well then, Vimaladattā permitted the two princes to leave their home and spread the Lotus Sutra,[74] and the *nāga* girl vowed, "I will open the teachings of the Mahāyāna and release all living beings from suffering,"[75] but neither promised to practice other sutras exclusively and not to practice the Lotus Sutra. Women today practice other sutras exclusively and do not know the practice of the Lotus Sutra. Quickly, quickly, they must change their ways. Namu Myōhōrengekyō. Namu Myōhōrengekyō.

1266/1/6   Nichiren

Written at 2 P.M. at Kiyozumidera

NOTES

1.   *STH*, pp. 391–405. Nichiren composed this essay in 1266, evidently for a laywoman. The signature, "Nichiren, disciple of Konpon Daishi" (Saichō), indicates that he still considered himself to be preaching doctrine introduced by Saichō. There are noticeable differences between the teachings found here and those in later letters and treatises, particularly Nichiren's tolerant attitude toward recitation of the *nenbutsu* and faith in rebirth in Amida's Western Paradise.

2.   *Kegonkyō*. The sources cited for Nichiren's allusions in *Hokke daimokushō* are given in Tokoro Shigemoto and Takagi Yutaka, *Nichiren*, pp. 112–122.

3.   *Kengukyō*. The four noble truths are the fundamental teaching of Śākyamuni: existence is suffering, desire is the cause of suffering, extinction of passion is possible, the Path is the way of extinction. The parrot of Anāthapindaka learned a verse from Ānanda and was reborn in the heavens of the four kings.

4.   *Ta chih tu lun*. A party of merchants, about to be swallowed up by a whale, recited "Homage to the Buddha, homage to the Dharma, homage to the community of monks" and were saved.

5.   In chapter 2, "Expedient Devices," Śākyamuni announces: "Frankly I cast aside my expedient devices and preach the Unexcelled Path." T9, p. 10a.

6.   Chapter 3, "Parable." The teaching is so difficult, the Buddha tells Śāriputra, that "even you can enter this sutra [only] by faith." T9, p. 15b.

7.   The fifty-two stages a bodhisattva passes through on the way to Buddhahood. The first ten are the stages of faith. Soothill, p. 115; Tokoro and Takagi, p. 112.

8.   *Nehangyō.* Evil friends led him into heretical beliefs and he went to hell.

9.   In the Lotus Sutra, chapter 8, "Announcement of Destiny of Five Hundred Disciples," Śākyamnni predicts the five hundred will all be reborn as buddhas with this name.

10.   Śāriputra is known as the wisest of the Buddha's disciples. Maudgalyāyana was the most proficient in supernatural powers. Maudgalyāyana's destiny is predicted in the Lotus Sutra, chapter 6, "Bestowal of Prophecy"; Śāriputra's in chapter 3, "Parable."

11.   Lotus Sutra, chapter 15, "Welling Up out of the Earth"; T9, p. 42a.

12.   Analogies from the *Nehangyō.*

13.   *Pao p'o tzu:* "Take a real horn more than one foot long and carve a fish from it. Hold it in your mouth as you enter the waters and they will part three feet for you to pass."

14.   The sandalwood is fragrant; the *erāvana* is the opposite and spreads its smell over a large area—here, forty *yojana.*

15.   *Nehangyō.*

16.   *Wen hsuan* contains the sentence: "It nests on the eyelash of a mosquito."

17.   Chapter 2; T9, p. 10a.

18.   Chapter 14; T9, p. 38c.

19.   *Ta chih tu lun:* "The Buddha Suśānta [Shusenta], because his disciples' practice was not fervent, forsook them and entered nirvana, halting for one *kalpa* the transformation of living beings to Buddhahood."

    "Prabhūtaratna [Tahō] could not preach the Lotus Sutra because of the requests of heavenly beings. He entered nirvana . . . . Since he was unable to preach the Lotus Sutra, it is said he was unable to preach at all."

20.   These analogies are found in the Lotus Sutra, chapter 27, "The Story of King Śubhavyūha"; T9, p. 60ab.

21.   Chapter 26, "Spells." The sentence from which Nichiren's quotation is taken promises happiness to the daughters of the *rākṣasas,* who vowed to protect those who "receive and keep the name of the Dharma Blossom."

22.   The version of the Lotus Sutra translated by Dharmarakṣa.

23.   The translation of the Lotus Sutra by Jñanagupta and Dharmagupta.

24.   This is the number of chapters and volumes in Kumārajīva's translation, the one most used by Nichiren.

25.   According to Chih-i, "Expedient Devices" is the nucleus of the first half of the Lotus, the *shakumon* or "manifest gate," which reveals the unity of the Dharma; "Life-span of the Tathāgata" is the nucleus of the second half, the *honmon* or "fundamental gate," which reveals the eternity of the Buddha. The *shakumon* is so called because it is preached by Śākyamuni in his human manifestation. In the *honmon* he is revealed in his fundamental nature.

26.   A magic wishing stone said to have been obtained from the dragon king, the head of a great fish, or the relics of the Buddha.

27.   The realms of desire, form, and formlessness.

28.   There are two results of past karma: the *shōhō,* being the resultant person, and the *ehō,* being the dependent conditions or environment—country, family, possessions, and so forth.

29.   The *vārsika,* or rainy season, a time of religious retreat.

30.   The first council which gathered to record the sutras after the Buddha's nirvana was said to have met at the Pippala cave at Rājagṛha.

31.   A.D. 67.

32.   A.D. 730.

33.   The sutras preached during the third and fourth periods of the Buddha's life,
        according to Tendai chronology.

34.   These five syllables each represent an element of the universe. A = earth, va =
        water, ra = fire, ha = wind, kha = space. Tokoro and Takagi, p. 115.

35.   Seed letters, in esoteric Buddhism, are Sanskrit letters which symbolize various
        deities and elements. Honored images are sacred images, and the emblems are
        jewels, swords, and so on, which represent the vows made by buddhas and bod-
        hisattvas.

36.   It consists of seven if the *Kuyōhōkyō* is considered part of the sutra.

37.   T9, p. 54ab.

38.   *Fa hua wen chu chi,* by the ninth patriarch of the T'ien-t'ai school, Miao-lo
        (711–782).

39.   The absolute that is free from, or rises above, all existence and concepts.

40.   Chapter 2; T9, p. 7b.

41.   *Miao fa lien hua ching hsuan i.*

42.   *Fa hua hsuan i shih ch'ien ts'ien.*

43.   The ten wonders of the manifest teaching are the universe which embraces all;
        the Buddha's all-embracing knowledge; his deeds; his attainment of the Buddha
        stages; his three laws of truth, wisdom, and vision; his response to appeals; his
        supernatural powers; his preaching; his supernatural retinue; his nirvana; his
        eternal life; his blessings. Those of the fundamental teaching are the fundamen-
        tal cause, the fundamental result, the realm, the fundamental response to appeal,
        the fundamental supernatural powers, the fundamental preaching, the funda-
        mental supernatural retinue, the fundamental nirvana, the fundamental life, the
        fundamental blessings. In each half of the teaching are the dharmas of the mind,
        of Buddha, and of living beings. These, multiplied by the above ten wonders,
        make thirty. Add the original ten to get forty. Meditation too has forty wonders.
        This is all based on Chih-i's commentaries on the Lotus Sutra.

44.   *Ta chih tu lun.*

45.   Common beings become buddhas just as poisonous substances may heal when
        properly used.

46.   *Mo ho chih kuan fu hsing chuan hung chüeh.*

47.   The *śrāvaka* (hearer) and *pratyekabuddha.*

48.   Ānanda was a disciple of Śākyamuni.

49.   *Jūhachihen* are eighteen supernatural transformations of which buddhas and
        bodhisattvas are capable.

50.   Killing an arhat, shedding the blood of a buddha, and destroying the harmony of
        the community of monks. The other two are patricide and matricide.

51.   The *Ta chih tu lun* tells of this disciple of Śākyamuni led astray by Devadatta.

52.   The circle of wind is beneath the circles of water and of metal on which the earth
        rests. The circle of wind rests on space.

53.   The descent of these four to hell is described in *Hsi yu chi.*

54.   The *devalokas* are the six heavens of desire directly above earth. The four
        dhyāna heavens are large divisions of the eighteen *brahmalokas,* or heavens of
        form, above the *devalokas.* The *rūpadhātu* is another name for the *brahma-
        lokas.* The *arūpadhātu,* heavens without form, are above the *rūpadhātu.*

55.   This is a lesser *kalpa:* the length of time it takes for a stone ten miles each
        dimension to be worn away by the robe of a god which brushes it every three
        years.

56.   Prehistoric Chinese rulers.

57.   Three early Chinese emperors met their downfall because of their love for a woman.

58.   *Yakṣas* are malevolent demons which devour human flesh. There is no such passage in the *Kegonkyō*. Tokoro and Takagi, p. 119.

59.   There is no such passage in the *Nehangyō*. Tokoro and Takagi, p. 119.

60.   Lotus Sutra, "Devadatta," describes the five obstacles as woman's inability to become Brahmā, Śakra, Māra, a *cakravartin,* or a Buddha in this body. The *Ta chih tu lun* lists the three followings: when young she follows her father; when youthful, her husband; when old, her son.

61.   Nichiren adduces the *Gonjikinyokyō* (p. 192), but the quotation has not been found. Tokoro and Takagi, p. 119.

62.   *Ta chih tu lun.*

63.   The story of the *nāga* woman who attained enlightenment is told in the "Devadatta" chapter of the Lotus Sutra. Mañjuśrī tells Śākyamuni how, as he expounded the Lotus Sutra in the kingdom of the *nāgas,* the daughter of the king was enlightened. The bodhisattva Prajñākuṭa refused to believe this: "I have seen how the Lord Śākyamuni, the Tathāgata, when he was striving after enlightenment, in the state of a bodhisattva, performed innumerable good works, and during many eons never slackened in his arduous task . . . . Afterwards he arrived at enlightenment. Who then would believe that she should have been able to arrive at supreme, perfect knowledge in one moment?" As he is speaking, the dragon girl appears before Śākyamuni and offers him a gem. Śāriputra then argues that she could not achieve enlightenment: "Thou hast conceived the idea of enlightenment, young lady of good family, without sliding back, and art gifted with immense wisdom, but supreme, perfect enlightenment is not easily won. It may happen, sister, that a woman displays an unflagging energy, performs good works for many thousands of eons, and fulfills the six perfect virtues, but as yet there is no example of her having reached Buddhaship, and that because a woman cannot occupy the five ranks . . . ." Suddenly the *nāga* woman changes sex and manifests herself as a bodhisattva. She then achieves Buddhahood. Prajñākuṭa and Śāriputra are silent. H. Kern, *Saddharma-Puṇḍarīka or the Lotus of the True Law* (New York: Dover, 1963), pp. 251–253.

64.   An Amidist element, accepted by the Tendai school, but later violently rejected by Nichiren, who promised "Buddhahood in this very body" to his educated followers and rebirth in Vulture Peak paradise to others.

65.   Nichiren seems to refer to a passage in the *Ōjō yōshū* by Genshin: "When the *chen* bird enters the water, fish and shellfish die. Any who touch the horn of the rhinoceros return to life. The yellow crane cried, 'Shian,' and Shian returned to life." The origin of the story of Shian (Tzu-an) seems to be in *Lieh hsien ch'uan.* The crane, which had been saved by Tzu-an, cried his name as he was dying and he returned to life.

66.   *Mo ho chih kuan.*

67.   *Hung chüeh.*

68.   *Kanmuryōgikyō:* "In forty years and more the truth has not been revealed." T9, p. 386b.

69.   Chih-i was considered a reincarnation of Yakuō, one of the bodhisattvas assembled to hear the Lotus Sutra preached.

70.   *Wen chu.*

71.   Saichō, 767–822, the founder of the Tendai school in Japan. Chih-i died in 597.

72.   *Hokkeshūku.*
73.   One of the Amida sutras, the *Kanmuryōjukyō.*
74.   Lotus Sutra, chapter 27, "The Story of King Śubhavyūha." The queen,
      Vimaladattā, permitted her two sons to take holy orders and helped them per-
      suade their father.
75.   Lotus Sutra, chapter 12; T9, p. 35c.

Letter to Tsuchirō Prison[1]

Tomorrow I am to cross to Sado. It is cold tonight and I pity you in jail. You, my lord, have read the Lotus Sutra with both body and mind and by virtue of this you will aid your father and mother, your family, and all living beings. When others read the Lotus Sutra, they read with their mouths only, with words only, and not with their minds. Even those few who do read with their minds do not practice what they read. How precious are those who read with both mind and body! The Buddha taught: "The children of the gods shall be his servants and messengers. Swords and staves shall not touch him, nor poison harm him,"[2] and it cannot be otherwise. When you are released from jail, come to me quickly. We must see each other.

Respectfully,

Nichiren

To Chikugo dono[3]

NOTES

1.   *STH,* pp. 509–510. Before he and his guards left Echi for Sado, Nichiren wrote this note on 1271/10/9 to his disciple Nichirō (1243–1320) and four others who had been jailed when he was arrested in Kamakura.
2.   Lotus Sutra, chapter 14, promises this protection to preachers of the Lotus. T9, p. 39b.
3.   Nichirō.

Letter from Teradomari[1]

On the tenth of this month we left Echi in Aikō district in Sagami[2] for an inn in Kumegawa in Musashi.[3] After twelve days' journey we arrived at the port of Teradomari in Echigo.[4] We are to cross to Sado from here, but the winds have been unsteady, and I do not know when we will sail.[5] The trip here was horrible; I cannot write of it.[6] Imagine my fear and suffering. But I was prepared for suffering from the beginning, so I won't complain of it now.

In roll four of the Lotus Sutra we read: "This scripture has many enemies even now when the Tathāgata is present. How much more so after his passage into extinction."[7] And in roll five we read: "All the world resents it and has difficulty believing."[8]

In roll thirty-eight[9] of the *Nehangyō* are these words:

At that time all those who believe in non-Buddhist teachings will say, "Great King, now there is one very evil man and that man is Gautama. All the evil men of the world congregate around him for their own profit. They join his household and do no good. By sorcery he has bewitched Kāśyapa, Śāriputra, and Maudgalyāyana."

Those who believed in other teachings, angry because the Buddha had refuted the teachings of their masters, the two gods and three immortals,[10] slandered Śākyamuni this way. But the Lotus Sutra does not make Śākyamuni the enemy. According to Chih-i the enemy are the Hearers, the Self-enlightened, and the bodhisattvas who seek near-enlightenment.[11] Those who do not wish to hear, or to believe, or to profit from the teaching for this age, though they may not speak words of disparagement, are enemies.

When we compare the age of Śākyamuni to the age after his nirvana, we see that the scholars of all the sects today are like the non-Buddhists. The man they call "the most evil man" is Nichiren. "All the evil men of the world who congregate around him" are Nichiren's disciples. The non-Buddhists of the past attacked Śākyamuni, failing to distinguish between his teachings and those of former buddhas. The scholars of the various sects today do the same. From the Buddhist teachings, they have produced wrong views. Men whose heads are spinning think the mountains are moving.[12]

Now the eight sects or the ten sects quarrel because there are many teachings.[13] In roll eighteen of the *Nehangyō* appears the parable of "exchanging a great treasure for life."[14] According to Chih-i, "life" is the Lotus Sutra. The "great treasure" is the three doctrines taught before the Lotus Sutra, which are described in the *Nehangyō*.[15] What is the perfect teaching according to the *Nehangyō*? It is the eternality of Buddha, which is also taught in the Lotus Sutra. The *Nehangyō* teaching of the perfection and eternality of Buddha supplements the Lotus Sutra. But the particular teachings of the *Nehangyō* are only the three earlier doctrines.

In roll three of Chih-i's *Hsuan i* we read, "The *Nehangyō* is the great treasure that saves lives. It is merely the second handclap."[16] In part three of the *Shih ch'ien* we read: "Now our sect understands the 'great treasure' to mean the *Nehangyō*."[17] In the *Szu nien ch'u*[18] Chih-i cites the words "although many paths are indicated,"[19] from the Lotus Sutra, and determines that the "great treasure" is the four earlier modes.[20] If this is true, all the sutras taught before and after the Lotus Sutra[21] are the "great treasure," which is given up for the sake of the Lotus.

The scholars of the world say this is only a doctrine of the Tendai sect, one not accepted by all the sects. But I, having considered this, say that the eight or ten sects came into being after the Buddha's nirvana and that they were created by theoreticians and preachers. We must not determine appropriate sutras for today by the teachings of sects which arose after the nirvana. Since Chih-i's judgments are in accord with the scriptures, they must not be rejected as belonging to only one sect.

Because the scholars of each sect cling to the errors of their masters, they insist that their teachings are appropriate to people whose capacity for enlightenment is slight,[22] that they themselves are not deviating from the teachings of the ancient masters, or that they have wise rulers backing them. The result is that those with evil minds flourish and provoke fighting. They bring suffering to innocent people and delight in doing it.

Among all the sects, the teachings of Shingon are particularly warped. Following the opinion of Subhakarasiṃha, Vajrabodhi[23] and their followers taught that " 'The teaching of three thousand dharmas in one thought,' is Chih-i's supreme truth and the essence of all the teachings of Śākyamuni's lifetime. This teaching of three thousand dharmas is to be regarded as the basis for both revealed and esoteric doctrine. But apart from this, the forming of mudras and the chanting of mantras is essential to Buddhist Teaching.'' Later priests of the Shingon sect, relying on this opinion, rejected the sutras which did not teach mudras and mantras as though they were non-Buddhist teachings.

According to one theory, the *Dainichikyō*[24] was not preached by Śākyamuni. According to another, it was the first sutra he preached. According to yet another, the Buddha appeared as Śākyamuni to preach the revealed sutras and as Dainichi to preach the esoteric sutras. Unable to discover the truth, these scholars conceive innumerable warped opinions.

These men are like the blind man who was unable to determine the color of milk and conceived various wrong ideas but could not guess the truth.[25] It is like the parable of the elephant.[26]

Now you must realize this: If the *Dainichikyō* preceded the Lotus Sutra, it is like the *Kegonkyō*. If it succeeded the Lotus, it is like the *Nehangyō*.[27]

Also, in the Lotus Sutra as it existed in India, there were mudras and mantras, but they were omitted by the Chinese translators. Kumārajīva omitted them and called his translation the Lotus Sutra. Subhākarasiṃha included mudras and mantras and called his version the *Dainichikyō*. Similarly, there are various other translations of the Lotus Sutra: *Shō Hoke, Tenbon Hoke, Hokezanmai, Satsuunfundari,* and so on.[28]

After the nirvana of the Buddha, the first man in India to understand this central point was the bodhisattva Nāgārjuna.[29] The first in China to understand was the Great Master Chih-i. While Subhākarasiṃha of the Shingon sect, Ch'eng-kuan of the Kegon sect, Chi-ts'ang of the Sanron sect, K'uei-chi of the Hossō sect, and the rest all had their own sects in name, in spirit they were descended from the Tendai sect. Their disciples do not realize this and malign the Lotus Sutra. How can they escape the consequences of slandering the True Teaching?

Some men criticize me: "He does not understand the times and preaches a crude doctrine, and so meets with adversity." Others say: "The teachings found in the chapter 'Fortitude'[30] are only for those bodhisattvas who have attained a high level. This is different from what is taught in the chapter 'Comfortable Conduct.' ''[31] Others say: "I too know the superiority of the Lotus Sutra, but I do not speak of it." Others say: "Nichiren's preaching is only theory." I am perfectly aware of this criticism.[32]

Pien-ho's legs were cut off.[33] Kiyomaro's name was changed to Kegaremaro, and he was almost put to death.[34] People laughed at them. But succeeding generations have not admired this ridicule. Your reasonless suffering is the same. In the chapter "Fortitude" are the words: "There are many ignorant men who revile us with foul mouths . . . . " I have seen my own situation described in this. Are not you too included in the word of this sutra? " . . . or attack us with swords and staves."[35] I have read this sutra. Will you not read the sutra too?

"Since within the great multitude they ever wish to ruin us, turning to kings and great ministers, to Brahmans and householders, they speak evil of us . . . . Foul language and scowling faces, repeated banishments."[36] "Repeated" means "again and again." I have been banished many times and exiled twice. The Lotus Sutra is Dharma preaching taking place in the past, the present, and the future. The chapter "Sadāparibhūta" of the past is the chapter "Fortitude" of the present; the chapter "Fortitude" of the present is the chapter "Sadāparibhūta" of the past.[37] The chapter "Fortitude" of today must be the "Sadāparibhūta" of the future. At that time I must become the bodhisattva Sadāparibhūta.[38]

I understand that the Lotus Sutra, which now consists of eight rolls of twenty-eight chapters, was one *yojana* long in India. It must have had many chapters, but the essence is contained in the twenty-eight chapters in China and Japan.

Leaving aside the main part of the sutra, let us turn to the section on propagation.[39] In "Apparition of a *Stūpa*"[40] are three pronouncements received by the assembly in midair above Vulture Peak.[41] I am a man of shallow understanding, but it seems that the "frightful and evil age"[42] during which the 20,000 and 80,000 and 80,000,000,000,000 bodhisattvas of the chapter "Fortitude" promised to propagate the sutra must be the beginning of the *mappō*.

The next chapter, "Comfortable Conduct," says, "in the latter age."[43] In a different version, the *Shō Hokekyō,* the same chapter has "this final latter age" and "this final latter age to come." The *Tenbon Hokekyō* says, "in this frightful and evil age."

At this time in this world there are assuredly the three types of enemies,[44] but not one of the 80,000,000,000,000 *nayuta*[45] of bodhisattvas has appeared. Does the tide wane and not wax, the moon diminish and not grow anew? If the water clears, the moon floats upon it. If a tree grows, birds nest in it. I speak as the representative of all those 80,000,000,000,000 *nayuta* of bodhisattvas. I invoke the divine protection of all those bodhisattvas.

This lay believer[46] says you ordered him to accompany me to Sado. That may be, but because of the expenses and various worries, I am sending him back. I cannot thank you enough for your kind intentions.

Please tell the others what I have written. What worries me is the fate of those who were jailed. Please send me word of them at the next opportunity.

10/22[47] 6 P.M.   Respectfully, respectfully,

                                             Nichiren

To Lord Toki

NOTES

1. *STH,* pp. 512–516. Waiting at Teradomari to sail for Sado, Nichiren wrote this letter on 1271/10/22 to Toki Tsunenobu (1220–1299).
2. Kanagawa Prefecture.
3. Saitama Prefecture.
4. Niigata Prefecture.
5. They finally sailed on the twenty-seventh, arriving at Matsugasaki on the twenty-eighth.
6. Nichiren feared he would be murdered as they traveled.
7. Chapter 10, T9, p. 31b.
8. Chapter 14, T9, p. 39a.
9. Actually, this appears in roll thirty-nine. T12, p. 592c.
10. Maheśvara and Viṣṇu, and Kapila, Ulūka, and Ṛṣabha.
11. "Hearers" *(śrāvaka)* are enlightened after listening to the Buddha. "Self-enlightened" *(pratyekabuddha)* attain enlightenment by individual practice. "Near-enlightenment" is contrasted to the eternal Buddhahood and original enlightenment of Śākyamuni, as revealed in the Lotus Sutra. This explication of Chih-i's teaching is found in *Fa hua wen chu chi,* commentary by Miao-lo.
12. Intoxicated, they think the world is spinning around them. The analogy is from the *Nehangyō.*
13. The eight "old" sects are: Kegon, Hossō, Sanron, Ritsu, Kusha, Jōjitsu, Tendai, Shingon; and the "new" sects are: Zen and Jōdo.
14. As in a kidnapping or robbery.
15. The Hīnayāna, teachings; the "intermediate" teachings, which were the first stage of Mahāyāna; the "separate" or "differentiated" Mahāyāna teachings. The fourth and final stage according to Tendai doctrine is the "perfect" teaching found in the Lotus Sutra.
16. It echoes the doctrine taught in the Lotus Sutra. T33, p. 704c.
17. T33, p. 858b.
18. A collection of Chih-i's lectures compiled by his disciple Chang-an.
19. There are many paths but the Lotus is the True Way. Chapter 2, T9, p. 9b.
20. Four corresponding to the four periods of the Buddha's teaching preliminary to the Lotus Sutra: Kegon, Agon, Hōdō, and Hannya.
21. The *Nehangyō* is considered, in Tendai chronology, to have been preached by the Buddha after the Lotus; all other sutras precede the Lotus.
22. Various Japanese sects believed the intellectual and moral capacity of beings in

the *mappō* to be diminished. New teachings and practices were devised for their salvation.

23. Indian masters who brought Tantric teachings to China.

24. The central sutra of the Shingon sect.

25. A parable from the *Nehangyō*. The blind man asked several people and, told milk was the color of shells, of rice, of snow, and of storks, was left confused as to its color.

26. This famous story is found in the *Nehangyō*: eight blind men each describe an elephant differently as they feel different parts of the animal.

27. And thus it should be given up for the Lotus Sutra.

28. The *Shō Hokekyō*, translated into Chinese in 286 by Dharmarakṣa, and the *Tenbon Myōhōrengekyō*, translated in 601 by Jñānaguptā and Dharmagupta, are still extant. The *Hokezanmaikyō*, said to have been translated in 427 by Chih-lou Chia-ch'an, and the *Satsuunfundarikyō*, said to have been translated by Dharmarakṣa (266–317) are not extant.

29. Founder of the Mādhyamika (Sanron) school, revered by Nichiren for his understanding of the Lotus Sutra.

30. Chapter 13, Lotus Sutra. This chapter stresses the difficulties of preaching in the latter ages.

31. Chapter 14, Lotus Sutra, tells of the rewards the Buddha will bestow on those who preach.

32. NKBT, p. 426, interprets this sentence as part of the previous quotation: "Nichiren's preaching is only theory; I know the true nature of things." NKBT, note 4 suggests the alternate reading, as does *STH*, p. 514.

33. The story of Pien-ho appears in *Han Fei tzu*. Pien-ho found a real jewel and presented it to the king, but it was believed fake and he was punished by having his legs cut off.

34. When Wake no Kiyomaro (Pure Man) (733–799) blocked the attempt of the priest Dōkyō to take the throne, his name was changed to Kegaremaro (Sinful Man), and he was exiled. *Zoku Nihongi*, Jingo-keiun 3 (A.D. 769)/9.

35. This quotation and the preceding one are from the Lotus Sutra, chapter 13, T9, p. 36b.

36. T9, p. 36b.

37. Chapter 20, tells the story of the bodhisattva Sadāparibhūta (Jōfukyō or Fukyō), who exemplifies the superiority of simple faith and pure-heartedness to worldly wisdom and skepticism. Sadāparibhūta endures persecution for practicing the teachings of the Lotus Sutra. In chapter 13, "Fortitude," the disciples and bodhisattvas promise to take on the difficult task of preaching the sutra after the Buddha's nirvana. Nichiren is saying that the situations and morals of both chapters are applicable in the past, present, and future and that devotees must model their lives on those described in the sutra.

38. Nichiren will live the "Sadāparibhūta" chapter, just as he is living the events of "Fortitude"; that is, carrying out the vow to spread the Lotus Sutra after the nirvana of Śākyamuni.

39. A sutra is divided into three parts: the introduction *(jobun)*, the main body *(shōshūbun)*, and the concluding section on the propagation of the sutra *(ruzūbun)*.

40. Lotus Sutra, chapter 11.

41. Three times Śākyamuni announces that he is seeking someone to propagate the sutra after his nirvana.

42.   Lotus Sutra, chapter 13, T9, p. 36b.
43.   Chapter 14, T9, p. 37a.
44.   Three types of enemies are predicted in chapter 13, "Fortitude": ignorant men, monks with twisted wisdom, and prideful hermits.
45.   A large number, ten million or one hundred million.
46.   A servant Toki had sent to accompany Nichiren. Exiles were given a small allowance for expenses. One of Nichiren's worries was how to feed the disciples that gathered around him in exile.
47.   1271.

Letter from Sado[1]

This letter is for Lord Toki[2] and his family, Lord Shijō Saburōzaemon,[3] Lay Priest Ōkuratō no Tsuji no Jūrō,[4] the Nun Sajiki,[5] and all others who should receive it. Please send me the names of those who have died in the skirmishes in Kyōto and Kamakura. Also, as soon as there is someone traveling to Sado, please send the non-Buddhist Anthology,[6] roll two of the *Wen chu,*[7] roll four of the *Hsuan i,*[8] the memorials to the court, and the Imperial pronouncements.[9]

In this world people fear fires, the shadow of the sword, and whatever causes death. Even oxen and horses fear death. How much the more do we humans cling to life! Even a leper clings to life. How much more so a healthy man!

The Buddha taught that three thousand myriad worlds filled with the seven treasures all given as alms are not worth one little finger sacrificed for the sake of the Buddhist Teachings.[10] Long ago, the Prince of the Himalayas gave up his life[11]; the Brahman Gyōbō stripped the skin from his body.[12]

These men did not cling to their lives but gave them as offerings in order to receive the Buddhist Teaching, by which they assuredly attained Buddhahood. Could he who would give up his life for the Buddhist Teaching regret giving up any other treasure? And how could a man who regrets giving up riches give up his life for the Teaching?

There are men who give up their lives to repay a great debt. And there are a surprising number of men who give up their lives for their lords. Men die out of shame. Women die for their men.

Fish cling to life, and when the pond is shallow they dig holes in the bottom in which to live. However, they may be beguiled by bait and bite the hook. Birds live in trees. They fear the low branches and live at the tips of the trees. However, they are beguiled by bait and caught in nets. Men, too, are like this. They lose their lives in the shallows of the world, but find it hard to sacrifice themselves for the precious Buddhist Teaching. This must be why no one today is attaining Buddhahood.

"Gentle persuasion" or "coercive subjugation" must be chosen to suit the times,[13] just as the martial or scholarly paths are chosen in the secular world. The great saints of the past practiced the Teachings according to the times. The Prince of the Himalayas and Prince Mahāsattva,[14] having been told that such was the practice of bodhisattvas, gave up their lives to learn the Teachings. If there were no object to the sacrifice, would anyone lay down his life? When there is no paper you must give your skin for paper, and when there are no brushes you must give your bones for brushes.[15]

We must deplore violations of the rules of discipline as well as their absence and hold steadfast to the precepts even in an age in which they are no longer followed. In an age of Confucianism or Taoism, when Buddhism is suppressed, we must debate the ruler fearlessly, like Tao-an,[16] Hui-yuan,[17] and Fa-tao.[18]

In the Buddhist Teachings, Hīnayāna and Mahāyāna, provisional teachings and the perfect teaching are all mingled. At times when pearls and pebbles are as little distinguished as cow's milk and donkey's milk,[19] we must divorce the Mahāyāna from the Hīnayāna, the provisional from the perfect, the revealed from the esoteric, just as did Chih-i and Saichō.

Beasts threaten the weak and fear the strong. The scholars of today are like beasts. They scorn the wise men who are weak and fear the unjust secular authorities. They are fawning retainers. When a man defeats a powerful enemy, he is then known as a brave warrior. At a time when evil kings take heretical monks as their allies and try to eject wise men in order to destroy the True Teaching, he who has the heart of a lion will surely become a buddha.

This is true in my case. I am not being vain. I am simply stouthearted enough to regret the loss of the True Teaching. When a vain man meets a powerful enemy, he is afraid. For example, the proud *asura* turned cowardly under the attack of Indra, and shrank so they could hide in the lotus blossoms in Lake Anavatapta.[20] If you obtain so much as one word or verse of the True Teaching which is propitious to the present age, you will surely attain the Path. Even though you study one thousand sutras and ten thousand commentaries, they will be to no avail if they do not suit the times.

The Hōji Battle took place twenty-six years ago,[21] and this year there was another battle from 2/11 to 2/17.[22] The evil non-Buddhists find it difficult to destroy the True Teaching of the Tathāgata, but the disciples of the Buddha will surely destroy it. It is the parasites in the body of the lion which kill it. It is difficult for enemies to destroy those who have amassed great merit, but those who are close to them plot and destroy them. The *Yakushikyō* calls this "uprisings within the country."[23] The *Ninnōkyō* tells us: "When the saints abandon the country, the seven disasters occur."[24] In the *Konkōmyōkyō* we read: "The thirty-three gods are angered and resentful because the ruler commits evil acts and does not govern."[25]

Although I am not a saint, I am like one in that I practice the teachings of the Lotus Sutra. And the events of our world are those predicted in these sutras. The predictions have come true in our world; we cannot doubt they will do so in the future.

When I incurred the displeasure of the *bakufu* last year on 9/12,[26] I cried out: "I am the pillar of the *bakufu,* I am the sun and moon, the mirror, the eyes. If I am sent away, the seven disasters will occur." Within sixty to one hundred fifty days "uprisings within the country" occurred. This is only retribution in the present life. When the true retribution comes, how they will suffer!

Yet the foolish men of the world ask, "If Nichiren has wisdom, why is he punished by the authorities?" I expected this punishment. There are children who strike their mother and father; Ajātaśatru was such a one.[27] There are those who murder buddhas and arhats and cause their blood to flow; Devadatta was such a one.[28] Ajātaśatru's six evil retainers praised him, and Devadatta's disciples, Kokālika and the rest, rejoiced.

I am the father and mother of the *bakufu* rulers; I am like the buddhas and arhats. How shameful that such a one should be exiled and the rulers and retainers rejoice! Those heretical priests, who feared *they* would be punished, must all be delighted! But they will yet suffer worse misfortunes than ours. Fujiwara Yasuhira struck down his younger brother and Kurō Hongan Yoshitsune and rejoiced.[29] The demons who will destroy the *bakufu* rulers have surely already entered the country. As the Lotus Sutra says, "Evil demons will enter their bodies."[30]

Well then, I have been punished in this way because of my actions in past lives. In "Sadāparibhūta" we read, "His penalty had been paid."[31] When the bodhisattva Fukyō was reviled and abused by innumerable slanderers of the Law, he was suffering in this life for actions committed in former lives.

Now I was born in this life into a poor and lowly family; I come from a family of outcasts. My heart seems to believe a little in the Lotus Sutra, but actually I am a beast in human form. In the blood of my mother and father, who were nourished by the flesh of birds and fishes, the spirit resided. It is as though the moon was reflected in muddy water or gold was found in excrement. Because I believe the Lotus Sutra in my heart, I fear neither Brahmā nor Indra; yet my body is the body of a beast. Because my body is not in accord with my heart, it is natural that ignorant men despise me. My heart is like the moon in muddy water or the gold in excrement.

Who can know that I slandered the Law in the past? Is my spirit that of the monk Shōi[32] or Mahādeva?[33] Am I one of those who reviled and abused Fukyō? Am I one of the tribe who went astray, or one of the five thousand arrogant,[34] or one of those unable to plant the seeds of Buddhahood in the time of the Buddha Daitsū[35]? It is difficult to judge karma from past lives.

Iron, forged, becomes a sword. When wise men and saints are abused and reviled, their value is tested. The official chastisement I have suffered is not due to my sins in this life. Exiled because of my sins in former lives, I will expiate those sins in this life and escape rebirth in the three evil realms in the future.

The *Hatsunaiongyō* says: "In future lives they will wear the priest's stole, leaving their homes and studying the Teachings, but they will be indolent and idle, and they will slander the Mahāyāna scriptures. Know that these men are the tribe who study non-Buddhist teachings today."[36] Those who read this scripture must be ashamed. Those today who leave their homes and wear priest's garments, but are indolent and idle, were disciples of the six non-Buddhist teachers[37] in the time of the Buddha. This the Buddha has written.

Hōnen's followers, and those of Dainichi,[38] call themselves the Nenbutsu sect and the Zen sect, respectively. They erect barriers to Buddhahood, saying "reject, combat, rebuff, and cast aside" the Lotus Sutra and recite the *nenbutsu* to Amida as taught in the provisional sutras; or preaching that the transmission of enlightenment is outside the scriptures and that the Lotus Sutra is but a finger pointing to the moon, they ridicule what they call reckoning up characters.[39] They are the descendants of the six non-Buddhist teachers who have now reappeared within Buddhism. How deplorable!

According to the *Nehangyō* the Buddha sent a beam of light that lit up the 136 hells beneath the earth, and there was not one sinner there. All had been saved by the chapter "The Life-Span of the Tathāgata"[40] in the Lotus Sutra. Only the *icchantika,* who had slandered the True Teaching, had been stopped by the guard. They bore children and peopled the Japan of today.

In the past I too was a man who slandered the True Teaching. For many years I recited the *nenbutsu* and looked upon those who live the Lotus Sutra and taunted: "Not one of these has yet attained Buddhahood" or "There is not one in a thousand who will attain Buddhahood."

Now sober after my intoxication with heresy, I look about and realize that those who, while drunk, gleefully strike their parents, awake to regret it. Their remorse is inexpressible. Their sin is difficult to cleanse. How much more difficult when the sin of slandering the Teaching in the past stains the heart! The scriptures say that the crow is black and the heron white because they are dyed by past karma.[41] This truth is unknown outside the Buddhist teachings; others believe the colors to be merely nature's way.

When I reveal to people of today their slander of the Teachings and try to save them from their sins, they insist they are innocent and hotly defend themselves, holding that Hōnen said to close the Gate of the Lotus Sutra. Even the Tendai and Shingon followers ally themselves with the reciters of the *nenbutsu.*

This year on the sixteenth and seventeenth of the first month, a man named Inshōbō, who is the leader of the several hundred *nenbutsu* chanters on Sado, came to my hut and said: Did not Hōnen write that we should cast aside the Lotus Sutra? He wrote that we are to teach all living beings to recite the *nenbutsu,* and "by its great virtue, there is no doubt of rebirth in paradise." Those priests sent to Sado from Mount Hiei and the priests of Miidera have seen this and praised it, saying, "Good! Good!" Why do you alone denounce it?[42]

These people are far inferior to the *nenbutsu*-ites of Kamakura and their arguments are quite pitiful. Seeing them, I am more and more horrified by my sin in slandering the Lotus Sutra both in former lives and, until recently, in this very life. For this sin I might have been born the disciple of such a man, in such a place as this. Who knows what might have happened?

In *Hatsunaiongyō* we read: "Good disciples! As retribution for innumerable sins and various evil acts performed in past lives, a man may be scorned by others, he may be born ugly of face or form, he may lack clothing, he may have only the meanest food, he may seek profit and be unable to gain it, he may be born to a poor family or a heretical family, or he may be chastised by the ruler."[43]

It also says: "That people in this world suffer only lightly in retribution for these many sins is due to the great merit of protecting this sutra."[44]

Had I not lived these words, the predictions of the Buddha would have gone unfulfilled. Scorned by others, born ugly of face and form, lacking clothing, having only the meanest food, seeking profit and unable to gain it, born into a poor or heretical family, chastised by the ruler: I alone have realized these eight phrases with my own body.

If you climb a tall mountain, you will fall. If you disparage others, you will find yourself scorned. If you slander a man who is handsome, you will be born ugly. If you steal clothing or food, you will be reborn as a hungry ghost. If you calumniate a family which believes the True Teaching, you will be born into a family of heretics. If you ridicule the five prohibitions or ten commandments, you will be born as a peasant and be punished by the ruler. This is the established law of retribution.

I am not suffering retribution for these acts, but for having reviled one who lived the Lotus Sutra in the past. The Lotus Sutra is the moon among moons, the star among stars, the Flower Mountain[45] among Flower Mountains, the jewel among jewels. At times I revered it, and at times I disparaged and scorned it, and so these eight troubles have come upon me.

The eight troubles were to have appeared one at a time, but so fiercely did I attack the Lotus Sutra that all have occurred at once. In the same way, as long as a peasant remains in the district, he may extend repayment of money owed to the *jitō* from year to year without being pressed. However, if he leaves, he must pay up all at once. This is what the sutra means when it says: "due to the great merit of protecting this sutra."[46]

The Lotus Sutra says: "There are many ignorant men who revile us with foul mouths or attack us with swords and staves . . . and we are repeatedly banished."[47] If the devils did not torture those in hell, they would never expiate their sins and escape; if the ruler and his ministers had not appeared in this life, I would have difficulty expiating my sin of slandering the Teaching.

I am like the bodhisattva Fukyō, and the people of this country are like the fourfold multitude who reviled him. The actors are different, but the cause of suffering is the same. Any person who kills his father or mother will fall into the deepest hell. Why should I not become the Buddha Śākyamuni like Fukyō?[48] The people of this country will be called Batsudabara.[49] They must suffer for one thousand *kalpas* in the deepest hell. I pity them, but what can I do?

Those who scorned the bodhisattva Fukyō later came to believe and follow him. Most of their sin was erased, but still they suffered as much as one who kills his father, mother, and one thousand others. The people of today have not recanted. Therefore, they must endure innumerable *kalpas* of long years in hell, as told in the chapter "Parable."[50] Three thousand dust mote *kalpas,* five hundred dust mote *kalpas* of long years will pass.[51]

But I have something else to say.

Some of those who seemed to believe in me have become doubters now that they have seen me exiled, and not only have they given up the Lotus Sutra, but they lecture me and think themselves wise. How unfortunate! Such hypocrites will burn in the deepest hell longer than those who chant the *nenbutsu*. Like the *asuras* who said Buddha was ruler of only eighteen worlds while they ruled nineteen, and like the non-Buddhists who said Buddha taught only one supreme path, while they preached ninety-five, these hypocrites say "Nichiren is a teacher, but he is too intransigent; we will spread the Lotus Sutra temperately." They are like the firefly that laughed at the moon, the ant hill that looked down on Flower Mountain, the well and the rivulet that scorned the torrent and ocean, the magpie that laughed at the phoenix.

Homage to the Sutra of the Lotus Blossom of the Wonderful Law.

1272/3/20   Nichiren

To my disciples and followers:

There is no paper in Sado and it is a worry to write to each of you. Anyone left out would be jealous. Gather those who are strong in their faith and discuss this letter and console yourselves.

A sorrow rare in the world has befallen us, and lesser sorrows are not worth considering. I have heard that some died in the recent battle,[52] and, true or not, how sad I am! What happened to Izawa *nyūdō* and Sakabe *nyūdō*? Please write and tell me about Kawanobe no Yamashiro and Lord Tokugyōji.[53] Without the non-Buddhist collection, *Chen kuan cheng yao,*[54] all the non-Buddhist tales, and the statements of doctrine of the eight sects, I cannot write my letters. Be sure to send them to me.

NOTES

1.   *STH,* pp. 610–619. This essay was composed 1272/3/20, four months after Nichiren was sent to Sado. Some followers had criticized Nichiren's intransigence and were urging him to modify his positions. This is Nichiren's reply, sent to his band of believers.

2.   Toki Tsunenobu (1220–1299) was a *bakufu* retainer employed in the Monchūjo, the Board of Inquiry. This list includes some of the most ardent of Nichiren's believers, those who had gathered followings themselves. Two other letters to Toki, *Teradomari gosho* and *Toki dono gosho,* appear in this book. See also *Toki ama gozen gosho,* herein.

3.   Shijō Yorimoto (1230–1296) was a retainer of Ema Mitsutoki. He had practiced Zen, but converted to Nichiren in 1256. Mitsutoki was a follower of Ryūkan, an opponent often mentioned by Nichiren, so there was conflict between lord and

retainer which Nichiren later helped to ease. A letter to Yorimoto's wife, *Shijō Kingo dono nyōbō gohenji,* is translated herein.

4. Okuratō no Tsuji was a Kamakura place name. Nothing else is known about this follower.

5. The name Sajiki also refers to a part of Kamakura. This woman was called Myōnichi-ni and Ben-dono-ni as well. She often sent servants with offerings to Nichiren at Sado and Minobu.

6. Evidently this is a collection of quotations from non-Buddhist writings. NKBT, p. 428, n. 7.

7. *Miao fa lien hua ching wen chu,* a collection of Chih-i's lectures.

8. *Miao fa lien hua ching hsuan i,* another collection of lectures by Chih-i.

9. This paragraph and the last are marginal notes, probably postscripts.

10. The bodhisattva Yakuō (Bhaiṣajyarāja) in the Lotus Sutra, chapter 23, sacrificed his arm to obtain the teaching. T9, p. 53c.

11. To hear a verse of the sutra, he sacrificed himself to a demon. This jataka story is found in the *Nehangyō.* T12, p. 450a.

12. He used the skin for paper to write Buddhist verses. The tale is found in *Ta chih tu lun,* where the name is Aihō (Ai-fa). T25, p. 178c.

13. *Shōju* and *shakubuku.* The *Shōmangyō* introduces the concept of gentle and forceful teaching methods; coercive subjugation is to be used against those whose evil is great and gentle persuasion applied to those whose evil is slight.

14. A jataka tale in the *Konkōmyōkyō* tells of this prince who sacrificed himself to a starving tigress to save her young.

15. As did Sibi in the *Ta chih tu lun.*

16. Tao-an (Chou dynasty) supported Buddhism in China at a time of repression by the Taoist Emperor Wu of the Northern Chou dynasty.

17. Hui-yuan (532–592) was also known for religious debates with Emperor Wu.

18. A priest of the Sung period (d. 1147), exiled for criticism of contemporary Taoist beliefs.

19. The analogy is from *Ta chih tu lun:* cow's milk and donkey's milk look alike, but donkey's milk will not make cheese when it curdles.

20. The *asura* are warrior demons, inhabitants of a realm which bears their name and is one of the three lower realms. The Hindu god Indra became a guardian god in the Buddhist pantheon. This tale appears in *Kanbutsuzanmaikyō* and in *Konjaku monogatarishū* 1-30.

21. In 1247 Hōjō Tokiyori defeated Miura Yasumura.

22. Hōjō Tokimune defeated Hōjō Tokisuke in this battle of 1272.

23. T14, p. 407c.

24. T8, p. 833a.

25. T16, p. 429c.

26. On 1271/9/12 Nichiren was arrested by Taira no Yoritsuna.

27. Ajātaśatru, deceived by Devadatta, imprisoned his father and killed his mother.

28. Devadatta, Śākyamuni's cousin, was his enemy and rival.

29. Yasuhira turned on Yoshitsune, who had sought refuge with him and his family, in June, 1189. Just months later Yasuhira was attacked and killed by Yoritomo, at whose behest he had destroyed Yoshitsune.

30. Chapter 13, T9, p. 36c. "Many evil demons will enter their bodies to malign and disgrace us."

31. "The men, having heard, held him lightly and maligned him, abused and reviled him, but the bodhisattva Never Disparaging [Fukyō] was able to bear this with

equanimity. When his penalty had been paid, and he faced the end of his life, he was able to hear this scripture, and his six faculties were purified." Hurvitz, p. 283; T9, p. 51b.

32. He reviled the bodhisattva Kikon and fell into hell. *Shohōmugyōkyō.*

33. Mahādeva slew both parents and a monk. *Ta p'i p'o sha lun.*

34. These left when Śākyamuni preached the Lotus Sutra. T9, p. 7a.

35. The story of this buddha is told in the Lotus Sutra, chapter 7, "Parable of the Conjured City."

36. T12, p. 877c.

37. Six preachers contemporary with Śākyamuni.

38. Dainichibō Nōnin, an early Kamakura priest of the Rinzai Zen sect, preached at the Sanbō temple in Settsu. He was murdered by his uncle, Taira Kagekiyo, in 1195.

39. A reference to the Zen teaching of nonreliance on written texts.

40. Chapter 16.

41. *Ryōgonkyō.* NKBT, p. 433, n. 22.

42. Nichiren's debate with Inshōbō at Tsukahara is described in more detail in "Hoke Jōdo montōsho" (1272/1/17), *STH,* pp. 518–522.

43. T12, p. 877c.

44. Hua-shan, the tallest mountain in central China, revered as one of the five sacred mountains of China.

45. T12, p. 877c.

46. *Hatsunaiongyō.* See quotation, *Sado gosho,* note 44. Suffering in this life erases evil karma, which would otherwise bring greater suffering in future lives. Nichiren is paying for all his sins at once, just as a peasant may pay all his debts at once and be relieved of his burden of repayments.

47. Chapter 13, T9, p. 36b.

48. In the Lotus Sutra, chapter 20, "Sadāparibhūta," Śākyamuni reveals that Fukyō was one of his former incarnations.

49. The bodhisattva Bhadrapāla led the five hundred bodhisattvas who held Fukyō in contempt.

50. Lotus Sutra, chapter 3.

51. See translation of *Kyōdaishō,* note 4, for a description of a three thousand dust mote *kalpa.* A five hundred dust mote *kalpa* is *kalpas* the number of the dust motes obtained by pulverizing 500,000,000,000,000,000 *nayutasaṃkhya* worlds and depositing one dust mote in a world after traversing as many worlds. All worlds traversed when the dust particles are exhausted are pulverized. The number of dust motes obtained is the number of *kalpas* in a five hundred dust mote *kalpa.*

52. The fighting of 1272/2.

53. These four disciples are otherwise unknown.

54. A T'ang collection on good government. The request reveals Nichiren's preoccupation with problems of church and state at this time. A copy in Nichiren's hand is kept at the Honmonji in Fujinomiya. NKBT, p. 515, n. 171.

Letter to Lord Toki[1]

I cannot describe my hunger and thirst. There is not a cup of rice for sale.[2] I am going to die of starvation. I am sending back the disciples who accompanied me, and I shall be alone. Tell this to the disciples with you.

The twelfth, I stayed in Sakawa[3]; the thirteenth, Takenoshita[4]; the fourteenth, Kurumagaeshi[5]; the fifteenth, Omiya[6]; the sixteenth, Nanbu[7]; the seventeenth, here. I am not yet sure, but if this mountain seems suitable, I may stay here awhile. At any rate, I am now alone, destined to wander through all parts of Japan. If I do settle anywhere, we shall see each other again.

17th

Respectfully,

Nichiren

NOTES

1. This letter to Toki Tsunenobu probably was written 1274/5/17, the day Nichiren arrived at Minobu. *STH,* pp. 809–810.
2. One *gō,* about 0.4 pint.
3. Present-day Kanazawa Prefecture, Sakawa.
4. Shizuoka Prefecture, Takenoshita.
5. Shizuoka Prefecture, Numazu.
6. Shizuoka Prefecture, Fujinomiya.
7. Yamanashi Prefecture, Minami Koma district.

Letter to the Wife of Lord Shijō Kingo[1]

Among the heretical teachings that are blinding the eyes and leading astray the souls of all the living beings of Japan, the Shingon school is foremost. I will not go into that in detail now though.[2]

The ten analogies[3] show us the superiority of the Lotus Sutra over all other sutras, but that was not the Buddha's main aim. He wanted to show that when we compare those who live the other sutras to those who live the Lotus Sutra, the devotees of the Lotus Sutra are like the sun and moon. He is saying that the devotees of the other sutras are like stars or lamps in comparison.

If you wonder how I know this, it is through the eighth analogy, the most important one. This passage says: "If anyone can receive and hold this scripture, he too, in the same way, shall be first among all living beings." These words are the heart of the whole sutra. They are like the eyes of a living being. They mean that the devotee of the Lotus Sutra is like the sun and moon, like Brahmā, like the Buddha. This passage says the devotee of the *Dainichikyō* is like the stars, the river, the common man.[4] Thus the men and women, priests and nuns of this world who keep the Lotus Sutra were seen by Buddha as the masters of all living beings. Indra and Brahmā should revere them and their happiness be indescribable.

If you meditate on this passage of the sutra noon and night and read it morning and evening, you will be an uncommon devotee of the Lotus Sutra. Do not think that the word "anyone" in "if anyone can receive and hold this scripture" refers to any nun or priest, layman or laywoman who believes in the Lotus Sutra. In the next passage the Buddha makes it clear that he is referring to women: "If there is a *woman*," he says.[5]

In reading all the other sutras, I have felt I would not want to be a woman. In certain sutras women are called the messengers of hell; in others they are called serpents; in others, warped wood; in others, those who dry up the seeds of Buddhahood. In non-Buddhist texts, too, among the three pleasures of Yung Ch'i-ch'i was the pleasure of *not* being a woman.[6] He also named the pleasure of *not* being reborn in heaven as a woman. There is also a saying that disasters were caused by three women.[7] Only in this Lotus Sutra are women who keep the sutra said to be superior to all other women and to men as well.

A woman does not mind being reviled by everyone if she is pitied by the man she loves. She does not care if she is hated by everyone if she is looked upon with compassion by Śākyamuni, Tahō, the buddhas of the ten directions, and even Indra, Brahmā, and the sun and moon. If she is praised by the Lotus Sutra, she need worry about nothing else. Since you have sent offerings to avoid the bad luck of your thirty-third year, I will tell Śākyamuni, the Lotus Sutra, and the sun god[8] of your faith.

People's bodies have left and right shoulders; by each stands a god. One is called Same-name; the other is called Same-birth.[9] These two gods are placed at your sides to protect you from the time you are within your mother's womb until your life ends. They follow you like a shadow, like an eye. They remember the bad you do and the good, and report everything, even the slightest act, to the gods. This is written in the *Kegonkyō* and can be read in roll eight of *Chih kuan* by Chih-i. Those women whose faith is weak will be abandoned by the gods, even though they keep the Lotus Sutra. If a general is weak, he will have no soldiers. If the bow is weak, the string is weak, too. And it is natural that when there is not much wind, the waves are small.

However, Saemon,[10] among all the lay brothers of Japan, is a step ahead as a believer in the Lotus Sutra. And the woman he married is the foremost among Japanese women. The Buddha is surely planning to enlighten you through the Lotus Sutra, just as he did the daughter of the *nāga* king.[11] The word "woman" implies "clinging."[12] The wisteria clings to the pine; woman clings to man. Take Saemon as your teacher and be led to the Lotus Sutra. The bad luck of your thirty-third year will turn into the good luck of your thirty-third year. "The seven troubles will disappear; the seven blessings be born."[13] You will grow younger and younger and your blessings increase. How marvelous this is!

1/27[14]   Nichiren

NOTES

1. This is a reply to the wife of Shijō Yorimoto, a samurai who corresponded with Nichiren often about his attempts to convert his liege lord. This letter was written, probably in 1275, to reassure his wife as she reached the age of thirty-three, one of the traditional unlucky ages for women in Japan, and to remind her of the Lotus Sutra promise of salvation for women. *STH,* pp. 855–859.

2. This letter is a reply. Presumably Nichiren is responding to a question or comment in Lady Shijō's letter.

3. Lotus Sutra, chapter 23, "Bhaiṣajyarāja," contains this passage announcing the superiority of the Lotus Sutra:

> Just as, for example, among all streams, rivers, and bodies of water the sea is first, this Scripture of the Dharma Blossom, also in the same way is the deepest and greatest among the scriptures preached by the Thus Come One. Also, just as among Earth Mountain, Black Mountain, the lesser Mount Iron-Rim, the greater Mount Iron-Rim, the Mount of Ten Jewels, and the whole multitude of mountains Mount Sumeru is the first . . . . Further, just as among a multitude of stars the moon, child of the gods, is first . . . . Further, just as the sun, child of the gods, can clear away all darkness. . . . Further, just as among lesser kings the wheel-turning sage-king is first . . . . Just as the divine Śakra is king among the thirty-three gods . . . . Further just as the great god king Brahmā is father of all living beings, this scripture also, in the same way, is father of all saints and sages, of all learners, and of those who having *[sic]* nothing more to learn, and of all who have launched bodhisattva-thought. Further, just as among all ordinary fellows the srota'āpanna, sakṛdāgāmin, anāgāmin, arhant, and pratyekabuddha are first, this scripture also, in the same way, is first and foremost among all scriptural dharmas, whether preached by the Thus Come One, or preached by bodhisattvas, or preached by voice-hearers. If anyone can accept and hold this scriptural canon, he, too, in the same way, shall be first among all living beings. Among all hearers and pratyekabuddhas the bodhisattva is first, and this scripture too, in the same way, is first and foremost among all scriptural dharmas. Just as the Buddha is the king of the dharmas, this scripture is also, in the same way, the king of the scriptures. Hurvitz, pp. 298–299; T9, p. 54ab.

4. In comparison to the sun, the ocean, and the enlightened being.

5. In this passage the Buddha announces that if any woman should grasp and keep this sutra, this existence will be her last as a woman, and she will be reborn in Amida's paradise. The Lotus Sutra does teach that women may attain salvation, but Nichiren is exaggerating the extent to which the passages he cites are intended to summon women converts. He also omits completely any mention of the promise of rebirth in Amida's Pure Land included in this passage.

6. In *Tales of Chuang Tzu,* Chuang Tzu meets a sage and asks what are his three greatest pleasures.

7. Three emperors of China were brought to their downfall by love for a woman.

8. Sūrya.

9. These gods have the same name and the same moment of birth as the person they protect.

10. Shijō Yorimoto, Lady Shijō's husband.

11. Lotus Sutra, chapter 12, "Devadatta."

12. "The character *onna* can also be read *kakaru.*"

13. *Ninnōkyō,* T8, p. 832b.

14. 1275?

Treatise on Brothers[1]

The Lotus Sutra is the heart of all eighty thousand scriptures; it is the backbone of the canon. The buddhas of the three worlds attained enlightenment with this sutra as their teacher; the buddhas of the worlds of the ten directions save living beings with the one vehicle. In the sutra libraries of today there are two groups of scripture and commentary which were brought to China between the Yung-ping era[2] of the Latter Han and the end of the T'ang dynasty. There are 5,048 rolls of old translations and 7,399 rolls of new translations.[3] Each of these sutras claims to be the first among all sutras, but when we compare the Lotus Sutra to the others, it is like comparing heaven and earth, or clouds and mud. The other sutras are the stars; the Lotus, the moon. The other sutras are lamps or torches, stars or moons, while the Lotus Sutra is the burning sun.

Turning from comparisons of entire sutras, we find twenty important points in the content of the Lotus Sutra. The first is the teaching of the three thousand dust mote *kalpas*. The second is the teaching of the five hundred dust mote *kalpas*.

The Buddha preached about the three thousand dust mote *kalpas* in the "Parable of the Conjured City" in the third roll of the Lotus Sutra:[4]

Suppose a man ground to dust all the earth of three thousand myriad worlds, and after carrying the dust through a thousand-times-three-thousand myriad worlds at last deposited a particle and then traveled another thousand-times-three-thousand myriad worlds and deposited another particle of dust, and so on, depositing them one at a time until all the particles were gone. Then suppose he ground together all those worlds with the worlds in which he had not deposited dust, and suppose each dust particle to equal a *kalpa*.

That number equals three thousand dust mote *kalpas*.

Now, long, long ago, Śāriputra, Kāśyapa, Ānanda, Rāhula, and all who were enlightened by hearing the three types of sermons[5] heard the Lotus Sutra from the bodhisattva who was the sixteenth son of the Buddha Daitsūchishō and who was none other than Śākyamuni, but they were led astray by ill fate and conceived the idea of giving up the Lotus Sutra.

Some fell back to the *Kegonkyō,* and then successively to the *Hannya-kyō,* the *Daishukkyō,* the *Nehangyō,* the *Dainichikyō,* the *Jinmitsukyō,* the *Kankyō,* and finally the Hīnayāna *Agon;* and at last the good deeds that brought them birth in the realms of god and men were exhausted and they fell into the three evil realms. As they fell, during three thousand dust mote *kalpas,* they were reborn most often in the deepest hell, but sometimes they were born into the seven great hells and sometimes in the more than one hundred other hells, and more rarely in the realms of beasts, hungry ghosts, or *asuras*. Then, after a great dust mote *kalpa,*[6] they were reborn in the realms of men and gods.

In roll two of the Lotus Sutra we read of such beings "dwelling in hell as if sporting in a garden; living in the evil realms as if in their own homes."[7] Those who commit the ten sins fall to the first or second of the eight hot hells and suffer there for five hundred lifetimes or a thousand years. Those who commit the five sins fall to the deepest hell, where they pass one medium *kalpa* before rebirth.

Abandoning the Lotus Sutra may not seem a sin as heavy as murdering a parent, but those who abandon the sutra fall to the deepest hell for many *kalpas*. Even if one were to kill one, two, ten, a hundred, a thousand, ten thousand, a hundred thousand, a million, or ten billion parents, one would not fall into hell for three thousand dust mote *kalpas*. Even if one were to kill one, two, ten, a hundred, a thousand, ten thousand, or ten million buddhas, one would not fall into the various hells for five hundred dust mote *kalpas*. For those enlightened by hearing the three types of preaching to fall into the hells for three thousand dust mote *kalpas* and for the great bodhisattvas to fall into the hells for five hundred dust mote *kalpas* just because they have abandoned the Lotus Sutra seems too harsh a punishment.

If you strike the air with your fist, you will feel no pain; but if you strike a stone, it will hurt. To slay a bad man is a light sin, but to slay a good one is a weighty sin. To kill a stranger is like striking mud with the fist, but to kill a parent is like striking stone. Dogs that bark at deer do not have their skulls split, but dogs that bark at lions have their entrails left to rot. Warriors who drink every day will have their heads crushed in battle, while Devadatta, who struck a buddha, found that the earth opened beneath him and he fell into hell. The weight of the sin depends on the victim.

Now then, the Lotus Sutra is the essential scripture among all the scriptures; the Teacher Śākyamuni is the original Teacher. If there is a person who gives up one word or one idea of the Lotus, his sin will surpass that of killing ten million parents or making the blood of a hundred thousand buddhas flow, and he will fall into the hells for the long ages of three thousand dust mote *kalpas* or five hundred dust mote *kalpas*.

But, it is very difficult to meet one who preaches the text of this sutra. To meet a preacher of this sutra is more difficult than for a one-eyed tortoise to find a floating log, more difficult than to suspend Mount Sumeru from the sky by a fiber of the root of a lotus. Tz'u-en,[8] who was a disciple of Hsüan-tsang, was the teacher of the T'ang emperor T'ai-tsung. He was a saint who had learned all the Sanskrit and Chinese sutras, who had filled his heart to overflowing with the scriptures, whose brush dripped mementos of the Buddha, whose teeth emitted light. People revered him as the sun and moon, and after his death he was worshipped as the pivot of the Teaching, but Saichō criticized him: "Though he said he admired the Lotus Sutra, he killed its spirit." Saichō meant that although Tz'u-en thought he adored the Lotus Sutra, his teachings destroyed it.

Śubhākarasiṁha[9] was a king of Udyāna in northwest India. He abdicated and took holy orders, traveling to the more than fifty states of India preaching the revealed and esoteric teachings. Later he went to China and became the teacher of the Emperor Hsüan-tsung. There is no Shingon priest of China or Japan who does not delve into his teachings. Yet this revered man died suddenly and was punished by Yama in hell. No one has been able to say why this happened. Pondering this, I realized it was because he originally practiced the Lotus Sutra, but came to believe the *Dainichikyō* to be superior.

The reason Śāriputra and Maudgalyāyana and the rest fell into the deepest hell and suffered for three thousand dust mote *kalpas* and five hundred dust mote *kalpas* was not because they committed the ten sins or the five sins. It was not because they committed the eight sins which include treason. It was because they came upon perverted wisdom and their faith in the Lotus Sutra was destroyed as they turned back to the provisional sutras.

Chih-i wrote: "If you keep evil companions, you will lose your own faith." "Your own faith" refers to faith in the Lotus Sutra. "To lose" means to abandon faith in the Lotus Sutra and turn to other sutras. Thus it says in the Lotus Sutra: "Although they are given the efficacious medicine, they will not swallow it."[10] Chih-i commented on this: "Those who have lost their faith will not take the efficacious medicine even though it is offered to them. They wander through cycles of life and death and flee to other lands."

Thus, a person who believes in the Lotus Sutra should fear not bandits, robbers, highwaymen, wild beasts, lions, or the Mongols who recently attacked Japan, but rather those people who would harm those who live the Lotus Sutra.

This world is the realm of Māra, and all living beings have been his since the beginningless beginning. In the six realms, twenty-five prisons of existence have been prepared. Living beings are locked in them, bound with the chains of wife and children and caught in the nets of parents and rulers. They are made drunk on the wines of ignorance, wrath, and stupidity and are made to lose their original Buddha-nature. Side dishes of wrongdoing are served with the wine, and they are pushed down into the hells of the three evil realms. When now and then there appears a man with a good heart, these lost beings serve as a hindrance to him. They try to entice those who believe in the Lotus Sutra into evil, and when that is impossible, they tempt them with the *Kegonkyō,* which resembles the Lotus Sutra.[11] Tu-shun, Chih-yen, Fa-tsang, and Ch'eng-kuan were such men.[12] Those who enticed men to the *Hannyakyō* were Chia-hsiang and Seng-ch'uan.[13] Those who tempted men to the *Jinmitsukyō* were Hsüan-tsang and Tz'u-en. Śubhākarasiṃha, Vajramati, Pu-k'ung, Kōbō, Jikaku, and Chishō led them to the *Dainichikyō.*[14] Those who led them into the Zen school were Bodhidharma and Hui-k'o. Shan-tao and Hōnen[15] tempted them with the *Kankyō.* In all these cases Yama, lord of the sixth heaven, entered the bodies of sages and deceived good men. This was foretold in the fifth volume of the Lotus Sutra: "Evil demons will enter their bodies."[16]

For example, even those bodhisattvas who have attained the stage at which they will become buddhas in the next life[17] may have evil demons called Radical Ignorance enter their bodies and obstruct enlightenment by the Lotus Sutra. How will it be for lesser beings?

King Māra also enters the bodies of wives and children and deceives parents and husbands. He enters the bodies of rulers and persecutes the one who lives the Lotus Sutra. He enters the bodies of fathers and mothers and chastises the filial child.

When Prince Siddhartha wanted to leave his family and take holy orders, his father Śuddhodana told him to wait until his eldest son, Rāhula, was born. Then Māra, to keep Siddhartha from entering the Path, kept the child in the womb for six years.

In the *mappō* of the Buddha Zentara, Śāriputra had completed sixty *kalpas* of religious practice and had only forty *kalpas* remaining when Māra, lord of the sixth heaven, appeared in the form of a Brahman and asked for one of his eyes to prevent his becoming a bodhisattva. Śāriputra gave him one of his eyes, but when he saw the Brahman trample the eye underfoot, he gave up his religious practice and, as a consequence, fell into the deepest hell for countless *kalpas.*[18]

In the *mappō* of the Buddha Daishōgon, sixty-eight trillion almsgivers were deceived by the four heretical monks led by Kugai, and they persecuted the monk Fuji and fell to the deepest hell for great world dust mote *kalpas.*[19]

In the *mappō* of the Buddha Shishionnō the men and women of the world trusted the monk Shōi, who observed monastic discipline, and laughed at the monk Kikon, who preached the truth that all beings will become Buddha, and as a result they fell into the deepest hell for innumerable *kalpas.*[20]

Nichiren's disciples and believers today are in similar situations. The Lotus Sutra says: "This scripture has many enemies even now when the Tathāgata is present. How much more so after his nirvana."[21] It also says: "All the world resents it and has difficulty believing."[22] The *Nehangyō* says: "If, because of good karma, you suffer the comparatively light retributions of death, torture, insult, whipping, imprisonment, starvation, or privation, you will not fall into hell." In the *Hatsunaiongyō* we read:

> If your clothing is insufficient and your food poor, if you are unable to obtain wealth, if you are born into a poverty-stricken family or a family of heretics, or if you are persecuted by the ruler or by other men, then you may conclude that your suffering in this world has been caused by virtue of your having protected the Law.

Even if we were enemies in past lives of those who practiced the True Law, if we believe the True Teaching in this life, our past sin of having hindered the enlightenment of others for which we should have suffered in hell in the future is outweighed by our present virtue, and instead of suffering greatly in future lives we suffer lightly in this one.

For having slandered the Law, among the retributions which are listed in the *Hatsunaiongyō* are being born into a poor family, being born into a family of heretics, and being persecuted by the ruler. "A family of heretics" means a family which slanders the True Teaching. "Being persecuted by the ruler" means being born in the reign of a bad ruler. You have suffered these retributions. Now each of you is persecuted by your parents; this will erase your past sin of slandering the Teaching. You have come across a ruler who oppresses those who practice the Lotus Sutra.

The sutras are clear and lucid. You cannot doubt that you slandered the Teaching in past lives. If you doubt this you will be unable to bear light suffering in this life. If you give up the Lotus Sutra because of your father's criticism, there is no doubt that not only will you fall into hell, but your loving mother and good father will also fall into the hottest of the hells where you will weep together.

This is what is called "conceiving the thought of supreme enlightenment." Because you believe so strongly in the Lotus Sutra, your great sins of the past are being expiated by persecution in this life. Cracks appear in iron when it is heated red hot, just as suffering is caused by sin. When stones are heated, they become dust, and when gold is heated it becomes pure gold. Now, with suffering, the virtues of your pure, faithful hearts will be revealed, and you will be protected by the ten *rākṣasī* of the Lotus Sutra.[23] The *rākṣasī* which appeared before the prince of the Himalayas was Indra.[24] The dove which was saved by King Sibi was Bishamonten.[25] Perhaps the ten *rākṣasī* have entered the bodies of your mother and father and chastised you to test your faith. In that case you will regret it, if your faith is shallow.

The capsizing of the lead carriage is a warning to later carriages. In today's world longing for enlightenment occurs naturally. This world is hateful, but we should not hate it, for I believe the people of Japan must suffer greatly, and we see that suffering now.

Outbreaks of fighting on 1272/2/11 were as numerous as flowers scattered by the breeze and spread like flames through gauze. Seeing that, how could we help but hate this world? In 1274/10 all the people of Iki and Tsushima died—an unthinkable atrocity! How miserable were those who went off to fight the Mongols! Aged parents, little children, and young wives were all left behind by the warriors who defended our shores. They imagined every cloud to be a banner of the enemy. They feared each fishing boat as an enemy ship. Every day the men climbed the mountains once or twice to look homeward, and three or four times each night they saddled their horses to flee. They experienced the world of the *asura* in this life.

The reason you are punished is that the ruler of this country is an enemy of the Lotus Sutra. The ruler became an enemy because of the slander of the Teaching by those who fast,[26] those who say the *nenbutsu,* and those who are masters of Shingon. Bear up under this persecution and put the divine grace of the Lotus Sutra to the test. I too will persist in praying to the gods of the heavens. Your fears and uncertainty will disappear. Since women are by nature frail, your wives may be swayed, but you must clench your jaws and persevere. Just as I unflinchingly spoke out to Hei no Saemonnojō,[27] you must have courage. Their path was different, but were not the children of Wada Yoshinori, the children of Miura Yasutoki, the family of Taira Masakado, and the followers of Abe Sadatō fearless?[28] They did not fear death. All men will die eventually. Do not be cowardly and be ridiculed by others. Because I worry about you, I want to tell you a story.

Pe-i and Shu-ch'i were the two sons of the King of Kuchu. The younger brother, Shu-ch'i, was named the King's successor. After their father died, Shu-ch'i refused to accept the office. Urged to do so by Pe-i, he in turn urged Pe-i to take the throne. "Would that not go against our father's wishes?" Pe-i argued.

"It may be against our father's wishes, but should he not have granted the rank to the elder son?" asked Shu-ch'i, and he refused. Together the brothers left the country of their parents and went to another country where they served King Wen of Chou. Within one hundred days of the death of King Wen, his son King Wu declared war against King Chou of Yin. Pe-i and Shu-ch'i clung to his bridle and told him it was a dishonor to his father to go to war before three years had passed. King Wu was incensed and was about to kill Pe-i and Shu-ch'i when his great-grandfather Wang stopped him. Pe-i and Shu-ch'i then left King Wu and hid in the Shou-yang Mountains, where they lived on wild plants. One day they met a man named Ma-tzu, who scolded them for eating plants that belong to King Wu, and they stopped. Because heaven does not abandon a sage, a white deer appeared to them and nourished them with its milk. After it had gone Shu-ch'i began to think how much more delicious its meat would be. Pe-i scolded him, but the heavens had heard and the deer did not reappear. The two brothers starved to death.

Even men who have been sages all their lives may die because of a thought. How worried I am about your thoughts!

When Śākyamuni was a prince, his father King Śuddhodana wanted him to stay at home and refused to allow him to become a monk. He placed two thousand guards at the four gates, but finally Śākyamuni defied him and took holy orders. In everything one ought to obey one's parents, but when it comes to the Buddhist Path, it is most filial not to obey.

In the *Shinjikangyō* we read that "severing ties of affection and duty to parents and entering the Buddhist Path is the true repayment of duty." This means that true repayment of duty to parents lies in disobeying their wishes, taking orders, and becoming a buddha. Even in worldly matters, the *Classic of Filial Piety* tells us that if one's parents should rebel, it is filial not to follow them in rebellion. When Chih-i meditated on the Lotus Sutra, it seemed his dead parents held fast to his knees to prevent his taking the Buddhist Path. Demons had appeared in the form of his parents to hinder him.

Here is another important story, like that of Pe-i and Shu-ch'i. The sixteenth emperor of Japan, Emperor Ōjin, who has been reincarnated as the bodhisattva Hachiman, had two children. The eldest was Nintoku and the second son was Prince Uji. The emperor, when he died, named Prince Uji his successor, but Prince Uji urged his elder brother to ascend the throne. "Why should we go against the wishes of our father?" Nintoku asked. For three years, as they deferred to each other, the throne was empty, and the people were sorely troubled. Everywhere in the country were disasters. Prince Uji, thinking it was his fault that his brother would not ascend the throne, committed suicide. Nintoku rushed to him and wept, but Prince Uji only survived long enough to exchange a few words. Nintoku became emperor, and not only was the country at peace, but Silla, Paekche, and Koguryo began to send eighty ships full of tribute each year.

There are many instances of bad relations between brothers, even those who were wise rulers. What karma led to the beautiful relationship between Nintoku and Prince Uji? Were they reincarnations of the Princes Vimalagarbha and Vimalanetra, whose story is told in the chapter "The King Śubhavyūha" in the Lotus Sutra?[29] Or were they reincarnations of the bodhisattvas Bhaiṣajyasamudgata and Bhaiṣajyarāja?[30]

Now, Lord Taifu no Sakan has been disinherited, and it seems possible that you, Lord Hyōe no Sakan, may not stand by him. If that is so, it will not be easy for your brother to return to your father's good graces, but if what the priest tells me is true, you sympathize with your brother. Marvelling at this, I have sent you a separate letter.[31] Your story will be one for posterity.

In the *Journey to the West* is the following story. In India, in the deer park at Vārānasī, there was a hermit of the forest who wanted to perfect the wizards' art. Already he had turned tiles and pebbles into treasure and changed the forms of men and beasts, but he had not been able to ride the wind to the Wizards' Palace. For this purpose, he persuaded a stalwart man to hold a long sword and stand at the corner of a platform holding his breath and not speaking. Provided he did not speak from dusk to dawn the hermit would perfect the wizards' art. The hermit sat in the center of the platform holding a sword and reciting a spell. Both vowed not to speak, even if it meant their death. Midnight had passed, and dawn was about to break when the warrior let out a yell. The hermit, now unable to perfect his art, turned to the warrior and lamented, "Why did you break your vow? This is terrible!"

The warrior replied, "I drifted off to sleep and the man I formerly served appeared and scolded me for not speaking. Because of my promise to you I bore his reproaches, but he became angry and said he would cut off my head. Still I did not speak and so he beheaded me. I grieved to see my body wander in purgatory, but still I did not speak. At last I was born to a Brahman family in southern India. During conception and birth, I bore the pain and still I did not breathe a word. Soon I was grown and married. My parents died and children were born. I had sorrows and joys, but still I did not speak. When I attained the age of sixty-five, still silent, my wife said she would kill the children I loved unless I spoke. I was an old man and would not be able to have more children if I lost those, and so, unthinking, I cried out. Startled by my cry, I awoke. You will never be able to forgive me for my weakness."

The hermit replied, "It was my fault for not having forewarned you." Nevertheless, they say the warrior died of remorse because he had not kept his vow to the hermit.

What is called the wizards' art in China is related to Confucianism.[32] In India it is part of the non-Buddhist teachings. Needless to say, it does not touch on even the Hīnayāna *Agon,* much less the partial or perfect teachings,[33] and least of all the Lotus Sutra. Still, perfecting even such a shallow art involved a fight with evil demons, who, in the end, prevented it. How much the more when you begin to adhere to the seven characters "Namu Myōhōrengekyō" which are the foundation of the Lotus Sutra. Those disciples and believers who first spread them throughout Japan will surely suffer indescribable, unimaginable hardship.

Master Chih-i's *Mo ho chih kuan* contains the essence of all that Chih-i taught and of all the holy teachings of the Buddha. After the Buddhist teachings were brought to China, the ten masters north and south of the Yangtze had wisdom brighter than the sun and moon and virtue renowned over the four seas, but they still did not know the depth or shallowness, the superiority or inferiority, or the order of the teachings the Buddha preached during his lifetime. However, the Man of Wisdom, Chih-i, not only followed the Buddha in illuminating the Teaching, but produced from the storehouse of the five characters Myōhōrengekyō that talismanic jewel "three thousand worlds in one thought," and presented it to the beings of the three countries. This doctrine originated in China and was not revealed by the Indian commentators. Thus, Master Chang-an's[34] commentary says: "The doctrine of meditation as preached by Chih-i has never before been heard," and "There is nothing comparable in the great commentaries of India."

The doctrine of "three thousand worlds in one thought" in roll five of *Mo ho chih kuan* seems deeper the further you penetrate it. If you preach that doctrine it is certain that demons will appear. If the demons did not fight it, we would know that it was not the True Teaching. In roll five Chih-i wrote: "As soon as you practice and comprehend, the three obstacles and the four demons will begin to fight you. You must not follow them or fear them. If you follow them, you will turn toward the evil ways. If you fear them, they will prevent your practicing the True Teaching." This commentary mirrors my life and also reflects the lives of my followers. Circumspectly learn and pass this on, and it will sustain you as you attain Buddhahood in the future.

The three obstacles mentioned in this commentary are passions, deeds, and retributions. The passions which are obstacles are covetousness, anger, and stupidity. The deeds which are obstacles are marrying and bearing children. The retributions which are obstacles come from ruler and parents, as well as from one of the four demons, the heavenly demon.[35]

Now in Japan there are many who insist that they practice the method of concentration and insight, but are the three obstacles and four demons opposing them? When he said, "If you follow them, you will turn toward the evil ways," Chih-i did not mean only the realms of hell, of beasts, and of hungry ghosts. All of the human and heavenly realms except that of the Buddha are evil ways. Therefore, *Kegon, Agon, Hōdō, Hannya, Nehan,* and *Dainichi* sutras, all the sutras except the Lotus Sutra, are evil ways. All those who lead people into any of the seven sects except Tendai are tormenting devils leading people into the evil paths. Even within the Tendai sect, there are men who lead people to the sutras anterior to the Lotus Sutra, while seeming to believe in the Lotus, and they too are tormenting devils who lead people into evil paths.

Now you two are like the hermit and the warrior. If one of you is lacking, neither will be able to attain perfection. You are like the two wings of a bird or the two eyes of a man. And your wives have faith in you. A wife is one who follows, one who accompanies. If the husband is happy, the wife too will thrive. If the husband is a thief, the wife will become a thief too. And this is so not only for this lifetime: in lives and worlds to come they will seek out marriage as the shadow accompanies the body and the flower accompanies the fruit. Insects which live in trees eat trees. Fish which live in water drink water. If the grass withers, the orchid weeps; if the pine flourishes, the oak rejoices. Even plants have close ties. The birds which are said to fly with wings united form one body but have two heads. The food which enters both mouths nourishes the one body. The fish called flounder share two eyes between each male and female pair so they cannot part during their whole lives. A husband and wife are the same.

Even if she is injured by her husband for the sake of the Lotus Sutra, a wife will not resent it. If they have the same faith, the wife will be able to follow the example of the *nāga* girl,[36] and will serve as a model to other women in attaining Buddhahood in the evil *mappō*. No matter what happens, I will tell the two saints,[37] the two gods,[38] the ten *rākṣasī*, Śākyamuni, and Tahō who guard the Lotus Sutra, and you will become buddhas in your next lives.

"Be master of your heart; do not allow your heart to be your master." This is written in the *Ropparamikkyō*. No matter what trials come your way, think of them as a dream and concentrate on the Lotus Sutra.

My words were difficult to believe, but now my predictions have come true and those who reviled me without reason must regret their actions. Men and women who come to believe in me in the future will not mean as much to me as you who believed me from the first. Many abandoned me in fear. Among them are some who revile me more than those who reviled me from the first. In the Buddha's lifetime the monk Sunakṣatra and others at first believed and later not only abandoned the Buddha but reviled him. They did not attain the Buddha power but fell into the deepest hell.

Be particularly sure to send this letter to Lord Hyōe no Sakan and read it carefully to the wives of Lord Taifu no Sakan and Lord Hyōe no Sakan.[39]

Namu Myōhōrengekyō.

Namu Myōhōrengekyō.

1275/4/16   Nichiren

NOTES

1.   *STH*, pp. 918–934. This letter to the Ikegami brothers is dated 1275/4/16. The two brothers, converts to Nichiren, were pressed by their father, a fervent Amidist, to give up their faith. Nichiren wrote often, trying to keep the wavering younger son, Hyōeshichirō, and his wife faithful and urging them to support the elder brother and convert their father. See also *Hyōe Sakan dono gohenji,* p. 283.

2.   A.D. 58–76. Reign of Emperor Ming.

3.   "Old translations" are those completed before the end of the T'ang dynasty in 907. Translations by Hsüan-tsang and later priests are called the "new translations."

4.   Chapter 7, T9, p. 22a.

5.   Sermons on the Dharma, parables, and tales of karma.

6.   *Kalpas* the number of the dust particles of three thousand myriad worlds ground to bits.

7.   Chapter 3. These are among the retributions visited upon those who cut off the Buddha seed. T9, pp. 15c–16a.

8.   632–682. Founder of the Fa-hsiang (Hossō) school.

9.   Subhākarasiṁha (d. 735), who arrived in China in 716, was preceded by his fame

as a Tantric teacher. He translated the *Dainichikyō,* or Mahāvairocanā sutra, into Chinese.

10. Lotus Sutra, chapter 16, T9, p. 43a.

11. It teaches that all beings have the Buddha-nature.

12. Chinese masters of the Hua-yen (Kegon) school of Buddhism. Fa-tsang (643–712) is generally considered the founder of the school in China.

13. Masters of the San-lun (Sanron) sect.

14. All are masters of the esoteric school of Buddhism. Nichiren blamed Jikaku (Ennin) and Chishō (Enchin) for introducing esoteric Buddhism at Enryakuji.

15. Masters of Pure Land Buddhism.

16. Lotus Sutra, chapter 13, T9, p. 36c.

17. *Tōgaku no bosatsu* who have attained the fifty-first stage of enlightenment.

18. *Nehangyō.*

19. *Nehangyō.*

20. *Shōhōmugyōkyō.*

21. Chapter 10, T9, p. 31b.

22. Chapter 14. T9, p. 39a.

23. Ten demons who appear in the Lotus Sutra, "Spells." In their evil state they were enemies of living beings; converted, they became enemies of evil and offered spells for the protection of preachers of the Lotus.

24. The prince's faith was tested by the god Indra in demon form.

25. Sibi's faith was tested by Bishamonten (Vaiśravana), one of the four heavenly kings, who appeared in animal form. This jataka tale appears in *Ta chih tu lun.*

26. Monks of the Ritsu school, who kept the rules of monastic discipline.

27. Taira Yoritsuna.

28. All four were rebels against the imperial court or *bakufu.*

29. Chapter 27. The two brothers performed miracles for their father, who had been an unbeliever, and converted him. They then persuaded their parents, again by means of amazing feats, to allow them to leave the household and join the Buddha.

30. Bhaiṣajyarāja was the elder of the brothers and the first to decide to become a bodhisattva of healing. He led his younger brother to adopt the same course.

31. See *Hyōe Sakan dono gohenji,* "Reply to Lord Hyōe no Sakan," p. 283.

32. Surely Nichiren means Taoism rather than Confucianism.

33. The four stages of the Buddhist teachings according to Chih-i were the Hīnayāna *Āgama,* the intermediate teachings, the differentiated teachings, and the perfect teachings. The last three are stages of Mahāyāna teachings culminating in the Lotus Sutra and *Nehangyō.*

34. Chang-an (561–632) was a disciple of Chih-i and recorded his lectures.

35. Māra, lord of the sixth heaven of desire.

36. Chapter 12 of the *Lotus Sutra* describes how the daughter of the *nāga* king attained Buddhahood.

37. Pradhānaśura and Bhaiṣajyarāja, protectors of the Lotus Sutra. Kino Kazuyoshi, *Nichiren* (Tokyo: Chūōkōronsha, 1970), p. 409.

38. The sun and moon gods Sūrya and Candra; Brahmā and Indra; or the gods who have the same name and same moment of birth as the individual. William Soothill and Louis Hodous, *A Dictionary of Chinese Buddhist Terms* (Kaohsiung, Taiwan: Buddhist Culture Service, n.d.), p. 24.

39. This paragraph is addressed to whichever of Nichiren's disciples was leading the lay followers in Ikegami.

Letter on Extending Your Allotted Life by the Lotus Sutra[1]

There are two types of illness. One is slight illness; the other, serious. Even with a serious illness, if a good physician attends you early, your life can be saved. This is certainly the case with a light illness. There are two types of karma. One is fixed karma; the other nonfixed. If you really repent, even fixed karma can be wiped out. This is certainly the case with nonfixed karma. In the seventh roll of the Lotus Sutra, we read: "This sutra is the efficacious medicine for the sickness of those in Jambudvīpa."[2] This is a passage from the Lotus. The saintly teachings of the Buddha's lifetime are all the golden words of the Tathāgata, and for innumerable *kalpas* there has been no falsehood in them. Moreover, it is said that this Lotus Sutra is the sutra in which Buddha "frankly casts aside expedient devices"[3]; it is the Truth among truths. The Buddha Tahō added clear proof[4]; all the buddhas stretched out their tongues to add testimony.[5] How *could* these words be false? Moreover, there is one supreme mystery. This passage from the sutra applies to women who may be ill during the last five hundred, twenty-five hundred or more years after Buddha's nirvana.[6]

When King Ajātaśatru[7] was in the fifteenth day of the second month of his fiftieth year, great boils appeared on his body. The famous doctor Jīva exerted all his strength, but Ajātaśatru was fated to die and go to the deepest hell in three months and seven days. The joys of his fifty years of life were extinguished all at once, and the suffering of a lifetime concentrated in thirty-seven days. Although his end was formulated by fixed karma, the Buddha repeatedly expounded the Lotus Sutra to him, as is told in the *Nehangyō*. The king's illness was immediately cured and the great sins which burdened his heart vanished at once like the dew.

Some fifteen hundred years after the Buddha's nirvana, there was a man called Ch'en Chen.[8] He had reached half a century and his life was extended by fifteen years to sixty-five. Besides it is said that the Bodhisattva Fukyō "increased his life-span yet further";[9] he extended his fixed karma by practicing the Lotus Sutra. These were all men, not women, but they did extend their lives by the practice of the Lotus. Moreover, Ch'en Chen did not live during the last five hundred years after the Buddha's nirvana,[10] so that efficacy of the Lotus in his time was like rice plants in winter or chrysanthemum blossoms in summer. For a woman of today to live the Lotus Sutra and extend her life would be like rice in autumn and chrysanthemums in winter—who would be surprised by it?[11] Thus, I prayed for my poor mother, who not only was cured, but also increased her life-span by four years.[12] Now, you have a woman's body and this body is afflicted. Try increasing your faith in the Lotus and see what will happen. Moreover, there is a good doctor available. Lord Nakatsukasa Saburōzaemonnojō lives the Lotus Sutra.[13]

Life is one's most precious treasure. To extend a life even one day is worth more than one million pieces of gold. The Lotus Sutra's splendid superiority over the other sacred teachings of Buddha's lifetime is due to the chapter, "The Life-Span of the Tathāgata."[14] Even the greatest prince in Jambudvīpa, if his life is short, is less important than the grass. Even if your wisdom is bright as the sun, if you die young, you are worth less than a dog which lives. Quickly, pile up the treasures of determination, and soon you will be cured.

I should introduce you to Lord Nakatsukasa, but there are those who think talking is good and those who suspect the speaker's sincerity. People's hearts are difficult to comprehend; there are many instances of misunderstandings. He does not like to have others rely on him, and I may offend him by writing to him. Just go to him without any intermediary, simply and without duplicity. He came here the tenth month of last year, and he was concerned about your illness. When I told him you were no worse than usual and you would surely recover by the first or second month of next year, that too caused him anxiety. "I rely on Lord Toki and on My Lady the Nun as a staff or a pillar," he said. He seemed considerably grieved. He is a person of indomitable spirit, and he takes your affairs very seriously.[15]

If you are stingy with your wealth, your illness will be hard to cure. One day of life is worth more than the treasures of three thousand worlds. You must first let your resolution be known. In regard to this, the seventh roll of the Lotus Sutra says that rather than offering up the treasures of three thousand myriad worlds, you should burn one finger and offer it up to the Buddha and the Lotus.[16] Your life is worth more than three thousand myriad worlds. Moreover, you are still young, and you have met the Lotus Sutra. Each day you live, your merit should increase. Ah, this precious life! This precious life! Write your name and age and send them. The gods of the sun and moon should be told about you.[17] Lord Iyo[18] also is concerned, and he is reciting the "I, myself" verse[19] to the gods of the sun and moon.

Reply to My Lady the Nun   Respectfully,

                                                            Nichiren

NOTES

1. *STH,* pp. 861–864. This letter was written from Minobu to the wife of Toki Tsunenobu, probably in 1275. The Nichiren who consoles a sick woman with the thought that the Lotus does offer benefit in this life is quite different from the Nichiren of other letters who urges his disciples, shrinking in the face of persecution, to relinquish the thought of benefit in this life and not to fear martyrdom.

2. Chapter 23. "O Beflowered by the King of Constellations! With the power of supernatural penetration, you are to protect this scripture. What is the reason? This scripture, for the people of Jambudvīpa, is a good physic for their sicknesses. If a man has an illness and can hear this scripture, the illness shall immediately vanish. He shall neither grow old nor die." Hurvitz, p. 301; T9, p. 54c.

3. Chapter 2, T9, p. 10a.

4. Chapter 11. Tahō (Prabhūtaratna) appeared in a jeweled stupa to testify to the truth of Śākyamuni's discourse. T9, p. 32bc.

5. Chapter 21, T9, p. 51c.

6. Just before the preceding passage in chapter 23 is this promise: "If a woman, hearing this Chapter of the Former Affairs of the Bodhisattva Medicine King, can accept and keep it, she shall put an end to her female body, and shall never again receive one. If after the extinction of the Thus Come One, within the last five hundred years there is a woman who, hearing this scriptural canon, practices it as preached, at the end of this life she shall straightway go to the world-sphere Comfortable . . . ." Hurvitz, p. 300. The last five hundred years are the years of the *mappō.*

7. The *Nehangyō* contains the tale of Ajātaśatru, led into sin by Devadatta but later converted to Buddhism.

8. *Mo ho chih kuan,* 8, contains this tale about Chih-i's brother.

9. Lotus Sutra, chapter 20. "Having attained this purity of the six faculties, he increased his life-span yet further by two hundred myriads of millions of nayutas of years, broadly preaching to others this Scripture of the Dharma Blossom." Hurvitz, p. 281; T9, p. 51a. Fukyō (Jōfukyō, Sadāparibhūta) was abused for his practice of the Lotus Sutra. Nichiren identified with him, and taught his followers a lesson based on Jōfukyō's story: persecution borne in this life erases past misdeeds and brings one nearer salvation.

10. The *mappō,* the period for which Nichiren believed the Lotus teachings were destined.

11. The Lotus Sutra is specifically designed to save beings in the *mappō.*

12. In 1264/11 Nichiren had returned to Awa because his mother was ill.
13. Shijō Yorimoto was one of the most fervent lay devotees. His skill as a physician evidently was one of the reasons his lord, Ema Mitsutoki, forgave him after confiscating his lands during the 1270s.
14. Chapter 16, which tells of the eternal existence of the Buddha. Because mankind shares in the Buddha-nature, Nichiren taught, human beings can also hope for eternal existence.
15. This paragraph is unclear in the original. Nichiren seems to be recommending Nakatsukasa as a doctor.
16. Chapter 23. "If there is one who . . . wishes to attain anuttarasamyaksambodhi, if he can burn a finger or even a toe as an offering to a Buddhastūpa, he shall exceed one who uses realm or walled city, wife or children, or even all the lands, mountains, forests, rivers, ponds, and sundry objects in the whole thousand-millionfold world as offerings." Hurvitz, p. 298, T9, p. 54a.
17. They protect devotees of the Lotus Sutra.
18. Son of Lady Toki by her former husband. As Nitchō he became one of the six disciples Nichiren named to continue his work when he died.
19. Considered the central verse of the Lotus Sutra in that it proclaims the eternal nature of the Buddha, this verse was recited as an act of devotion in the same way as the title. "Since I attained Buddhahood, throughout the number of kalpas that have passed, incalculable hundred thousands of myriads of million times asaṃkhyeyas . . . ." Hurvitz, p. 242; T9, p. 43b.

Reply to Lord Hyōe no Sakan[1]

The two messengers have delivered your gifts.

I have written to Lord Ben[2] about your resolve, and I will now tell you what should be most important to you.

During the time of the True Teaching and the Imitation Teaching, the world was not so degenerate. Wise men and saints were born one after the other, while the gods protected mankind. Now that the Latter Days of the Teaching have begun, the greed of mankind is growing. There is no pause in the squabbling between lord and retainer, parent and child, or brother and brother, much less in quarrels among people not bound by any of these relationships.

Because of this, the gods have abandoned the country, and the three calamities and seven disasters will occur.[3] As many as seven suns will appear at one time, plants will wither, rivers and streams will dry up, the earth will burn like charcoal, and the seas become as viscous as oil. Finally, flames will shoot up from hell and fire will fill the universe to the heaven of Brahmā. When all this happens, the earth will gradually crumble away.

Everyone believes children should obey their parents, retainers their lords, disciples their masters. This is known to wise and foolish alike. However, we constantly see men drunk with greed, wrath, and stupidity, fighting their lords, condescending to their parents, and denigrating their masters. In my previous letter I wrote: "Follow parent, lord, and master and remonstrate when they are wrong." You should keep this always before you.

Now, Lord Uemon Tayū no Sakan[4] has again been disinherited. As I told your wife, this was certain to happen. I told her I was worried about you and that she, too, should be concerned. It seems you have given up your faith, and my words are not likely to sway you, but you must not hate me when you are in hell. All the reeds cut in a thousand years can be reduced to ashes in an hour. One hundred years of meritorious deeds can be destroyed by a word—this is the truth of the Dharma.

Your father, Lord Saemon Tayū, has definitely become an enemy of the Lotus Sutra, but your elder brother lives the Lotus Sutra's teachings. You think only of the present and are possessed by filial duty. Ignorant men will praise you.

Munemori followed his father's example of bad deeds and was beheaded at Shinohara.[5] Shigemori did not follow his father's example and died young,[6] but how filial he was! Is it filial to obey your father, who is an enemy of the Lotus Sutra, and abandon your elder brother, who lives the one vehicle? You must make up your mind to follow your brother in perfecting the Buddha path.

Were your father the king Śubhavyūha, you brothers should admonish him as did Vimaladatta and Vimalagarbha.[7] Past and present are different, but the Truth of the Lotus Sutra is the same. More recently, was there not the example of the Governor of Musashi,[8] who gave up his great estates and his retainers and became a hermit? You are currying favor for the sake of a little property. Do not hate me when you fall into the evil destinies because of your lack of faith: over and over I have warned that you are bound to fall. Until now you have wanted to be a devotee, and it will be a pity if your weak conviction causes you to fall to the evil paths. I fear there is but one chance in a hundred or one in a thousand that you will listen to me, but I must tell you I think you should announce your faith to your father. Tell him that a father should be obeyed in all things, but if he becomes an enemy of the Lotus Sutra, it is unfilial to stand by him. You must turn from him and cleave to your brother. Tell him that if he disinherits your brother, he must disinherit you as well. Do not be afraid. There are those who have believed in the Lotus Sutra since long, long ago, but who have never attained Buddhahood because of fear.

There are differences between full tide and ebb tide; between the new moon and the full moon; among summer, fall, winter, and spring. The difference is as striking when a common man becomes a buddha. When the three obstructions and four *maras* appear,[9] sages delight in encouraging him, and ignorant men retreat in fear.

I have been wanting to tell you this as soon as I had the opportunity, so I was grateful to welcome your messenger. If you had completely given up your faith in the Lotus Sutra, you would not have sent anyone. Since you did, I am writing this letter.

It is more difficult to become a buddha than to pass a thread from one Mount Sumeru straight through the eye of a needle set upright on this Mount Sumeru.[10] Imagine how difficult it would be in a gale! The Lotus Sutra tells us:[11]

> After millions and millions of myriads of incalculable *kalpas,* at last they were able to hear this Lotus Sutra. In millions and millions of myriads of incalculable *kalpas,* the buddhas, the world-honored ones, occasionally preach this scripture. For this reason, the practitioner is not to give way to doubt when he hears a scripture like this one after the Buddha's nirvana.

Of the twenty-eight chapters of the Lotus Sutra, this passage is the most marvelous. In the chapters between the "Introduction" and chapter 10, "Preachers of the Dharma," many beings from bodhisattvas who have achieved Buddha-enlightenment[12] down through humans and gods, the four classes of religious beings,[13] and the eight types of supernatural beings appear,[14] but the only Buddha is Śākyamuni. This section seems to have deep import, but actually it is shallow in some ways. The twelve chapters from "Apparition of the Jeweled Stupa" to the twenty-second chapter, "Entrustment," contain deep areas with deep import. This is because the jeweled stupa of the Buddha Tahō has sprung up before Śākyamuni like the sun rising in front of the moon, and the buddhas of the ten directions are seated beneath the trees, glowing as brightly as if they had set fire to all the grasses and trees of all the worlds of the ten directions, and Śākyamuni preaches this section of scripture before them all.

The *Nehangyō* tells us:

> All living beings have suffered for innumerable, incalculable *kalpas.* Each being has piled up skeletons as high as Mount Vipula of Rājagṛha during one *kalpa,* has drunk as much mother's milk as there is water in the four oceans, has lost more blood than the waters of the four oceans, has wept more tears at the deathbeds of fathers, mothers, sisters, brothers, wives, children, and household than the waters of the four great oceans, and has had more parents in more lives than you could count with counters made from five-inch lengths of all the grasses and trees of the world.

Śākyamuni preached this scripture as he lay beneath the *śāla* trees before his nirvana, so we should attend to it most carefully. We read that the parents who gave birth to us during uncountable *kalpas* cannot be numbered with counters made of five-inch lengths of all the grasses and trees of the worlds of the ten directions. Although we have been able to find so many parents, we have been unable to find the Lotus Sutra. It is easy to find parents, but difficult to find the Lotus Sutra. Now, if you turn your back on your parents (you will have parents in every life) and stand by the friend of the Lotus Sutra (for such a man is rarely met in the cycle of births and deaths), not only will you become a buddha, but you will lead the parents you abandoned to Buddhahood as well.

Prince Siddhārtha was King Śuddhodana's heir, but when King Śuddhodana wanted to place his son on the throne, Siddhārtha disregarded his father's wishes, left the palace at night, and became a monk. He was called unfilial, but when he became a buddha he led Śuddhodana and Māyā to Buddhahood first of all.

There is no parent worthy of the name who tells his child to leave home and become a buddha. In your case, there are many who fast[15] or say the *nenbutsu* who would divert you from your faith in the Lotus Sutra by leading your parents astray. I have heard that Ryōkan[16] is plotting to cut off the seed of the Lotus Sutra and hinder faith among the members of your family by urging the practice of the million repetitions of the *nenbutsu*.

Lord Shigetoki, lay priest of the Gokurakuji, was an awesome man, but he was tricked by those who advocate the *nenbutsu* and became my persecutor. He and his family have fallen; only the Governor of Echigo is left.[17] Those who believe Ryōkan seem impressive, but remember what became of the Nagoe family after they built the Zenkōji, the Chōrakuji, and the Daibutsuden. Look what has happened to their descendants.[18] Tokimune is ruler of all Japan, but he has enemies as numerous as all the beings of Jambudvīpa.

If you desert your brother and take his place in your family, can you prosper for a thousand or ten thousand years? You will have fallen before you know it. Think about your next life. I fear this letter will come to naught and this makes it hard to write, but I hope you will remember it.

11/20[19]   Respectfully,

                                                           Nichiren

Reply to Lord Hyōe no Sakan

NOTES

1. Among Nichiren's believers was a young samurai who was disinherited twice by his father for his faith. In 1275, Nichiren wrote to Ikegami Munenaga (the Hyōe Sakan of the title), pleading with him to stand by his elder brother and to help convert their father. *Kyōdaishō,* translated herein, also urges the two to remain steadfast. *STH,* pp. 1401–1407.

2. Ben Ajari Nisshō, one of Nichiren's six chief disciples.

3. Nichiren most commonly cites the seven disasters found in the *Ninnokyō.* See translation of *Risshō ankokuron,* herein: eclipses, irregularities in the constellations, fire, flood, wind storms, drought, and brigands. Another set, which Nichi-

ren also cites in *Risshō ankokuron,* is that found in *Konkōmyōkyō:* pestilence, invasion, rebellion, misplaced stars, eclipses, early monsoons, and late monsoons. The three disasters are interpreted differently in different texts; they may be flood, fire, and warfare; or the warfare, plague, and famine said to mark the end of a *kalpa.* Nichiren has adopted discriptions of the end of a *kalpa* and presents them as warnings that worship of the Lotus Sutra has declined.

4. The elder Ikegami brother is generally called Munenaka although there is no source for this in Nichiren's letters.

5. Taira no Munemori, son of Kiyomori, was appointed by him as his successor. He was taken prisoner by Yoshitsune after the battle of Yashima in 1185.

6. Shigemori was Kiyomori's favorite son. He died young, of grief, it was said, at his father's treatment of his opponents. Nichiren contends that he was filial in trying to remonstrate with his father, rather than in joining in his misdeeds.

7. Lotus Sutra, chapter 27.

8. Hōjō Yoshimasa.

9. The three obstructions are passions, deeds, and retributions. The four *māras* are devils who block the path to salvation. These obstacles must be overcome to attain Buddhahood.

10. Mount Sumeru is the central mountain of every world system.

11. Chapter 20. The passage concludes with an exhortation to preach the scripture throughout the ages of the various buddhas. T9, p. 51c.

12. The stage preceding Buddhahood.

13. Monks, nuns, and men and women lay devotees.

14. Eight classes of supernatural beings in the Lotus Sutra: *deva, nāga, yakśa, gandharva, asura, garūḍa, kinnara, mahoraga.*

15. Not eating after noon was one of the rules of discipline which Nichiren had discarded and which were being reemphasized by the Ritsu movement.

16. Also known as Ninshō (1217–1303), a leader of the Shingon-Ritsu movement and also an Amidist. He was one of Nichiren's chief opponents in Kamakura.

17. Shigetoki died in 1261. The Governor of Echigo was Naritoki.

18. The Nagoe family had sided with Hōjō Tokisuke in his rebellion of 1272 and was defeated.

19. *STH* dates this letter 1277. More recent studies all date it 1275, based on reconstruction of the chronology of events from the letters.

Letter to My Lady the Nun Toki[1]

I have received the string of coins[2] and the bamboo container[3] you sent.

An arrow flies by the strength of the bow, clouds move by strength of the dragon,[4] men act by the strength of women. The visit Lord Toki paid me recently was due to My Lady the Nun.

When you look at smoke, you see fire; when you look at rain, you see the dragon; when you look at a man, you see a woman. Seeing Lord Toki was like seeing My Lady.

Lord Toki told me with joy: "While we were grieving over the approaching death of my mother, the nun took such great care and nursed her so well that I shall not forget my gratitude in any coming life."

My greatest concern now is your illness. As I have insisted for these three years that you have been ill, you should burn moxa to recover your health. Even those without sickness cannot escape impermanence, but you are still young. You live the Lotus Sutra, so you are unlikely to die an untimely death.[5] Yours surely is not illness due to bad karma, but even if it were, you could rely on the power of the Lotus Sutra.

King Ajātaśatru kept the Lotus Sutra and extended his life by forty years.[6] Ch'en Chen had fifteen years added to his life.[7] My Lady the Nun is also a practitioner of the Lotus Sutra. Your faith is like the waxing moon, like the rising tide. Think that your illness will disappear and your life be lengthened, and be heartened. Take care of yourself and do not worry.

When we do worry, it should be about Iki and Tsushima and about Dazaifu.[8] The warriors of Kamakura have enjoyed pleasures like those of heaven, but now they must depart for Kyūshū. The parting of the husband who leaves and the wife who stays is as painful as stripping off their skins. They press their faces together and weep eye to eye, but they must soon separate. Yui Beach, Inabura Hill, Koshigoe, Sagawa, Hakone Hill.[9] One day, two days pass, as walking, walking, walking farther and farther away, they are cut off now by rivers and mountains, and by clouds, too. Tears accompany them and grief is their companion. How unhappy they must be! If the Mongols attack while they are lamenting, they will be taken prisoner, whether in the mountains or on the sea, and will come to grief on shipboard or in Korea.

Though I have committed no fault at all, I, the practitioner of the Lotus Sutra, father and mother to all the living beings of Japan, have been reviled and attacked and led through the back streets by men gone mad.[10] They will be punished by the ten *rākṣasī,* and suffer things a hundred thousand million times worse than the invasion of the Mongols.

You have been able to see such events with your own eyes, yet nothing can harm you if you do not doubt the Buddha. To become an empress or be reborn in heaven is nothing. Instead, follow the footsteps of the daughter of the *nāga*[11] and ally yourself with the nun Mahāprajāpatī.[12] How joyful! How joyful! Recite "Namu Myōhōrengekyō," "Namu Myōhōrengekyō."

3/27[13]   Respectfully,

                                                                 Nichiren

To My Lady the Nun

NOTES

1.   *STH,* pp. 1147–1150. Toki Tsunenobu had journeyed to Minobu to hold funeral services for his mother the month before this letter was written in 1276/3/27. Nichiren was very close to Toki and his wife, who had taken religious vows. They converted their home to the Hokekyōji after his death.

2.   *Gamoku* was a type of coin with a hole in the center. One *kan* is one thousand *gamoku* strung together.

3.   A length of bamboo for storing grain or soy sauce. These often were beautifully polished and highly valued.

4.   Dragons were believed to ride clouds and bring rain.

5.   *Higo* is death not determined by karma, early death.

6.   Ajātaśatru murdered his father and took the throne. Later he converted to Buddhism. See *Kaen jōgō sho,* for a fuller recounting of his story.

7.   His life was extended when he learned meditation from Chih-i.

8.   Iki and Tsushima islands were in the front line of the Mongol attack and sustained heavy damage, as did Dazaifu, the military headquarters on Kyūshū.

9.   Places soldiers would pass going south from Kamakura toward Kyūshū.

10. This paragraph explains the reason for the misery described in the preceding

paragraph. The leaders of Japan, "the men gone mad," are bringing punishment on Japan by their treatment of the prophet Nichiren.

11.   The story of the *naga* woman who attained enlightenment is told in the "Devadatta" chapter of the Lotus Sutra.

12.   The aunt of Śākyamuni, whose enlightenment is predicted in "Fortitude," the thirteenth chapter of the Lotus Sutra.

13.   1276.

Reply to the Nun Niiama[1]

The package of nori you sent arrived safely, and I am very grateful for that sent by Ōama as well. I am now in a place called Minobu Peak, which adjoins Suruga province on the south. The Ukishima Plain of Suruga stretches more than two hundred fifty miles from the seacoast to Mount Minobu here in the Hakii district in Kai. A hundred leagues over this road are more difficult to travel than a thousand on any other. Here the swiftest river in Japan, the Fuji, plunges from north to south. On either side rise towering mountains. The valleys are deep, bordered by huge boulders aligned like folding screens. The water rushes past like an arrow shot through a tube by a stalwart warrior. At times the water is so swift and the rocks are so numerous that boats following along the banks or crossing the river are smashed to bits. Beyond these rapids is the peak called Minobu. To the east is Tenshi Peak; to the south is Mount Takatori; to the west is Mount Shichimen; and, to the north, Minobu Peak. The mountains encircle the valley like screens. When I climb the mountain to look around, the forest is dark and dense. Descending into the valleys, I find boulders ranged in rows. The howls of huge wolves fill the mountains, while monkeys' screams echo in the valleys. Over the clamorous shrilling of the cicadas, cries of deer longing for their loved ones touch the heart.

Spring flowers bloom in summer; autumn fruits ripen only in winter. When I chance to see a human figure, it is a peasant gathering wood. My infrequent visitors are old friends, fellow believers. The Four White-haired Recluses, who fled the world to Shang Mountain, and the Seven Sages of the Bamboo Grove, who hid their traces from the vulgar world, must have lived like this.

When I clamber eagerly up the mountain, thinking I have seen *wakame* (seaweed) growing, it is only bracken that grows there, row upon row. When I climb down to the valleys thinking I have seen nori growing, again I am mistaken: it is only parsley that sprawls in thick clumps. I had long forgotten my native village, but the nori you sent brought sad memories rushing over me. This is the nori I saw long ago on the beaches at Kataumi, Ichikawa, and Kominato. Its color, appearance, and taste are unchanged, yet my parents are both gone. My regrets bring tears to my eyes.

But enough of this. I have been worrying for some time about your request for a *honzon* for Ōama.[2] This *honzon* I worship is not mentioned in the writings of any of the many monks who traveled from India to China, nor is it mentioned by the Chinese scholars who traveled to India. If you look into such books as *Journey to the West*,[3] the *Tz'u en ch'uan*,[4] or the *Ch'uan teng lu*,[5] there is a mention of the *honzon* of every temple in each of the five regions of India. There are also the *honzon* of the many temples described by the saints who crossed from China to Japan and the wise men who left Japan to go to China. Because all the temples of Japan, beginning with the oldest, Gangōji and Shitennōji, have appeared in various works since the time of the *Annals of Japan*,[6] surely no *honzon* has been omitted. Among them all, there is no *honzon* such as this.

Someone questioned me saying, "If it does not appear in the texts, it should at least have been painted or carved by the sages of old." But, the Lotus Sutra is right before their eyes. Doubters should check carefully to see whether it really is in the sutras. To think that the existence of no previous replica is a shortcoming is unjust. To take another example, no one in the world except Maudgalyāyana knew that Śākyamuni hid for a time in Trayastṛmsā Heaven to preach the Teaching to his mother.[7] This *honzon*, also, I know of through the power of the Buddha. Although the teachings of the Buddha are right before our eyes, unless the opportunity comes, they are unseen. Unless it is time for their propagation, they do not spread. This is the Law. This is as immutable as the rise and fall of the tides, as the waxing and waning of the moon.

Our spiritual leader Śākyamuni held this teaching in his mind for five hundred eons. Then, for forty some years after he appeared in this world and while he preached the first half of the Lotus Sutra, he still kept it to himself. But he prepared for it in the eleventh chapter, "Apparition of a Stūpa," revealed it in the sixteenth chapter, "The Life-Span of the Tathāgata," and culminated his explication in the chapters on "The Supernatural Powers of the Tathāgatas" and on "Spells."[8] Monju in his Gold-hued World, Miroku in the Tuṣita heavenly palace, Kannon on

Mount Potalaka, and such disciples of the Buddha Nichigatsujōmyōtoku as the Bodhisattva Yakuō all fought to be allowed to deliver the message but were not acceptable. Though these were said to be the wisest of men, they had studied the Lotus Sutra only briefly and would have had trouble enduring the persecutions of the Latter Days. These words the Buddha set down in the fifteenth chapter, "Issuing of Bodhisattvas from the Earth"[9]: "I have true disciples who were hidden away in the depths of the earth five hundred eons ago. I now call forth Jogyō and the other bodhisattvas to deliver this teaching to them and to entrust to them the words, Myōhōrengekyō,[10] which are the essence of the Original Gate[11] to Buddhahood. This doctrine must not by any means be propagated during the thousand years of the True Law after my death, nor during the thousand years of the Imitation Law. At the beginning of the Latter Days when heretics fill the land, all the heavens will be angered, comets will shoot across the sky, and the earth will rumble like waves crashing on shore. Such terrible disasters as droughts, fires, floods, high winds, epidemics, plagues, famines, and armed riots will occur without number. At that time when every man will wear armor and carry a bow and arrows, when all buddhas, bodhisattvas, and good gods of heaven will have exhausted their powers, if you gird your body with this five-word mandala and lodge it in your heart, rulers will be able to aid their countries and the people will escape tribulation. Moreover, in future lives they will escape the great fires of hell."

While Nichiren is not the bodhisattva Jogyō, it is, I believe, the plan of that bodhisattva that I should know all this. I have spoken thus the past twenty years or so. Of the one who is to propagate this teaching it is said: "This scripture has many enemies even now when the Tathāgata is present. How many more will there be after his nirvana"[12]; and "All the world resents it and has difficulty believing."[13] The first enemies of the teaching and its bearers are rulers of nations, of districts and towns, stewards and proprietors and all the people. The second and third are priests who bring complaints, and ascetics who slander or abuse the prophet of the teaching or who attack him with swords and sticks.

Although the Tōjō district of Awa is remote, it may be thought of as the center of Japan. This is because the great goddess, Amaterasu, appeared there. Long ago she manifested herself in Ise province, but the ruler's deepest devotion was turned to the Hachiman and Kamo shrines, and his devotion to Amaterasu was shallow. At that time, when Amaterasu was angered, there lived a man called Minamoto Yoritomo, General of the Right. He wrote a pledge of faith in Amaterasu and presented it to a priest, Ōka Kodayū, who secreted it in the Outer Shrine at Ise. It is because this pleased Amaterasu that Yoritomo became the general who took all Japan into his grasp. Did this great goddess leave Ise to settle in Tōjō of Awa when he decided on that district as her dwelling? There is another such example: the bodhisattva Hachiman long ago dwelt in the West, then moved to Otoko Mountain in Yamashiro province and now dwells in Tsurugaoka in Kamakura, Sagami province.

Of all the places in the world, Nichiren first preached the True Teaching in the same Tōjō of Awa province in Japan. Consequently, the steward of that area became my enemy. He and his followers attacked me and half his forces were lost. Your family is given to foolish lies, sometimes believing me, sometimes attacking me—thoroughly inconstant. When I was in disfavor, they soon abandoned the Lotus. This is why I have always preached that the Lotus is "difficult to believe, difficult to understand" on every occasion.[14] If I should send a *honzon* because of my debt to your family the ten *rākṣasī* would surely think this favoritism on my part. If in accordance with the Sutra I do not give the *honzon* to unbelievers, I will avoid favoritism, but Ōama will not understand her misdeed, I fear, and will bear a grudge against me. Therefore, I have written my scruples to Suke no Ajari and had him take the letter to Ōama.

Although you have been sympathetic to your mother-in-law in her vacillations, let your faith be known. While I was in Sado and during the time I have been here, you have corresponded with me now and then, and never have you shown signs of faltering. Therefore, I am sending you a *honzon*. I feel as though I am treading on thin ice or confronting a great sword.

Let me make my reasoning a little more clear. When I was in disfavor in Kamakura, 999 out of 1,000 followers lost faith, but now that the persecutions have lessened, these people have come back in repentance. Of course, your mother-in-law means more to me than these, but, while I am very sorry, I cannot return flesh to the bones. I shall forever say that one must not turn one's back on the Lotus Sutra.

2/16[15]

Respectfully,

Nichiren

Niiama gozen gohenji

NOTES

1.   *STH,* pp. 864–870. This letter was written to a woman follower in Awa, Nichiren's home province. The family had been allies of Nichiren's family in their struggles with the *jitō* Kagenobu.

2.   While in exile in Sado, Nichiren had conceived an object of worship which was to be a mystic representation of the universe: a mandala. It consisted of the words

"Homage to the Sutra of the Lotus Blossom of the Wonderful Law," surrounded by the names of the Buddhas Śākyamuni and Tahō, and of bodhisattvas, of men, gods, and all other beings.

3. The record of the travels in India of the Chinese pilgrim, Hsüan-tsang, who left China in A.D. 629 and returned seventeen years later bearing numerous sutras and relics.

4. A biography of Hsüan-tsang by the T'ang dynasty monk Hui-li.

5. A Sung dynasty work compiled by Tao-yuan, which traces the lineage of the masters of Zen.

6. *Nihongi.*

7. Since Śākyamuni's mother died seven days after his birth, she never benefited by his teachings. A story tells how he transported himself in trance to heaven to preach to her. The earthly king feared he would not return. Gathering the best artists in the land, he sent them to heaven. The image they created of the Buddha preaching in heaven is, of course, not extant, but copies were supposedly carried to China and thence to the Seiryōji in Kyōto.

8. "Apparition of a Stupa" contains the revelation of Śākyamuni's existence in times past, while "Life-span of the Tathāgata" reveals the Buddha is not limited to this human life-span, but is eternal. Chapters 21, "The Supernatural Powers of the Tathāgatas," and 26, "Spells," reveal the saving power of the Lotus Sutra ("Any who receive and keep this scripture after my passage into extinction shall have no doubts about the Buddha Path"; T9, p. 52c) and the holiness of the title *(daimoku)* ("All of you who do no more than protect those who receive and keep the name of the Dharma Blossom, shall have incalculable happiness"; T9, p. 59b).

9. In this chapter of the Lotus Sutra myriads of bodhisattvas rise from the earth led by these four: Jogyō (Viśiṣṭacāritra); Muhengyō (Anantacāritra); Jogyō (Viśuddhacāritra); Anryūgyō (Supratiṣṭhitacāritra). Jogyō was supposed to have been a convert of the Buddha ages ago and to come into the world in evil times to bring the Dharma. Nichiren at times proclaimed himself a reincarnation of this bodhisattva, come to proclaim the teaching in the Latter Ages. This passage is not a citation from the Lotus, but a summary and elaboration of certain points by Nichiren.

10. Sutra of the Lotus of the Wonderful Law (the Lotus Sutra).

11. *Honmon,* used to designate the saving teaching of a sect, and in the more specific sense of the doctrine taught in the second half of the Lotus Sutra.

12. Lotus Sutra, chapter 10, T9, p. 31b.

13. Lotus Sutra, chapter 14, T9, p. 39a.

14. Lotus Sutra, chapter 10, T9, p. 31b.

15. 1275.

Reply to My Lady the Nun, Mother of the Lord of Ueno[1]

I have recorded the gifts you sent on behalf of Lord Nanjō Shichirōgorō on the forty-ninth day after his death—the two strings of coins, the horse-load of white rice, the load of sweet potatoes, the grated bean curd,[2] the *konnyaku*,[3] the basket of persimmons, the fifty citrons, and so on.

For his enlightenment, I have recited the whole of the Lotus Sutra once, the "I myself" verse several times, and the Title a hundred thousand times.

The sutra which is called the Lotus does not resemble any of the other holy teachings of the Buddha's life. Moreover, it is written that "only a buddha and a buddha can fathom its reality"[4]; it was not suited for any other beings from the highest level of bodhisattva down to common men. However, Nāgārjuna, in his *Treatise on the Great Perfection of Wisdom,*[5] gave the opinion: "Those lower than buddhas need only believe to become buddhas." In the tenth chapter of the Lotus Sutra, "Preachers of Dharma," it is written: "Yakuō, now I proclaim to you, of all the sutras I preach, the Lotus is the foremost."[6] In the fifth roll,[7] Buddha says: "Monjushiri, this Lotus Sutra, the secret treasure house of the Tathāgatas, is placed on top of all the sundry sutras." In the seventh roll,[8] Buddha says: "The Lotus Sutra is exactly like this: among all the sutras it is supreme." He also says: "It is the brightest," and "It is the most sacred." These passages from the scripture are not my own opinion, but the words of the Buddha; they cannot be untrue. For people born into common families to say "I am the equal of a samurai" is certainly an offense. How much worse to say "I am the equal of a king" or even "his superior." In this case the blame falls not only on the individual, but on his father and wife and children, who will suffer for it too. A raging fire will level his home, just as a great tree crushes smaller trees as it falls.

The Buddha's teachings are like this also: when people believe whatever they want without exercising any discrimination, and depend on the *Kegon, Agon, Hōdō, Hannya, Dainichi,* or *Amida* sutras,[9] and someone insists that their Amida sutra, or some other sutra, is the equal of the Lotus Sutra or, even worse, its superior, others of his ilk rejoice to have their sutra valued in this fashion; but they are committing a sin. Master, disciple, and lay devotee will all fall into the evil destinies, as swiftly as arrows. However, there is nothing to stop you from saying the Lotus Sutra is superior to all the other sutras. Rather, this brings great merit, for the sutra itself says this is true.

At the beginning of the Lotus Sutra is the sutra called *Muryōgikyō.*[10] It is like the advance party sent by the shogun to quiet all disorder when the emperor makes an imperial journey.[11] In the *Muryōgikyō* it is written[12]: "In forty years and more the truth has not yet been revealed." The *Muryōgikyō* serves as the shogun who shoots arrows at the enemies of the emperor or cuts them down with a sword. This proclamation is like an efficacious sword which will strike down all those who do not accept the Lotus Sutra: those who read the *Kegonkyō,* the Ritsu priests who cling to *Agon* sutras, the reciters of the *nenbutsu* who accept the *Kankyō,* and the Shingon teachers who believe the *Dainichikyō.* In the same way Sadatō was defeated by Yoshiie,[13] and Kiyomori was defeated by Yoritomo.[14] The passage "Forty years and more," of the *Muryōgikyō* is Fudō's sword and rope, Aizen's bow and arrow.[15] Therefore, Lord Nanjō Gorō, when you climb Shide Mountain and cross the Sanzu rivers,[16] quell the bandits of carnal desire and the pirates of bad karma, take as your bodyguard the *Muryōgikyō* passage, "In forty years and more the truth has not yet been revealed"; and travel without obstacle the road to Vulture Peak Heaven. In the first roll of the Lotus Sutra, "Expedient Devices,"[17] it says: "After the World-honored One's Dharma has long been in effect, he will at last preach the truth." It also says[18]: "Frankly casting aside my expedient devices, I preach the Unexcelled Path." In the fifth scroll it says[19]: "Only the bright jewel in my topknot . . . ." It also says: "Only a king's topknot has such a jewel." It also says: "like this powerful king who long guarded this bright jewel, but now presents it." The meaning of these passages is that all the sutras brought to Japan, all of the 7,399 rolls are subordinate to the Lotus Sutra. In just this way, although there are more than 4,994,828 men and women in Japan, all of them are the subjects of one king. All the other sutras are like the momentary idle musings of an uneducated woman.

When a pagoda is built, first many small sticks are gathered for scaffolding which is raised a foot or two at a time. Then the pagoda itself is erected and the scaffold cut down. The scaffold is all the other sutras; the great pagoda is the Lotus Sutra. The Buddha preached that all the other sutras are scaffolding for the Lotus Sutra. Those who believe in the Lotus, "casting aside expedient devices," tear down and throw away the "Namu Amida Butsu" of the Amida sutras, the Shingon school of the *Dainichikyō,* and the two hundred fifty rules of the priests of the Ritsu school who keep the *Agonkyō.* Then they keep the Lotus Sutra. Although a scaffold is necessary to build a great pagoda, when the pagoda is erected, the scaffold is torn down. The meaning of the passage "casting aside expedient devices" is this. Although the pagoda is a result of the scaffold, no one tears down the pagoda and worships the scaffold. The people who turn to religion today pass their whole lives fervently reciting "Namu Amida Butsu." Those who do not recite "Namu Myōhōrengekyō" even once discard the pagoda and keep the scaffold. They are called clever in this world, but their cleverness is in vain.

The late Lord Shichirōgorō did not resemble the people of Japan of today. Although he was young, he followed in the footsteps of his wise father. Not yet twenty years old, he has become a buddha by reciting "Namu Myōhōrengekyō." "All, without doubt, achieve Buddhahood."[20] As a mother who loves her children, you should recite "Namu Myōhōrengekyō," so that you may be reborn with Lord Nanjō and Lord Gorō. Different seeds produce different plants. If you plant the seed of "Namu Myōhōrengkyō" in your heart, you will be reborn in the country of that same "Namu Myōhōrengekyō."[21] When you three see each other there, how great your joy will be!

Well then, if you open the Lotus Sutra and look in it, it says: "He is covered with the robe of the Tathāgata and is protected by all the present buddhas of the ten directions."[22] The essence of this passage of the sutra is that in the east, west, south, and north, in all the eight directions of the compass, the uncountable *nayutas* of countries outside the thousand-millionfold worlds are completely filled with buddhas of the ten directions. They are numerous as stars in the sky, thick as rice and hemp on the earth. They protect those who live the Lotus Sutra as a great prince protects his retainers. The protection of the four heavenly kings is welcome, but it does not equal the protection of all the heavenly kings, all the constellations, the suns and moons, Indras, Brahmās, and the other gods of all the worlds. Nor does it equal all of the bodhisattvas—Miroku in his Tuṣita palace, Jizō on Karada Mountain, Kannon on Mount Potalaka, Monju on Shōryō Mountain—who arm their retainers and defend the practitioner of the Lotus Sutra. We cannot express our gratitude to

Śākyamuni, Tahō, and all the buddhas of the ten directions, who come personally and offer protection with their own hands during the twelve hours of the day and the twelve hours of the night.

The late Lord Gorō believed in this marvelous scripture and became buddha. Today, the forty-ninth day after his death, all the buddhas have gathered in the Vulture Peak Pure Land where they hold him in their hands, stroke his head, embrace him, and delight in him as in the new moon or a newly opened blossom.

Why do the buddhas of the ten directions of the three worlds protect the Lotus Sutra? It is only right, for that which is called the Lotus Sutra is the father and mother of all the buddhas of the ten directions of the three worlds. It is their nurse. It is their lord. The frog is nourished by its mother's voice. It feeds on the wind. Fish must have water. Birds build their nests in trees. The buddhas depend on the Lotus Sutra for their life, their sustenance, and their home. Fish live in water; the buddhas live in this scripture. Birds dwell in trees; the buddhas dwell in this scripture. The moon lodges in the water; the buddhas lodge in this scripture. You must realize that in countries where this scripture does not exist, there are no buddhas.

Long ago, there was a king called Lun To.[23] He was lord of all Jambudvīpa. When he was asked what he would eat, he heard a white horse whinny and replied that that nourished him. When the horse whinnied, this king became young, his complexion was ruddy, his spirit was high, his strength mighty, and his rule splendid. Therefore, everyone in that country rounded up and raised white horses, just as the king of the Wei collected many cranes,[24] and Emperor Te-tsung loved fireflies.[25] The white horse whinnied because the white bird sang, so they also gathered many white birds. Then something happened. All the white birds disappeared and the white horses did not whinny, so the king had nothing to eat. He was like a flower in full bloom wilting in the dew, like the full moon covered by clouds. The king was near death, and the queen, crown prince, ministers, and the whole country were like children separated from their mother. They grew pale; dew soaked their sleeves.[26] What should they do? What should they do? In the country were many who were not Buddhists. Compare these to the Zen, Jōdo, Shingon, and Ritsu schools of today. There were also disciples of Buddha. Compare them to the followers of the Lotus Sutra today. The two groups were incompatible as water and fire. They were like the states of Wu and Yueh.[27] The great emperor issued a statement saying: "If any non-Buddhist causes this horse to whinny, I will proscribe Buddhism and turn to the other religions with the full faith with which all the gods revere Indra. If a disciple of Buddha causes this horse to whinny, I will cut off the heads of all non-

Buddhists, dispossess them of their lands, and give the lands to the disciples of Buddha.'' The non-Buddhists paled and the disciples of Buddha bewailed this. They could not, however, let the situation pass, so the non-Buddhists first prayed for seven days. No white birds came, and the white horses did not whinny. The next seven days it passed to the disciples of Buddha to pray. Among them was a young priest named Horse-whinny.[28] For seven days he prayed, holding the Lotus Sutra which all the buddhas revere, whereupon a white bird flew up to the altar. It sang one note; one horse whinnied. The king heard the horse and rose from his bed. The queen and all the rest of the people turned to Horse-whinny and bowed down. White birds appeared, one, two, three, ten, a hundred, a thousand, and filled the country. The white horses whinnied endlessly. One, two, a hundred, a thousand whinnied. The king was nourished, and his face and form became those of a man of thirty, his mind became bright as the sun, his government became so righteous that sweet dew rained from the sky, the imperial breeze caressed the people, and endless hundred-year generations began.

The buddhas are like this, too. The buddha called Tahō achieved nirvana without coming across the Lotus Sutra, so he reappears when it is read. It was the same with Śākyamuni and all the buddhas of the ten directions. Since it is a sutra of such miraculous virtue, those who keep it can be secure in the knowledge that Amaterasu Ōmikami, the bodhisattva Hachiman, and the Fuji Sengen bodhisattvas will not forsake them.[29] In those countries which are enemies of this sutra, no matter how piously they pray, the seven calamities will occur, and at last the country will be destroyed by other countries, like a ship in a typhoon or grasses and trees in a drought. Today, my followers who practice the Lotus Sutra are ridiculed, and no matter how many prayers are said in Japan, all are useless. We will be attacked by the great Mongol nation and quickly destroyed. Look around you! Is it not so? You must believe that this is because everyone is now an enemy of the Lotus.

Well now, it is forty-nine days since the late Lord Gorō passed away. Although early death is a common occurrence, all who have heard of this are heartbroken. How much the more the mother and wife must suffer! I sympathize with you. There are childish and mature children, ugly and beautiful—but all are loved. He was a boy satisfactory in every way, truly lovable. When the late Lord Ueno died in his prime, your grief was strong, and you were ready to commit suicide by fire or by water, although pregnant with this child. But you decided to wait until the baby was safe and entrust him to someone else before taking your life. Comforted by this thought, you passed fourteen or fifteen years. Thinking that your coffin would be borne by your two sons, you were sustained, but in the ninth month of this year, the sun and moon were hidden by clouds, flowers were lashed by the wind. You wept, hoping it was only a long nightmare. But you were not dreaming, and the forty-nine days of mourning rushed by. "If it is true, what shall I do?" The full-blown flower lingers, while the bud has withered. The aged mother remains, while the young child is gone. Oh, pitiless, transient world! Give up this heartless world and serve the Lotus Sutra that Lord Gorō believed in. Help him go to the indestructible, unchanging Vulture Peak Pure Land. The father is on Vulture Peak. The mother remains behind in this world. Think with sympathy and love of the late Lord Gorō who is midway between the two. Though I have much more to say, I will stop here.

10/24[30]   With respect,

                                                       Nichiren

Reply to My Lady the Nun, Mother of Lord Ueno

NOTES

1.   Nanjō Hyōe Shichirō was the lord of Ueno manor in Fuji district, south of Mount Fuji. He died around 1267, and his widow became an ardent supporter of Nichiren. She and her two sons were members of an ardent group of believers south of Mount Fuji. After Nichiren's death, his disciple Nikkō left Minobu and worked to build up the congregation in Ueno. With the help of Nanjō Shichijirō Tokimitsu, the oldest son of Shichirō, he built the Taisekiji. This letter was written to Nanjō's wife forty-nine days after the death of the younger son. The brothers had visited Nichiren at Minobu in 1280/6. The boy died 1280/9/5, at about fourteen years of age. *STH*, pp. 1810–1818.

2.   *Suridōfu*. Commentators suggest this may resemble *kōyadōfu*.

3.   A gelatinous vegetable paste.

4.   Lotus Sutra, chapter 2, T9, p. 5c.

5.   *Ta chih tu lun.*

6.   T9, p. 31b.

7.   Chapter 14, T9, p. 39a.

8.   Chapter 23. T9, p. 54a. These phrases are taken from a paragraph of analogies Nichiren calls the "ten analogies" (see Shijō Kingo dono nyōbō gohenji, herein).

9.   The *Kegonkyō* and the *Agon, Hōdō,* and *Hannya* classes of sutras include all sutras "before" the Lotus. Nichiren mentions the *Dainichi* and *Amida* sutras specifically to emphasize that the Shingon and Amidist sects are the main objects of his criticism.

10. *The Sutra of Innumerable Meanings* is usually considered the preface to the Lotus, as the *Kanfugengyō (Sutra of Meditation on the Bodhisattva Samantabhadra)* is its conclusion.

11. Thus the *Muryōgikyō* comes to prepare the way for the Lotus.

12. T9, p. 386b. Śākyamuni preached forty years before revealing the Lotus Sutra.

13. The campaign against Abe Sadatō and his father Yoritaki is called the Early Nine Years' War. Sadatō surrendered to Minamoto Yoshiie in 1062.

14. Taira no Kiyomori was defeated by Minamoto no Yoritomo in 1180.
15. Fudō and Aizen are two of the fierce kings who guard Buddhism.
16. The steep mountain and treacherous rivers of hell.
17. Chapter 2, T9, p. 6a.
18. Chapter 2, T9, p. 10a.
19. Chapter 14. Buddha compares his supreme teaching to the jewel in a king's topknot, which is his most precious possession and the last thing he would give away. T9, pp. 38c–39a.
20. Lotus Sutra, chapter 2. "If Hearers or bodhisattvas hear the Dharma I preach, so much as a single verse, all, without doubt, achieve Buddhahood." T9, p. 9b.
21. Vulture Peak Heaven. Taken literally the idea of heaven conflicts with Nichiren's teaching of the identity of nirvana and samsara, but it is, like the Pure Land teaching, easier for the unlearned to comprehend.
22. Chapter 10. "He" is anyone who hears and reveres the Lotus Sutra after the Buddha's nirvana.
23. This is a version of the tale of the origin of the name Aśvaghoṣa. Nichiren's detail is original.
24. Perhaps Nichiren is referring to I Kung, whose story is told in the *Shih Chi, Jikkinshō,* and *Kōkonchōmonjū.*
25. 742–805. The ninth emperor of the T'ang dynasty.
26. A standard metaphor for tears.
27. Two competing states of the Spring and Autumn Period in China.
28. Aśvaghoṣa.
29. The Sengen Shrine is in Fujinomiya in Shizuoka. It enshrines the *kami* Konohanasakuyahime, Ninigi, and Ōyamamatsumi, who, in line with Ryōbu Shintō beliefs, were considered to be bodhisattvas. The shrine was near the Ueno estates.
30. 1280.

Reply to My Lady the Nun Ueno[1]

I received the load of white rice and the basket of potatoes you sent as alms and have chanted "Namu Myōhōrengekyō" for your father.

The Buddha named the sutra "Lotus of the Good Law" after the lotus blossom. In heaven the great *mandara* flower is most marvelous and on earth the cherry blossom, but the Buddha did not choose them. Comparing other blossoms to the lotus, we find that sometimes the flower appears first and then the fruit, or the fruit may come first and then the flower. There are plants which produce a single flower and many fruits, some which produce many flowers but only one fruit, and still others which produce fruit without flowers. Only the lotus bears fruit and flower at the same time.

According to other sutras, one piles up good deeds first and later obtains Buddhahood. Thus they are uncertain. However, if you but take the Lotus Sutra in your hand, that hand will soon become Buddha, and if you chant the Lotus Sutra, your mouth will soon become Buddha, just as the reflection of the moon floats upon the water the moment the moon rises from east of the mountains and just as sound and echo ring out simultaneously. Thus it is that the Lotus Sutra promises, "All who hear will attain Buddhahood,"[2] and by this we know that of one hundred or one thousand who keep this sutra there will be not even one who fails to attain Buddhahood.

I understand from your letter that this is the anniversary of the death of your father, the *nyūdō* Matsuno Rokurōzaemon. It is only to be expected that with so many descendants there would be considerable variation in the filial duties which they perform on behalf of their late ancestor. Should any of them, however, not have faith in the Lotus Sutra, they must be reckoned among the enemies of the True Law.

The Buddha Śākyamuni vowed, "At last I will preach the Truth in this sutra."[3] And the Buddha Tahō testified that "all that you preach is wholly true,"[4] while the buddhas of the ten directions rolled their tongues out to Indra's heaven in verification.[5]

If you cross the great sea to the southwest of Japan, you will come to the country called China. In that country there were men who believed in Buddha but not the gods, and there were men who believed in the gods but not the Buddha. In the beginning it was the same in Japan.

In China there was a man named Wu-lung who was the greatest calligrapher in the country. He was as famous as Michikaze or Yukinari in Japan. This man hated Buddhism and vowed that never in his life would he copy a sutra.

He became very ill, and on his deathbed he turned to his son. "You are my son. You must succeed me and work to become an even greater calligrapher than I. But no matter what the circumstances you must never copy the Lotus Sutra," he enjoined. With his last words blood gushed from his eyes, ears, nose, mouth, and skin like water from a spring. His tongue split into eight parts and his body disintegrated. The relatives and family at his bedside knew nothing of the three evil destinies. They did not realize this horrible death was a sign that he was falling into hell.

The son I-lung became the most famous calligrapher in China. In accordance with his father's dying wish he vowed never to copy the Lotus Sutra. The king, a man named Ssu-ma, was a Buddhist and especially revered the Lotus Sutra. He summoned I-lung because he wished to have the best calligrapher in the country make him a copy of the Lotus Sutra to keep and worship. I-lung said, "My father made this last request," and told the king of his father's command. Since it had been his father's dying wish, the king summoned another calligrapher to copy the sutra for him. But, when it was done, he was not satisfied.

Once more he summoned I-lung. "You say you cannot copy the sutra because of your father's dying wish. So I order you to copy just the *daimoku* on the eight rolls of the sutra." Again and again I-lung refused. The king was enraged. "Your father was my retainer. How can you fear to break your vow to your father, and yet refuse to obey your lord's command, a far worse sin?"

I-lung did not want to be unfilial, but he could see no way to refuse the royal command. He wrote the titles, gave them to the king, and returned home. Immediately he went to his father's grave where, weeping tears of blood, he confessed that, unable to refuse the king's order, he had written just the title of the Lotus Sutra. There was no apology he could make for his disobedience. Three days he stood by the grave, refusing all food and bewailing his unfilial conduct. Around five on the morning of the third day, he fell to the ground as if dead. In a vision he saw a god in the sky. The god looked like pictures of Indra. His retinue surrounded him.

"Who are you?" I-lung asked.

"Don't you recognize me? I am your father. In my former life I clung to the non-Buddhist teachings and hated Buddhism and especially the Lotus Sutra. When I died I fell into the deepest hell where every day my tongue was torn out hundreds of times. When I died I was reborn to suffer again. I cried out to heaven; I bent down to the earth and wept, but to no avail. I wanted to warn people in the human world of this misery, but I could not. As long as you obeyed me, my words turned into flames which roared around me and into swords which fell upon me like rain. Your unfilial behavior is unheard of, but your disobedience saved me. I was weeping over my fate when a golden Buddha appeared before me in hell, and chanted 'Even if you pile up many sins in the human world, there is no doubt you will attain Buddhahood if you but hear the Lotus Sutra.' When this Buddha appeared in hell, it was as though water had been dashed on the flames. My pain was gone.

"I pressed my palms together and asked his name. 'I am the character Wonderful from the sixty-four characters of the titles which your son is writing now.'

"My son, you wrote the characters eight times on eight scrolls and the sixty-four characters became buddhas. They lit up the darkness of hell like the full moon. The deepest hell became paradise; it became the bright abode of Buddha. All the sinners in hell were transformed into buddhas on lotus blossoms. Now I am going to the palace in Tusita heaven, but I wanted to tell you this first."

I-lung asked, "How could the titles which I wrote have saved you, for I wrote the characters without faith?"

"Your hand is my hand," his father explained. "Your body is my body. The characters you wrote were characters written by me. You did not believe in the Lotus Sutra, but you saved me by writing the title. This is like a child who, playing with fire, burns something by accident. Faith in the Lotus Sutra is the same. You can have faith without realizing it and still be saved. Do not slander the Buddhist teachings, for you may come to regret the things you say while in the world."

I-lung told his dream to the king, who rejoiced. "My prayers have been answered," he said. I-lung was favored by the king and soon the entire country had come to believe in the Lotus Sutra.

Now the late Lord Gorō[6] and the *nyūdō* were your father and son. You

are the daughter of the *nyūdō*. Your faith in the Lotus Sutra has undoubtedly already guided your father and child to the palace of Tusita
heaven.

11/15[7]   Respectfully,

                                                           Nichiren

Reply to My Lady the Nun Ueno

NOTES

1.   *STH,* pp. 1890–1894. The lay nun was wife of Nanjō Shichijirō Tokimitsu. See
        also *Ueno dono no haha amagozen gohenji,* herein.
2.   T9, p. 9b.
3.   T9, p. 6a.
4.   T9, p. 32b.
5.   T9, p. 51c.
6.   Gorō had died some years earlier.
7.   1281.

Letter from Mount Minobu[1]

Truly Minobu is a dwelling place sent from heaven by the grace of the earth-shaking gods.[2] Even the lowly and insensitive man or woman is arrested by its beauty. In late autumn, that touching season, the dew settles thickly on the grass-thatched hut and strings jewels on the tangle of spider webs. The trees on the mountain peaks startle with their sudden color. Their reflection in the trickle of water in the flume calls to mind the waters of the Tatsuta River.[3] In the background the rugged mountains tower. At the tips of the branches the fruit of the one vehicle[4] grows; on the lower branches the cicadas shrill. When the water rises, the moon of ultimate truth is reflected there. When the deep unlit darkness lifts, there is no cloud in the sky of enlightenment.

In this tranquil setting, we discuss the Law of the Marvelous Sutra of the One Vehicle[5] in my hut all the day long, and voices chanting the central passages of the sutras hum through the night. The renowned Vulture Peak,[6] where Śākyamuni dwelled, has been transplanted to Japan.

Enveloped in fog or buffeted by storms, I go into the mountains to cut firewood. Through dewy grass I descend into the valleys to gather herbs. When I rinse vegetables in the rapids of the swift mountain streams, my dampened sleeves remind me that Hitomaro sang of a fisherman who passed his life with tear-drenched sleeves as he dried salt from seaweed at Poetry Bay.[7] The life I lead here resembles that of Buddha when he was seeking the Law.

Long ago when Śākyamuni appeared in the world as the Brahman Gyōbō,[8] he stripped off his skin and made paper, extracted his marrow and used it to liquify his ink, pulverized his flesh for ink, and broke up his bones for brushes, all to meet the Buddha Kasho and learn the verse: "You must practice the Teaching; do not practice heresy. He who practices in this life and the next will be at peace." As Prince Mahāsattva he fed his body to a starving tiger.[9] As the Prince of the Himalayas he threw himself from a cliff to obtain half a verse of scripture.[10] When he was King Sibi, he cut up his flesh to save a dove.[11] He plucked out an eye for the Brahman who begged for it.[12]

Long ago, when the Buddha became king of a great country, although he was the master of countless officials and a large army, he allowed himself to neglect the affairs of government, presuming on his store of good karma.[13] The ten pleasures[14] were to him like sparks before the wind, fleeting as a dream on a spring night, evanescent as morning glories blooming on a brushwood fence. Though he had become king of a great country as a reward for keeping the commandments in the past, he lived this life in vain, led on by the demon of evanescence, performing no good deeds, and at last he fell into the flames of hell where there are no distinctions between warriors and peasants.[15] He was burned by the fires of the three torments,[16] bound at the knees, elbows, and head by cables of iron, and silenced with a gag made of the three torments. His body was tortured by roaring *rākṣasa*,[17] with tridents in their hands. He lifted his voice in a piercing scream to the heavens and bent down and wept to the earth, but the courtiers and warriors were unable to come and save him. His relatives and family could not come and rescue him.

Then, knowing that not even his wife, with whom he had slept for so many nights within the brocade curtains, and whom he loved so much that they might have been birds who shared a wing or pines whose branches intertwined, not even she and their children could save him, he opened his storehouses himself and gave the gold and silver and all the seven treasures to priests as alms. He gave elephants and horses, and even his wife and children. Later he blew the conch for the Law. He beat the drum for the Law. He sought the Law in the four quarters.

At that time there was a hermit named Aji who came to the king and said, "If you truly desire to seek the Law, serve me as I tell you." The king rejoiced and went to the mountains, where he gathered fruit, cut firewood, picked herbs, and drew water for a thousand years. All this time he recited, "Because my heart cherishes the Law, my body and mind know neither sloth nor fatigue." Because he expected to learn the wonderful Law, he could work without becoming fatigued in body or mind.

The teaching which he learned in this way was the Sutra of the Lotus of the Wonderful Law. That king was the Buddha Śākyamuni. There is a verse in Japan which tells how the Buddha served and obtained the Wonderful Law. When a sutra is copied and present this verse is intoned: "The Lotus Sutra—I obtained it cutting firewood, gathering herbs, drawing water." Hearing this, we realize our own sins and feel sympathy.

To walk the Path to Buddhahood, you must serve a teacher. In roll four of the *Hung chüeh,* Miao-lo wrote: "If there is a disciple who finds fault with his teachers, whether real or not, he will lose all the great merit of the teaching." This means that a disciple who finds fault with his teacher, whether that fault is real or not, will himself lose the merit of the teaching.

In roll one of the *Chih kuan*[18] are these words:

Because the Tathāgata warmly praised this wonderful Law, those who heard it rejoiced. The bodhisattva Jōtai sought the Law in the East[19] and Zenzai sought it in the South.[20] The bodhisattva Yakuō sought for 7,200 years, and burned his arm to find the Law.[21] King P'u Ming was decapitated for the sake of the Law.[22] Though you sacrifice as many lives as the innumerable sands of the Ganges three times in one day, you cannot repay the benefaction of one verse. Even though you bear the Buddha on your shoulders during a hundred thousand million *kalpas,* you cannot requite his mercy.

In roll five of the *Chih kuan* we read that a seeker pulverized his bones in the scented castle,[23] and another threw his body from the snowy peaks, but they could not repay the grace of the Buddha's teaching.

In roll four of *Hung chüeh* we read that long ago in the great country P'i-mo a fox pursued by a lion fell into a dry well. The lion leapt over the well and ran on, but when the fox tried to climb out it was too deep. After several days the fox was about to starve and cried: "What suffering! I am going to die miserably in this dry well. The lives of all living beings are fleeting. It is a shame I was not eaten by the lion. Oh buddhas of the worlds of the ten directions, know the purity of my heart."[24] At that time, the god Brahmā heard the fox's cry and came down himself to lift the fox from the well and ask it to preach him the Law.

"That's backwards," said the fox. "The disciple is on top and the teacher on the bottom." All the gods laughed.

When Brahmā, acknowledging that the fox was correct, nevertheless sat at his feet and asked him to preach, the fox said, "This is backwards. It is not right for disciple and teacher to sit down together." Thereupon Brahmā removed the robes of all the gods, piled them up and placed the fox upon them, and again asked him to preach the Law. The fox said: "There are those who hope to live and hate death. There are those who hope to die and hate life."[25] Ignorant people do not know about future lives and so they hope to be born and hate to die. Good people know the truth of the workings of karma and retribution and so they hope to die and hate to be born. Brahmā learned this and followed the fox as his teacher.

Chih-i commented: "The Prince of the Himalayas served a demon and begged for half a verse; Brahmā revered an animal and made it his teacher. No one throws away money because the purse stinks."[26] No matter how humble, if a man has the Teaching, you must not belittle him.

Roll eight of the Lotus Sutra says: "If a man sees a person who holds this sutra and makes known his faults and evils, whether they be fact or not, that man in the present age shall get white leprosy."[27] That is, if one makes known the faults and evils of one who lives the Lotus Sutra, whether those faults are real or not, one will contract white leprosy in this life and fall into the deepest hell in the next life. Thinking about this, we realize that it is more difficult for a thread sent from Indra's heavenly palace to pass cleanly through the eye of a needle set upright upon the earth than for us to be born as men. And even though an endless period of a trillion trillion unbelievably long *kalpas* should pass, it is difficult to come upon the teachings of the Tathāgata. Even when one is at long last reborn as a human and comes upon the teachings which are so rarely heard, if one should also come upon evil knowledge, one will surely fall into the three evil realms, for the sutra tells us that if the teacher falls into hell, the disciple will follow, and if the disciple falls, the lay believers too will follow.[28]

Now, happily, you have met the one who lives the one vehicle, and, without stripping off your skin, grinding up your flesh, or serving for a thousand years, you learn these teachings: "three thousand worlds in one thought,"[29] "ten essential qualities in the ten worlds,"[30] "one true middle path,"[31] and "universal path to enlightenment."[32] If we had not piled up good karma in past lives, we would not have been born in the *mappō,* the age when the marvelous Law is transmitted, and it would have been difficult to attain enlightenment in the eternity of the future.

Look at the world around us. There are many who profess profound faith, but there is not one in a thousand whose faith touches his heart. It is true, as the *Nehangyō* says, that: "Those who do not believe and fall into evil paths are as abundant as the dirt on the earth; those who believe and attain Buddhahood are as scarce as the dirt piled on a fingernail."

Long ago the Buddha, wishing to repay his debt to his mother Māyā, slipped up to Trayastṛmsā Heaven on the fifteenth of the fourth month.[33] While he was there, everyone in the five regions of India from great kings to humble men and women, wept and sorrowed at his absence, like parents grieving for a child who has died. Even separation from a loving mother or a father you rely upon is unbearable. How much more unbearable a separation from the enlightened Tathāgata with the thirty-three marks and eighty signs, whose color is a beautiful copper-gold, and whose voice is that of the bird of paradise, and who preaches that all beings will attain Buddhahood. Because his mercy and compassion are infinite, the longing and grief for him cannot be described. It surpassed the sorrow of the beautiful woman shut up in the Shang-yang Palace.[34] It was stronger than the grief of O-huang and Nu-ying, daughters of Emperor Yao, at parting from Emperor Shun.[35] It surpassed the longing of Su Wu, exiled to the land of the barbarians, living nineteen years amidst the snow.[36]

A man who loved the Buddha took wood to make an image, but he was unable to carve the likeness of even one of the thirty-two marks of the Buddha. At that time the great King Udayana[37] called Viśvakarman,[38] the Carpenter, down from Trayastṛmsā Heaven and had a statue made from red sandalwood. That statue greeted the original Buddha in Trayastṛmsā Heaven, because of King Udayana's profound faith. This was the first statue of the Buddha carved in this human world.

Again, there was a rich man called Sudatta.[39] When the Buddha was to descend to India from Trayastṛmsā Heaven on the fifteenth of the seventh month,[40] Sudatta wished to build a temple, but he had no land on which to build. Prince Jeta, son of King Prasenajit, owned a park called Jetavana, which was about one hundred miles wide. It had been invaded by men with swords and knives and plundered. When the rich Sudatta asked for the park in which to build his temple, the prince demanded in payment gold sufficient to cover the park four inches deep. Sudatta agreed to the terms, but the prince then said, "It was only a joke. I cannot sell this park."

Sudatta insisted, "A prince does not equivocate. How could you lie, even for a moment?" and he told King Prasenajit what had happened.

"Prince Jeta will succeed me on the throne. How could he even flirt with an untruth," wondered the king. Prince Jeta had no recourse but to give up the park.

Well now, when the rich man Sudatta paid for the park with gold piled four inches thick as promised and joyfully prepared to build the temple, Śāriputra appeared and stretched a rope across, surveying the land. Looking at the sky, he laughed and laughed.

"A great saint is always dignified. Why are you laughing?" wondered Sudatta.

"Battles are taking place in the six heavens of desire because you are going to build this temple. Each of the gods wants the man who is planting such wholesome roots in his heaven. I am laughing at them for fighting. When your life-span is over, you will be born in the palace of Tuṣita.''[41]

Thus the temple was built and named Jetavana. On the night of the fifteenth of the seventh month when the Buddha was to enter the temple, Indra and Brahmā built gold, silver, and quartz bridges from Trayastṛmsā Heaven. The Buddha entered by the middle bridge, while Indra on his left and Brahmā on his right held a canopy. Behind the Buddha came monks, nuns, laymen, and laywomen; gods, dragons, *yakśas, gandharvas, asuras, garūḍas, kinnaras,* and *mahoragas;* twelve hundred arhats led by Kaśyāpa, Kātyayāna, Maudgalyāyana, and Subhūti[42]; twelve thousand hearers; and eighty thousand bodhisattvas.

All the people of the five regions of India lit lanterns according to their status; some lit ten thousand, some lit one thousand, some lit one hundred, and some lit one lantern. Among them was one poor woman, incomparably poor. She had nothing to cover her but a mat woven of reeds even coarser than rush. She searched everywhere but was unable to find the money to buy even one lamp. Had her tears been oil they could have fueled one hundred or one thousand or ten thousand lamps or more. Finally, she cut off her own blue-black hair, and made a wig which she sold to buy a lantern. Perhaps because her devotion was accepted by the Buddha and gods, the three treasures, the gods of heaven, and the gods of earth, her lamp alone was not extinguished by the fierce winds that blow at the beginning and end of a *kalpa,* and it lit the way as the Buddha entered Jetavana.

As you see, even though a man be rich and give great treasure as alms, if his faith is weak he cannot attain Buddhahood. Even though a man be poor, if his faith is strong, there is no doubt of salvation.

A boy named Mushōtokushō presented mud pies to the Buddha, and by virtue of this was reborn as King Aśoka. Finally, having built eight billion four thousand stupas and sent them to various countries, he resolved to attain enlightenment.

In the Lotus Sutra a woman who had been chosen during the forty years of preaching achieved Buddhahood,[43] and even Devadatta, who was called an *icchantika* and who broke the five prohibitions, became a buddha. Thus there is no doubt that in this polluted *mappō* those men and women, religious and lay, who are *icchantika* because they have broken the five commandments and slandered the Law, will all attain Buddhahood by the Lotus Sutra. Moreover, we must trust these words from roll seven of the Lotus Sutra: ''After my passage into extinction, any who receive and keep this scripture shall assuredly walk the Buddha path.''[44]

As I sit on my meditation mat, I begin to dream. Awakened by a deer crying for his mate, I understand that in me the moon of "three teachings are one"[45] and "three meditations are one mind"[46] has been shining brightly all along, but because the moon was covered by the cloud of ignorance and disbelief I have suffered rebirths and death in the nine worlds until today.[47] I thought:

These gathering clouds
On Mount Minobu also
Shall be swept away,
Mountain wind on Vulture Peak
Of the everlasting law.[48]

NOTES

1.   *STH*, pp. 1915–1924.
2.   *Chihayaburu*, a *makura-kotoba* (fixed poetic epithet) for the gods. Nichiren's style is especially literary and lyrical in this essay. There are numerous references to the Japanese poetic tradition.
3.   Famed in poetry for the beauty of the autumn leaves floating on its waters.
4.   The Lotus Sutra teaches that there is only one true way to attain Buddhahood, one vehicle.
5.   The Lotus Sutra.
6.   Śākyamuni preached the Lotus Sutra on Vulture Peak.
7.   Possibly this is a reference to *Kokinshū* no. 962, which is attributed not to Kakinomoto Hitomaro, fl. 670–700, but to Ariwara Yukihira, 818–893:

wakuraba ni	If from time to time
tou hito araba	Any should ask for me,
suma no ura ni	Answer them this:
moshio tarutsutsu	At Suma Bay with tear-drenched sleeves
wabu to kotaeyo	I dry the salt from seaweeds.

8.   The tale is from *Ta chih tu lun*. T25, p. 178c.
9.   This story is found in the *Konkōmyōkyō*.
10.   The story is told in the *Nehangyō*.
11.   King Sibi saw a hawk about to eat a dove and sacrificed his own flesh to save it, weighing out an equal measure for the hawk. The story is found in *Ta chih tu lun*.
12.   *Ta chih tu lun*.
13.   The Lotus Sutra, chapter 12, contains the germ of Nichiren's story:
    I was ever king of the realm, [and as king] I vowed to seek unexcelled bodhi, my thought never receding. Wishing to fulfill the six pāramitās, I strove to confer gifts, in my mind never begrudging elephants, horses, or the seven jewels; nor realms or walled cities; nor wife and children, slaves and servants; nor head, eyes, marrow, trunk and flesh, arms and legs; not begrudging bodily life itself. At that time, the people of the age had incalculable length of life. For Dharma's sake, I abandoned realm and title, leaving the government to my heir, and to the beat of a drum I announced to the four quarters that I was seeking Dharma: "Whoever can preach the Great Vehicle to me, for him I will render service and run errands for the rest of my life!" At that time there was a

seer *(rṣi)* who came and reported to the king, saying, "I have a great vehicle; its name is the Scripture of the Lotus Blossom of the Fine Dharma. If you can obey me, I will set it forth for you." When the king heard the seer's words, he danced for joy, then straightway followed the seer, tending to whatever he required: picking his fruit, drawing his water, gathering his firewood, preparing his food, even making a couch of his own body; feeling no impatience, whether in body or in mind. He rendered him service for a thousand years, bending all efforts to menial labor for Dharma's sake and seeing to it that he lacked nothing.

Hurvitz, p. 195; T9, p. 34bc.

14. Rewards for keeping the ten commandments in past lives.

15. *Setsuri (ksatriya)* are the second caste, warriors and rulers. *Suda (sudra)* are the fourth caste, cultivators and peasants.

16. The three torments of hell are fiery heat, fierce winds, and the *garūḍa* bird, which eats flesh.

17. Demons who torment beings in hell.

18. *Mo ho chih kuan.*

19. His story is told in the larger *Hannyaharamikkyō.*

20. *Kegonkyō.*

21. Lotus Sutra, chapter 23; T9, p. 53c.

22. *Ta chih tu lun.*

23. The story is told in the larger *Hannyaharamikkyō.*

24. Nichiren cites this passage in Chinese and then translates into Japanese. The retelling is omitted.

25. Here again a repetitious translation is omitted.

26. *Mo ho chih kuan.*

27. Chapter 28, T9, p. 61c.

28. *Chu wei mo ching,* by Seng-chao.

29. These are fundamental Tendai doctrines. The universe is divided into ten realms: Buddha, bodhisattva, *pratyekabuddha,* hearer, god, demon, human, hungry ghost, beast, and hell. Each realm has the other nine, which makes one hundred realms in all. Each possesses ten essential qualities: form, nature, substance, force, action, condition, effect, reward, cause, and ultimate state. Thus there are one thousand worlds. Each has three divisions: living beings, the five aggregates, and the space we live in. The three thousand worlds thus enumerated are encompassed by one thought; this indicates the interpenetration of all dharmas. Ch'en, pp. 311–312.

30. The ten essential qualities are in each of the ten worlds.

31. Every dharma is empty and temporary, real and unreal.

32. The Lotus Sutra promises salvation to all.

33. The day before the summer retreat.

34. The story is from the poem "White-haired Woman of Shang-yin" in *Hakushi monjū (Po shih wen chi).*

35. When Shun died, their tears dyed the brushwood fences red.

36. Su Wu was exiled during the Han dynasty.

37. A contemporary of Śākyamuni, said to have had the first image of the Buddha made.

38. The all-doer or maker, architect of the universe.

39. Anāthapindaka.

40. The end of the summer retreat.

41.   Realm of the Buddha Miroku (Maitreya).
42.   Four of the Buddha's ten chief disciples.
43.   The daughter of the *nāga*. Chapter 12, "Devadatta."
44.   Chapter 21, T9, p. 52c.
45.   Things are in their essential nature unreal, while their derived forms are real; yet real and unreal are one.
46.   The three meditations are meditations on the nature of things as real, unreal, and both.
47.   The nine realms below the Buddha realm.
48.   tachiwataru
       mi no ukigumo mo
       harenubeshi
       taenu minori no
       washi no yamakaze
       The first two lines refer to both the clouds which gather around the peak of Mount Minobu and the clouds of ignorance preventing the enlightenment of the person who is to "cross over," that is, "be enlightened."

Message to Lord Hakii[1]

Respectful greetings! We reached Ikegami[2] without incident. The journey, with mountains and rivers to cross, was not easy but your sons helped me and I am happy to think my safe arrival is due to your care. I had thought I would return over this same road, but I am so ill that is uncertain. However, I cannot express my gratitude to you for your protection of one who has found Japan too much to handle and for your faith these past nine years. Wherever I die, I would like to be buried in the valley at Minobu.[3]

I enjoyed riding your chestnut horse immensely, and I hate to part with him. I would like to take him as far as the waters in Hitachi, but I am worried that someone might steal him so I am going to leave him with Lord Mobara[4] in Kazusa until I return. Since I worry about leaving him to an unfamiliar groom, I intend to leave the groom too. Hoping you approve, I am writing to let you know of my decision.

9/19[5]

Respectfully,

Nichiren

To Lord Hakii
My illness prevents my affixing my seal. Please forgive me.[6]

NOTES

1.   This is the last letter Nichiren wrote before his death on 1282/10/13. Hakii Sanenaga, the *jitō* of Minobu, had provided a hermitage in the mountains since 1274. *STH,* pp. 1924–1925.

2.   Nichiren and Hakii's sons left Minobu on 9/8 and were about eleven days on the road to Ikegami in present-day Tokyo, home of the Ikegami family with whom Nichiren had often corresponded about the conflict of filial duty and faith.
3.   The tomb is in the valley near the temple Kuonji near the remains of Nichiren's hermitage.
4.   Mobara Kanetsuna lived at Mobara in modern Chiba prefecture.
5.   1282.
6.   Nichiren dictated the letter to Nikkō.

List of Sutras and Classes of Sutras

Agonkyō 阿含経, Āgama sūtras.

Amidakyō 阿彌陀経, Sukhāvativyūha sūtra, T 366.

(Daibon) hannyaharamikkyō 大品般若波羅密経, Pañcaviṃśatisāhasṛikā prajñapāramitā sūtra, T 223.

(Daihōdō) daishukkyō 大方等大集経, Mahāsaṃnipāta sūtra, T 397.

(Daihōkōbutsu) kegonkyō 大方広仏華厳経, Avatamsaka sūtra, T 279.

Dainichikyō 大日経, Mahāvairocanā sūtra, T 848.

(Ge) jinmitsukyō 解深密経, Saṃdhi nirmocana sūtra, T 676.

Hatsunaiongyō 般泥洹経, Mahāparinirvāna sūtra, T 376.

Hōdōkyō 方等経, Vaipulya sūtras.

Hōjōjukyō 法成就経, T 819.

Hokezanmaikyō 法華三昧経, T 269.

Jūjūbibasharon 十住毘婆沙論, Daśabhūmi vibhāṣa śāstra, T 1521.

Kanbutsuzanmaikyō 観仏三昧経, Buddha dhyāna samādhisāgara, T 643.

(Kan) fugenkyō 観普賢経, T 277.

Kan (muryōju) kyō 観無量壽経, Amitāyur dhyāna, T 365.

Kengukyō 賢愚経, Damamūka nidāna sūtra, T 202.

Konjikinyokyō 金色女経.

Konkōmyō (saishōō) kyō 金光明最勝王経, Suvarṇaprabhāsa, T 663.

Kuyōhōkyō 供養法経.

Kyakuon'ōjinjukyō 却温黄神呪経.

Muryōgikyō 無量義経, Ananta nirdeśa, T 276.

Muryōjukyō 無量壽経, Sukhāvativyūha sūtra, T 360.

Myōhōrengekyō (Hokekyō) 妙法蓮華経, Saddharmapuṇḍarīka sūtra, T 262.

Nehangyō 涅槃経, Mahāparinirvāna sūtra, T 374.

Ninnōkyō 仁王経, T 245, 246.

Ropparamikkyō 六波羅密経, Mahāyāna nayasatpāramitā sūtra, T 261.

Ryōgonkyō 楞厳経, Carye samudra deśa buddheṣṇisa śuraṅgama, T 945.
Satsuunfundarikyō 薩曇分陀利経, Saddharmapuṇḍarīka sūtra, T 265.
Shinjikangyō 心地観経, T 159.
Shōhokekyō 正法華経, T 263.
Shohōmugyōkyō 諸法無行経, T 650.
Shōmangyō 勝鬘経, Śrīmālādevī siṃhanāda sūtra, T 353.
Sōkangyō 双券経, see Kanmuryōjukyō.
Tenbon myōhōrengekyō 添品妙法蓮華経, T 264.
Yakushi (nyōraihongan) kyō 薬師如来本願経, Bhaiṣajyaguru sūtra, T 449.
Yuimakyō 維摩経, Vimalakīrti nirdeśa sūtra, T 474, 475.

List of Japanese Terms and Corresponding Kanji

busshin 仏心
chingo kokka kyō 鎮護国家経
daimoku 題目
ehō 依報
gyōja 行者
higō 非業
hijiri 聖
hōbō 謗法
hōnan 法難
honmon 本門
honzon 本尊
inja 隠者
inzudai 院宗代
jiga 自我
jikkyō 実教
jikyōsha 持経者
jitō 地頭
jobun 序分
jōdo 浄土
kaidan 戒壇
kōshi 講師
mappō 末法
mikkyō 密教
mukai 無戒

myōshu 名主
nenbutsu 念仏
nyūdō 入道
rensho 連署
ruzubun 流通分
samuraidokoro 侍所
sendara 旃陀羅
setsuwashū 説話集
shakubuku 折伏
shakumon 迹門
shidosō 私度僧
shikken 執権
shōbō 正法
shōdō 唱導
shōen 荘園
shōju 摂受
shōhō 正報
shōkan 荘官
shōshūbun 正宗分
sokushin jōbutsu 即身成仏
wakankonkōbun 和漢混淆文
zazen 座禅
zōbō 像法
zuihitsu 随筆

Chinese and Japanese Religious Figures

Chang-an 章安 (Kuan-ting), 561–632
Ch'eng-kuan 澄観, 737–838?
Chih-i 智顗, 538–597
Chih-yen 智儼, 602–663
Chishō 智證 (Enchin), 814–891
Chi-ts'ang 吉蔵 (Chia-hsiang), 549–623
Dōgen 道元, 1200–1253
Dōryū 道隆 (Rankei), 1213–1278
Eisai 栄西, 1141–1215
Enchō 円澄 (Jakkō), 771–836
Fa-tao 法道, d. 1147
Fa-tsang 法蔵, 643–712
Genshin 源信 (Eshin), 942–1017
Gishin 義真, d. 833
Gyōchi 行智, thirteenth century
Hōnen 法然 (Genkū), 1133–1212
Hsüan-tsang 玄奘, 602?–664
Hui-k'o 慧可, 486–593
Hui-yüan 慧遠, 523–592
Ippen 一遍, 1239–1289
Jikaku 慈覚 (Ennin), 794–864

Kakuban 覚鑁, 1095–1143
Kakumyō 覚明
K'uei-chi 窺基 (Tz'u-en), 632–682
Kūkai 空海 (Kōbō), 774–835
Miao-lo 妙楽 (Chan-jan), 711–782
Nen'a 念阿 (Ryōchū), 1199–1287
Ninshō 忍性 (Ryōkan), 1217–1303
Nōan 能安
Nōnin 能忍 (Dainichi), early
   Kamakura
Pu-k'ung 不空, 705–774
Ryōkan 良観 (Ninshō), 1217–1303
Ryōnin 良忍, 1072–1132
Saichō 最澄 (Dengyō), 767–822
Seng-chao 僧肇, 384–414
Shan-tao 善道, 613–681
Shinran 親鸞, 1173–1262
T'an-luan 曇鸞, 476–542
Tao-an 道安, sixth century
Tao-ch'o 道綽, 562–645
Tu-shun 杜順, 557–640?

Japanese and Chinese works Cited by Nichiren

Chen kuan cheng yao 貞観政要, Wu-ching.
Cheng yuan hsin ting shih chiao mu lu 貞元新定釈教目録, Yuan-chao, T 2157.
Chu wei mo ching 註維摩経, Seng-chao.
(Fa hua) hsuan i 法華玄義, Chih-i, T 1716.
(Fa hua) hsuan i shih ch'ien 玄義釈籤, Miao-lo, T 1717.
(Fa hua) wen chu 文句, Chih-i, T 1718.
(Fa hua) wen chu chi 文句記, Miao-lo, T 1719.
Han fei tzu. 韓非子.
(Hokke) shūku 法華秀句, Saichō.
Hsi yu chi 西域記, Hsüan-tsang.
Kuan ching shu 観経疏, Shan-tao.
Lieh hsien ch'uan 列仙伝.
Mo ho chih kuan 摩訶止観, Chih-i, T 1911.
(Mo ho chih kuan fu hsing chuan) hung chueh 輔行伝弘決, Miao-lo, T 1912.
Nihongi 日本記.
Ōjōyōshū 往生要集, Genshin, T 2682.
Pan chou san mei tsan 般舟三昧讚, Shan-tao, T 47.
Pao p'o tzu 抱朴子.
Senjaku (hongan nenbutsu) shū 巽択本願念仏集, Hōnen.
Shih chi 史記, Ssu-ma Ch'ien.
Szu nien ch'u 四念処, Chih-i.
Ta p'i p'o sha lun 大毘婆沙論, Hsüan-tsang, T 1545.
Ta chih tu lun 大智度論, Nāgārjuna, T 1509.
Tso chuan 左伝.
Wang sheng lun chu 往生論註, T'an-luan.
Wen hsuan 文選, Hsiao T'ung.

APPENDIX E

Chapters of
the Lotus Sutra

Bibliography

WORKS IN JAPANESE AND CHINESE

Akamatsu Toshihide 赤松俊秀. *Kamakura bukkyō no kenkyū* 鎌倉仏教の研究, 2 vols. Kyoto: Heirakuji shoten, 1957–1966.

Akiyama Ken, ed. 秋山虔. *Chūsei bungaku no kenkyū* 中世文学の研究. Tokyo: Tokyo daigaku shuppankai, 1972.

Andō Toshio 安藤俊夫. *Tendaigaku* 天台学. Kyoto: Heirakuji shoten, 1968.

Araki Yoshio 荒木良雄. *Chūsei Kamakura Muromachi bungaku jiten* 中世鎌倉室町文学事典. Tokyo: Shunshūsha, 1966.

———. *Chūsei kokubungaku ron* 中世国文学論. Tokyo: Seikatsusha, 1944.

Asai Yorin 淺井要鹿. *Shōwa shinshū Nichiren shōnin ibun zenshū* 昭和新修日蓮聖人遺文全集, 3 vols. Kyoto: Heirakuji shoten, 1962–1964.

Bukkyō bungaku kenkyū kai, ed. 仏教文学研究会. *Bukkyō bungaku kenkyū*. Tokyo: Hōzōkan, 1963.

Enami Bunzō 江南文三. *Nihongo no Hokekyō* 日本語の法華経. Tokyo: Daizō shuppan, 1968.

Fujita Kōtatsu 藤田宏達. *Hokke shisō* 法華思想. Kyoto: Heirakuji shoten, 1969.

Fukui Kyūzō 福井久蔵. *Kokubungaku to bukkyō* 国文学と仏教. Tokyo: Sanseidō, 1939.

Hisamatsu Sen'ichi 久松潜一. *Shinpan Nihon bungakushi* 新版日本文学史, volume 3, *Chūsei* 中世. Tokyo: Shibundō, 1971.

Hung, William, et al., eds. *Fo tsang tzu mu yin tê* 仏蔵子目引得. Peiping: Harvard-Yenching Institute, 1933.

Ichiko Sadatsugu 市古貞次. *Chūsei bungaku kenkyū nyūmon* 中世文学研究入門. Tokyo: Shibundō, 1965.

Ichimura Sonosaburō 市村其三良. "Nichiren no shingon haigeki" 日蓮の真言排撃. *Shigaku zasshi*, Vol. 39, 7 (1928), pp. 56–71.

Ienaga Saburō 家永三郎. *Chūsei bukkyō shisōshi kenkyū* 中世仏教思想史研究. Kyoto: Hōzōkan, 1960.

————. "Nichiren no shukyō no seiritsu ni kansuru shisōshiteki kenkyū" 日蓮の宗教の成立に関する思想史的考察. In *Chūsei bukkyō shisōshi kenkyū* 中世仏教思想史研究. Kyoto: Hōzōkan, 1955.

————, ed. *Nihon bukkyō shisō no tenkai* 日本仏教思想の展開. Kyoto: Heirakuji shoten, 1956.

Iwama Tanryō 岩間湛良. *Minobusan kuonji* 身延山久遠寺. Tokyo: Kyoiku shincho sha, 1961.

Iwano Shin'yū 岩野真雄, ed. *Kokuyaku issaikyō* 国訳一切経. Tokyo: Daitō shuppansha, 1958–1962.

Kabutogi Shōkō 兜木正享. *Hokekyō to Nichiren shōnin* 法華経と日蓮上人. Kyoto: Heirakuji shoten, 1956.

Kadokawa Motoyoshi 角川源義 and Sugiyama Hiroshi 杉山博, eds. *Nihon bungaku no rekishi* 日本文学の歴史, volume 5, *Ai to mujō no bungei* 愛と無常の文芸. Tokyo: Kadokawa shoten, 1967.

Kageyama Gyōyū 影山尭雄. *Nichiren kyōdanshi gaisetsu* 日蓮教団史概説. Kyoto: Heirakuji shoten, 1959.

Kamakura shishi hensan iinkai 鎌倉市史編纂委員会. *Kamakura shishi* 鎌倉市史, 6 volumes. Tokyo: Yoshikawa Kōbunkan, 1967.

Kanakura Enshō, ed. 金倉圓照. *Hokekyō no seiritsu to tenkai* 法華経の成立と展開. Kyoto: Heirakuji shoten, 1970.

Kawazoe Shōji 川添昭二. *Nichiren: sono shisō, kōdō to mōko raishū* 日蓮: その思想行動と蒙古来襲. Tokyo: Shimizu shoin, 1971.

————. *Nichiren*, volume 2 of "Kōza gendai ronri" 講座現代論理. Tokyo: Chikuma shobo, 1959.

Kikuchi Ryōichi. 菊地良一. *Chūsei no shōdō bungei* 中世の唱導文芸. Tokyo: Kōshobō, 1968.

Kino Kazuyoshi 紀野一義. *Nichiren* 日蓮, volume 8 of "Nihon no meicho" 日本の名著. Tokyo: Chūōkōronsha, 1970.

————. *Nichiren: hairyū no michi* 日蓮配流の道, volume 4 of "Nihon no tabibito" 日本の旅人. Kyoto: Tankosha, 1973.

———— and Umehara Takeshi 梅原猛. *Eien no inochi* 永遠のいのち, volume 12 of "Bukkyō no shisō" 仏教の思想. Tokyo: Kadokawa shoten, 1969.

Kiyomizu Ryūzan 清水龍山, ed. *Genbun taishō kōgoyaku Nichiren shōnin zenshū* 原文対照口語訳日蓮上人全集, 7 volumes. Tokyo: Ryūbunkan, 1921–1925.

Kobayashi Ichirō 小林一郎. *Hokekyō daikōza.* 法華経大講座 12 volumes. Tokyo: Nisshin shuppan, 1964–1965.

Kobayashi Iichirō 小林猪一郎. *Nichiren shōnin ibun daikōza* 日蓮上人遺文大講座. Tokyo: Heibonsha, 1936–1937.

Kubota Jun 久保田淳. *Chūsei bungaku no sekai* 中世文学の世界. Tokyo: Tokyo University Press, 1972.

Kubota Shōbun 久保田正文. *Nichiren: sono shōgai to shisō* 日蓮: その生涯と思想. Tokyo: Kōdansha, 1967.

Masutani Fumio 増谷文雄. *Nichiren: shokan o tōshite miru hito to shisō* 日蓮: 書簡を通してみる人と思想. Tokyo: Chikuma shobō, 1967.

―――. *Shinran Dōgen Nichiren* 親鸞道元日蓮. Tokyo: Shibundō, 1956.

Miyasaka Yusho 宮坂宥勝. *Kana hōgoshū* 仮名法語集. Tokyo: Iwanami shoten, 1964.

Miyazaki Eishū 宮崎英修. "Nichiren shōnin ibun no bunkenteki kenkyū" 日蓮上人遺文の文献的研究. In Mochizuki Kankō 望月歓厚, ed. *Kindai Nihon no Hokke bukkyō* 近代日本の法華仏教. Kyoto: Heirakuji shoten, 1968.

―――. *Nichirenshū* 日蓮宗. Tokyo: Hōbunkan, 1961.

―――. *Nichiren to sono deshi* 日蓮とその弟子 Tokyo: Mainichi shinbunsha, 1971.

Miyazaki Enjun 宮崎円尊. *Chūsei bukkyō to shomin seikatsu* 中世仏教と庶民生活. Kyoto: Heirakuji shoten, 1951.

Mizuno Kōgen 水野弘元. *Shin butten kaidai jiten* 新仏典解題事典. Tokyo: Shunshusha, 1966.

Mochizuki Kankō, ed. 望月歓厚. *Kindai Nihon no Hokke bukkyō* 近代日本の法華仏教. Kyoto: Heirakuji shoten, 1968.

―――. *Nichiren kyōgaku no kenkyū* 日蓮教学の研究. Tokyo: Heirakuji shoten, 1961.

―――. *Nichiren shū gakusetsu shi* 日蓮宗学説史. Kyoto: Heirakuji shoten, 1968.

Mochizuki Shinkō 望月信享. *Bukkyō daijiten* 仏教大辞典, 5 volumes. Tokyo: Sekai seiten kankōkai, 1932–1936.

Motai Kyōkō 茂田井教享. *Nichiren shokan ni kiku* 日蓮書簡に聞く. Tokyo: Kyōiku shinchōsha, 1966.

―――. *Nichiren shū* 日蓮宗. Kyoto: Daizō shuppansha, 1958.

Nabata Ōjun, et al. 名畑應順. *Shinranshū Nichirenshū* 親鸞集日蓮集. Volume 82 of "Nihon koten bungaku taikei" 日本古典文学大系. Tokyo: Iwanami shoten, 1964.

Nagai Yoshinori 永井義憲. *Nihon bukkyō bungaku* 日本仏教文学. Tokyo: Kōshobō, 1963.

―――. *Nihon bukkyō bungaku kenkyū* 日本仏教文学研究. Tokyo: Hotō shobō, 1966.

Nakajima Shōshi 中島尚志. *Nichiren* 日蓮. Tokyo: San'ichi shobō, 1970.

Nakao Takeshi 中尾堯. *Nichiren shū no shomondai* 日蓮宗の諸問題. Tokyo: Yūzankaku, 1975.

Nichiren kyōgaku kenkyūjo, eds. 日蓮教学研究所. *Nichiren kyōdan zenshi* 日蓮教団全史. Kyoto: Heirakuji shoten, 1964.

Nichiren shōnin zenshū kankōkai, eds. 日蓮上人全集刊行会, *Nichiren shōnin zenshū* 日蓮上人全集, 7 volumes. Tokyo: Nichiren shōnin zenshū kankōkai, 1925–1926.

Nihon bukkyō gakkai, eds. 日本仏教学会. *Kamakura bukkyō keisei no mondaiten* 鎌倉仏教形成の問題点. Kyoto: Heirakuji shoten, 1969.

Nishio Kōichi 西尾光一. *Chūsei setsuwa bungakuron* 中世説話文学論. Tokyo: Hanawa shobō, 1963.

Nomura Hachirō 野村八良. *Kamakura jidai bungaku shinron* 鎌倉時代文学新論. Tokyo: Meiji shoin, 1922.

Oda Tokunō 織田得能. *Oda bukkyō daijiten* 織田仏教大辞典. Tokyo: Daizō shuppansha, 1954.

Ogawa Yukio. *Nichiren: sono shōgai to ashiato* 日蓮その生涯と足跡. Tokyo: Kinseisha, 1961.

Ono Genmyō 小野玄妙. *Bussho kaisetsu daijiten* 仏書解説大辞典, 12 volumes. Tokyo: Daitō shuppansha, 1933–1936.

Ōno Tatsunosuke 大野達之助. *Nichiren* 日蓮. Tokyo: Yoshikawa kōbunkan, 1958.

Ōshima Nakatarō 大嶋仲太郎. *Myōhōrengekyō sakuin* 妙法蓮華経索引. Kyoto: Heirakuji shoten, 1941.

Risshō Daigaku Nichiren kyōgaku kenkyūjo 立正大学日蓮教学研究所. *Nichiren kyōdan zenshi* 日蓮教団全史. Kyoto: Heirakuji shoten, 1964.

―――. *Nichiren shū tokuhon* 日蓮宗読本. Kyoto: Heirakuji shoten, 1961.

Risshō Daigaku shūgaku kenkyūjo, eds. 立正大学宗学研究所, *Shōwa teihon Nichiren shōnin ibun* 昭和定本日蓮聖人遺文, 4 volumes. Minobu: Minobu Kuonji, 1959–1965.

Ryūkoku Daigaku, ed. 竜谷大学. *Bukkyō daijii* 仏教大辞彙. Tokyo: Fuzanbō, 1935–1936.

Sakamoto Yukio 坂本幸男, ed. *Hokekyō no chūgokuteki tenkai* 法華経の中国的展開. Kyoto: Heirakuji shoten, 1972.

―――. *Hokekyō no shisō to bunka* 法華経の思想と文化. Kyoto: Heirakuji shoten, 1965.

――― and Iwamoto Yutaka 岩本格. *Hokekyō* 法華経, 3 volumes. Tokyo: Iwanami shoten, 1962, 1965, 1967.

Satomi Kishio 里見岸雄. *Nichiren: sono hito to shisō* 日蓮その人と思想. Tokyo: Kinseisha, 1963.

Shigyō Kaishu 執行海秀. *Nichiren shōnin to sono shisō* 日蓮上人とその思想. Kyoto: Heirakuji shoten, 1955.

————. *Nichiren shū kyōgakushi* 日蓮宗教学史. Kyoto: Heirakuji shoten, 1960.

Shimura Kunihiro 志村有弘. *Chūsei setsuwa bungaku kenkyū josetsu* 中世説話文学研究序説. Tokyo: Ōbūsha, 1974.

Shioda Gison 塩田義遜. *Nichiren shōnin goshōsokubun zenshū* 日蓮聖人御消息文全集. Kyoto: Heirakuji shoten, 1968.

Suzuki Ichijō 鈴木一成. *Nichiren shōnin ibun no bunkengakuteki kenkyū* 日蓮上人遺文の文献学的研究. Tokyo: Sankibō, 1965.

————. *Nichiren shōnin seiden* 日蓮上人正伝. Kyoto: Heirakuji shoten, 1948.

Takagami Kakushō 高神覚昇. *Mikkyō gairon* 密教概論. Tokyo: Daiichi shobō, 1937.

Takagi Yutaka 高木豊. "Inseiki ni okeru chiho besso no seiritsu to katsudō" 院政期における地方別所の成立と活動. In Kasahara Kazuo 笠原一男, ed., *Hōken kindai shakai ni okeru Kamakura bukkyō no tenkai* 封建近代社会における鎌倉仏教の展開. Tokyo: Hōzōkan, 1965.

————. *Nichiren: sono kōdō to shisō* 日蓮その行動と思想. Tokyo: Hyōron-sha, 1970.

————. *Nichiren to sono montei* 日蓮とその門弟. Tokyo: Kōbundō, 1965.

Takahashi Mitsugu 高橋貢. *Chūko setsuwa bungaku kenkyū josetsu* 中古説話文学研究序説. Tokyo: Ōbūsha, 1974.

Takakusu Junjirō 高楠順次郎 and Mochizuki Shinkō 望月信享, eds. *Nihon bukkyō zensho* 日本仏教全書. Kyoto: Sekai seiten kankō kyōkai, 1948–.

Takakusu Junjirō et al., eds. *Taishō shinshū daizōkyō* 大正新修大蔵経. Tokyo: Taishō issaikyō kankōkai, 1924–1933.

Takayama Rinjirō 高山林次郎. *Chōgyū zenshū* 樗牛全集, volume 4. Tokyo: Hakubunkan, 1924.

Tamura Yoshirō 田村芳朗. *Kamakura shinbukkyō shisō no kenkyū* 鎌倉新仏教思想の研究. Kyoto: Heirakuji shoten, 1965.

————, ed. *Nichiren shū* 日蓮集. Volume 4 of "Nihon no shisō" 日本の思想. Tokyo: Chikuma shobō, 1969.

————. *Yogenja no bukkyō* 予言者の仏教. Tokyo: Chikuma shobō, 1967.

———— and Miyazaki Eishū, eds. 宮崎英修. *Koza Nichiren* 講座日蓮, 5 volumes. Tokyo: Shunshōsha, 1972–1973. I. *Nichiren to hokekyō* 日蓮と法華経, 1972. II. *Nichiren no shōgai to shisō* 日蓮の生涯と思想, 1972. III. *Nichiren shinkō no rekishi* 日蓮信仰の歴史, 1972. IV. *Nihon kindai to Nichiren shugi* 日本近代と日蓮主義, 1972. V. *Nichiren goroku* 日蓮語録, 1973.

Tokoro Shigemoto 戸頃重基. *Kamakura bukkyō* 鎌倉仏教. Tokyo: Chūō-kōronsha, 1967.

————. "Nichiren." In *Gendai shūkyō kōza* 現代宗教講座, volume 1.

Tokyo: Sōbunsha, 1954.

―――. *Nichiren no shisō to Kamakura bukkyō* 日蓮の思想と鎌倉仏教. Tokyo: Fuzanbō, 1965.

――― and Takagi Yutaka 高木豊. *Nichiren* 日蓮. Volume 14 of "Nihon-shisō taikei" 日本思想大系. Tokyo: Iwanami shoten, 1970.

Uesugi Fumiho 上杉文秀. *Nihon Tendai shi* 日本天台史 (正, 続), 2 volumes. Tokyo: Kokusho kankōkai, 1972.

Yamaguchi Kōen 山口光円. *Tendai gaisetsu* 天台概説. Kyoto: Hōzōkan, 1967.

Yamakawa Chiō 山川智応. *Nichiren shōnin kenkyū* 日蓮聖人研究, 2 volumes. Tokyo: Shinchōsha, 1929–1931.

Yasuraoka Kōsaku 安良岡康作. *Chūseiteki bungaku no tankyū* 中世的文学の探求. Tokyo: Yūshōdō, 1970.

WORKS IN WESTERN LANGUAGES

Anesaki, Masaharu. *History of Japanese Religion.* Rutland, Vermont: Charles E. Tuttle Company, 1963.

―――. *Nichiren, The Buddhist Prophet.* Cambridge, Mass.: Harvard University Press, 1916.

Bharati, Agehananda. *The Tantric Tradition.* Garden City, N.Y.: Doubleday & Company, Inc., 1965.

Birch, Cyril. *Studies in Chinese Literary Genres.* Berkeley and Los Angeles, Calif.: University of California Press, 1974.

Ch'en, Kenneth. *Buddhism in China.* Princeton, N.J.: Princeton University Press, 1972.

Del Campana, Pier P. "*Sandaihihō-shō* by Nichiren." *Monumenta Nipponica* 26, nos. 1–2 (1971): 205–224.

des Longrais, F. Jouon. *Âge de Kamakura.* Paris: Maison Franco-japonaise, 1950.

Dykstra, Yoshiko K. "Miraculous Tales of the Lotus Sutra: The *Dainihonkoku Hokkegenki*." *Monumenta Nipponica* 32, no. 2 (Summer, 1977): 189–210.

Eliot, Charles. *Japanese Buddhism.* London: Edward Arnold & Co., 1935.

Frederic, Louis. *La vie quotidienne au Japan a l'époque des samourai, 1185–1603.* Paris: Librairie Hachette, 1968.

Fridell, Wilbur M. "Notes on Japanese Tolerance." *Monumenta Nipponica* 27, no. 3 (Autumn, 1972): 253–271.

Fung Yu-lan. *A History of Chinese Philosophy*, volume 2. Princeton, N.J.: Princeton University Press, 1953.

Hall, John W., and Mass, Jeffrey P., eds. *Medieval Japan: Essays in Institutional History.* New Haven, Conn.: Yale University Press, 1974.

Hurvitz, Leon, "Chih-i, An Introduction to the Life and Ideas of a Buddhist Monk." *Mélanges chinois et bouddhiques* 12 (1960–1962): 1–372.

————. *Scripture of the Lotus Blossom of the Fine Dharma*. New York: Columbia University Press, 1976.

Iwano Shinyū. *Japanese-English Buddhist Dictionary*. Tokyo: Daitō-shuppansha, 1965.

Katō, Bunnō et al. (trans.). *The Threefold Lotus Sutra*. New York: Weatherhill, 1975.

Kelsey, W. Michael. "Konjaku Monogatari-shū: Toward an Understanding of Its Literary Qualities." *Monumenta Nipponica* 30, 2 (Summer, 1975): 121–150.

Kern, H. *Saddharma-Puṇḍarīka or the Lotus of the True Law*. New York: Dover Publications, 1963.

Kitagawa, Joseph M. *Religion in Japanese History*. New York: Columbia University Press, 1966.

Lee, Edwin B. "Nichiren and Nationalism: The Religious Patriotism of Tanaka Chigaku." *Monumenta Nipponica*, 30, no. 1 (Spring, 1975): 19–35.

Lieteau, Haruyo. "The Yasutoki-Myōe Discussion: A Translation from *Tōgano-o Myōe Shōnin Denki*." *Monumenta Nipponica* 30, no. 2 (Summer, 1975): 203–210.

Liu Wu-chi. *An Introduction to Chinese Literature*. Bloomington, Ind.: Indiana University Press, 1966.

Mass, Jeffrey P. *Warrior Government in Early Medieval Japan*. New Haven, Conn.: Yale University Press, 1974.

————. *The Kamakura Bakufu*. Stanford, Calif.: Stanford University Press, 1976.

Mills, D. E. *A Collection of Tales from Uji*. Cambridge, England: Cambridge University Press, 1970.

Nakamura, Kyoko Motomochi. *Miraculous Stories from the Japanese Buddhist Tradition*. Cambridge, Mass.: Harvard University Press, 1973.

Petzold, B. "The Chinese Tendai Teachings." *Eastern Buddhist* 4 (1927–1928): 299–347.

Reischauer, E. O., trans. *Ennin's Diary: The Record of a Pilgrimage to China in Search of the Law*. New York: Ronald Press Company, 1955.

————. *Ennin's Travels in T'ang China*. New York: Ronald Press Company, 1955.

Renondeau, Gaston. "Traité sur le stabilité du pays par l'établissement de l'orthodoxie." *T'oung Pao*, 40, nos. 1–3, 1950.

————. *La doctrine de Nichiren*. Paris: Presses universitaires de France, 1953.

Ruch, Barbara. "Medieval Jongleurs and the Making of a National Literature." *Japan in the Muromachi Age*. Eds. John Whitney Hall and Toyoda Takeshi. Berkeley and Los Angeles, Calif.: University of California Press, 1977, pp. 279–309.

Sansom, George. *A History of Japan to 1334*. Stanford, Calif.: Stanford University Press, 1958.

Soothill, William E., and Hodous, Lewis. *A Dictionary of Chinese Buddhist Terms*. Kaohsiung, Taiwan: Buddhist Culture Service, n.d.

Steenstrup, Carl. "The Gokurakuji Letter." *Monumenta Nipponica* 32 (Spring, 1977): 1–34.

Suzuki Teitarō. *The Kyōgyōshinshō*. Kyoto: Shinshū Ōtaniha, 1973.

Wright, Arthur F. *Buddhism in Chinese History*. Stanford, Calif.: Stanford University Press, 1959.

Yampolsky, Philip B. *The Zen Master Hakuin: Selected Writings*. New York: Columbia University Press, 1971.

Index

Index preparation by Jane P. Bigg, Deanna G. Black, Donna R. Breslauer, Elaine M. Dietz, Jean L. Flom, Pamela L. Phillips, Sarah H. Preble, Rose Ringo, Joann D. Ryding, Abdua Sattar, Cathy G. Scovel, Marilyn M. L. Wong, with special thanks to Frances F. Enos, Colette H. Gomoto, John P. Hoover, Gloria A. McClanahan, Joann D. Ryding, and Professor Sarah K. Vann.

Laurel Rasplica Rodd is Assistant Professor of Japanese at Arizona State University where she teaches Japanese language, literature, and culture. She began her study of Japanese at the East-West Center and received a B.A. in French from DePauw University. She received her M.A. and Ph.D. degrees from the University of Michigan, and is currently working on studies and translations of the *Kokinshū* and the poetry of Yosano Akiko.

Asian Studies at Hawaii

No. 13 *Nanyang Perspective: Chinese Students in Multiracial Singapore.* Andrew W. Lind. June 1974.

No. 14 *Political Change in the Philippines: Studies of Local Politics preceding Martial Law.* Edited by Benedict J. Kerkvliet. November 1974.

No. 15 *Essays on South India.* Edited by Burton Stein. February 1976.

No. 16 *The* Caurāsī Pad *of Śrī Hit Harivaṁś.* Charles S. J. White. 1977.

No. 17 *An American Teacher in Early Meiji Japan.* Edward R. Beauchamp. June 1976.

No. 18 *Buddhist and Taoist Studies I.* Edited by Michael Saso and David W. Chappell. 1977.

No. 19 *Sumatran Contributions to the Development of Indonesian Literature, 1920–1942.* Alberta Joy Freidus. 1977.

No. 20 *Insulinde: Selected Translations from Dutch Writers of Three Centuries on the Indonesian Archipelago.* Edited by Cornelia N. Moore, 1978.

No. 21 *Regents, Reformers, and Revolutionaries: Indonesian Voices of Colonial Days, Selected Historical Readings, 1899–1949.* Translated, edited, and annotated by Greta O. Wilson, 1978.

No. 22 *The Politics of Inequality: Competition and Control in an Indian Village.* Miriam Sharma. October 1978.

No. 23 *Brokers of Morality: Thai Ethnic Adaptation in a Rural Malaysian Setting.* Louis Golomb. February 1979.

No. 24 *Tales of Japanese Justice.* Ihara Saikaku. Translated by Thomas M. Kondo and Alfred H. Marks. January 1980.

No. 25 *Mandarins, Gunboats, and Power Politics: Owen Nickerson Denny and the International Rivalries in Korea.* Robert R. Swartout, Jr. March 1980.

No. 26 *Nichiren: Selected Writings.* Laurel Rasplica Rodd. 1980.